AVID
READER
PRESS

THE PHILOSOPHER IN THE VALLEY

ALEX KARP, PALANTIR, AND THE RISE
OF THE SURVEILLANCE STATE

MICHAEL STEINBERGER

AVID READER PRESS

New York   Amsterdam/Antwerp   London
Toronto   Sydney/Melbourne   New Delhi

Avid Reader Press
An Imprint of Simon & Schuster, LLC
1230 Avenue of the Americas
New York, NY 10020

For more than 100 years, Simon & Schuster has championed authors and the stories they create. By respecting the copyright of an author's intellectual property, you enable Simon & Schuster and the author to continue publishing exceptional books for years to come. We thank you for supporting the author's copyright by purchasing an authorized edition of this book.

No amount of this book may be reproduced or stored in any format, nor may it be uploaded to any website, database, language-learning model, or other repository, retrieval, or artificial intelligence system without express permission. All rights reserved. Inquiries may be directed to Simon & Schuster, 1230 Avenue of the Americas, New York, NY 10020 or permissions@simonandschuster.com.

Copyright © 2025 by Michael Steinberger

All rights reserved, including the right to reproduce this book or portions thereof in any form whatsoever. For information, address Avid Reader Press Subsidiary Rights Department, 1230 Avenue of the Americas, New York, NY 10020.

First Avid Reader Press hardcover edition November 2025

AVID READER PRESS and colophon are trademarks of Simon & Schuster, LLC

Simon & Schuster strongly believes in freedom of expression and stands against censorship in all its forms. For more information, visit BooksBelong.com.

For information about special discounts for bulk purchases, please contact Simon & Schuster Special Sales at 1-866-506-1949 or business@simonandschuster.com.

The Simon & Schuster Speakers Bureau can bring authors to your live event. For more information or to book an event contact the Simon & Schuster Speakers Bureau at 1-866-248-3049 or visit our website at www.simonspeakers.com.

Interior design by Carly Loman

Manufactured in the United States of America

1 3 5 7 9 10 8 6 4 2

Library of Congress Control Number: 2025945130

ISBN 978-1-6680-1295-6
ISBN 978-1-6680-1297-0 (ebook)

To Kathy, James, and Ava
(and Patches, too)

CONTENTS

	Prologue	1
ONE	The Schmattes Factory	15
TWO	Spun from a Different Orbit	35
THREE	The Silicon Valley Start-up with a Chip on Its Shoulder	59
FOUR	Seeing Stones and Prying Eyes	89
FIVE	The Commercial Break	111
SIX	The War Against the Army	127
SEVEN	The Peter Problem	147
EIGHT	Proof of Concept	181
NINE	The Batshit-Crazy CEO	213
TEN	A Survival Situation	233
ELEVEN	The Rebels Win	255
	Epilogue	277
	Acknowledgments	291

PROLOGUE

MAKING THE WORLD SAFE FOR HIMSELF

"There must be a meth lab around here."

Alex Karp was out for a jog. It was a Tuesday afternoon in September 2021, and while it was still warm in northern New Hampshire, there was a hint of autumn in the air—a slight chill to the sun. Karp, dressed in biking shorts and a T-shirt, was moving at a very slow clip along the road that abutted his property. The gentle pace was deliberate, part of a conditioning regimen prescribed by the former Norwegian commandos who served as his bodyguards and who also helped him train for cross-country skiing, a sport that he pursued obsessively. Before his run, Karp had done a tai chi session with his longtime instructor, Grandmaster Yang Yang, who was visiting from New York, and had eaten a quick lunch of pretzels slathered with peanut butter.

Karp was at the base of a hill when a beat-up car appeared in front of him. It was traveling at a crawl, too, as if the driver were lost or looking for a difficult-to-find address. A man was behind the wheel and a woman was in the front passenger seat. They appeared to be in their late twenties or early thirties, and their gaunt faces suggested hard living. Karp was in the business of noticing things: he ran a company whose work revolved around pattern recognition, and he had recently observed a couple of mystery cars driving through the sparsely populated neighborhood, which prompted him to make the comment about the meth lab. As the car drew closer, Karp raised his hand to say hello. The couple didn't respond but just eyed him warily.

The suspicion was understandable: here they were, on a twisting country lane three miles from the nearest town and maybe an hour south of the Canadian border, and suddenly in front of them was a wiry man with a huge knot of salt-and-pepper hair trotting down the middle of the street, followed by some burly guys on bicycles, and trailed by a black Chevy Suburban with tinted windows. While Karp had reason to wonder why they were there, they had even more reason to wonder about him and his entourage. Narcs laying a trap? Someone in witness protection? A drug lord? If the couple was indeed en route to making an illicit purchase, the curious encounter was doubtless unnerving. Had they known Karp's true identity, they might have floored the accelerator. Instead, though, they drove by him cautiously, as if to signal that they didn't want trouble.

With the car behind him, Karp continued his run. Ambling along, he talked about the $180,000 donation that he had recently made to a local hermit known as "River Dave," whose cabin had burned down. It was an act of kindness, but also a gesture of solidarity, one introvert to another. The gift drew national headlines. Some articles noted that Karp had been awarded a compensation package worth $1.1 billion in 2020, making him the highest-paid chief executive officer of a publicly traded company that year.

After pausing for a moment to watch some foxes darting across the road, Karp segued into a discussion about the prospect of war with China and the importance of maintaining America's dominance in computer software. This jag led to a brief diatribe against the "wokeness" of Silicon Valley and what he saw as the tech industry's indefensible ambivalence about working with the U.S. military. And as was often the case, the subject of wokeness brought the conversation around to our alma mater, Haverford College, its failure to invite him to speak on campus, and what he considered its lackluster effort to cultivate him as a potential donor, which he found both insulting and insane.

After maybe a half hour of running, Karp came to an intersection that marked the end of his route. He toweled off, took a sip of water, and climbed into the front passenger seat of the Suburban. (Karp had never learned to drive.) During the short ride back to his house, he ripped into Facebook, calling it a "parasitic business," and confided that its chairman and chief executive officer, Mark Zuckerberg, had recently called their mutual friend Peter Thiel to complain about Karp's broadsides against his company. Karp's five-hundred-acre property sat on a gently sloping hillside. His home, surrounded by pine and birch trees, offered a commanding view of the White Mountains. Karp walked inside, where he was met by Günter, one of four Austrians who were his executive assistants. The others were Gabriel, Hermann, and Agnes. A Swiss, Martin, was also part of his personal staff. Karp and Günter spoke briefly, in German; he conversed with his assistants almost exclusively in German. Several members of Karp's security detail, which included five Norwegians, a handful of Americans, a couple of Austrians, an Irishman, and a Scot, were eating a late lunch at the kitchen table. It was a slightly surreal scene that called to mind a Bond villain's lair. However, Karp's company worked with British intelligence, not against it. Plus, the mezuzah on the front door wasn't something you were likely to see in a Bond flick.

Karp suggested going to the shooting range in his backyard to take target practice, but sensing my lack of enthusiasm, he dropped the idea. As we walked into the living room, he put his phone into a Faraday cage and asked me to do the same. "The Chinese would be crazy not to try to listen to my calls," he explained. A lifelong bachelor now in his mid-fifties, Karp owned multiple homes in the United States and Europe. The New Hampshire house was his primary residence. He had a sentimental attachment to northern New England (he also owned a place in Vermont); he had spent childhood summers there, when his parents were still together, before the acrimonious divorce that upended his life for a time.

The home was sparsely furnished; it had a couch and some chairs, but otherwise felt unoccupied. This was a reflection of Karp's asceticism and also his peripatetic schedule; before Covid-19 grounded him, he spent roughly three hundred days a year on the road and rarely stayed in the same place for more than a night or two. He insisted that his job required all the travel, but some of his colleagues were skeptical. "The guy's clearly running from something," one said with a laugh. Books were scattered around the house. A German-language biography of Albert Einstein lay on the dining room table, alongside a set of John le Carré novels. That might have seemed like a peculiar juxtaposition, but in a home owned by Alex Karp, it had a certain logic.

Karp was the chief executive officer of Palantir Technologies, a company that specialized in data analytics. Named after the seeing stones in J. R. R. Tolkien's *Lord of the Rings*, Palantir built software that could sift through enormous quantities of data to identify connections and trends that might take human analysts days, weeks, or even months to find. It was started after 9/11 for the purpose of helping the American government combat terrorism and was financed in part by In-Q-Tel, the CIA's venture capital arm. A number of clandestine services now used Palantir, including the Mossad. Speculation that its technology had played a part in the 2011 raid that killed Osama bin Laden had conferred on Palantir an enduring mystique.

The company's work, however, was not limited to counterterrorism. All six branches of the U.S. military had deployed its technology. More than three dozen federal agencies were Palantir clients, among them the FBI, the IRS, and the National Institutes of Health, or NIH. Major corporations like BP, the energy giant, used Palantir to make sense of the flood tide of data that they generated every day. Although Palantir was a relatively small company, with only around four thousand employees, its reach was tentacular. From terrorism to climate change to famine to immigration to human trafficking to financial fraud to the future of warfare, Palantir was at the nexus of the most consequential issues of the twenty-first century, a point illustrated vividly during the pandemic, when over a dozen countries utilized the company's software to try to track and contain the novel coronavirus. The United States and Britain also turned to Palantir for help with distributing vaccines.

But even as the company's business evolved, its core mission remained unchanged: according to Karp, Palantir existed to defend the West (a mandate that was known internally as "saving the Shire," a nod to Palantir's literary roots; company management was also fond of referring to employees as "hobbits"). The explicitly ideological agenda made Palantir an oddity in the corporate world. From the start, it refused to do business in China and Russia because it saw both countries as adversarial. This decision was ultimately vindicated, but in the mid-2000s it struck some potential investors as bizarre: Why would any company forswear China's booming market? At Palantir, however, the pursuit of profitability—a goal that would prove frustratingly elusive—was always subordinate to what Karp and his colleagues saw as their higher purpose: making Palantir a sword and shield for America and for the West more broadly.

Palantir seemed especially anomalous in Silicon Valley, which was dominated by companies selling consumer products and services. But the Palantirians took pride in being different; instead of making gadgets and games, they believed they were on the front line of a battle to preserve America's way of life. And although the company was based in Palo Alto, Karp and his colleagues bore a deep animus to the Valley and its culture—Facebook became an object of particular scorn—and drew additional motivation from their own sense of estrangement. (In 2020, Palantir formally broke with the Valley by relocating its headquarters to Denver.)

Karp, certainly, was an outlier in the tech industry. He had no training in computer science or business, and with his personal background, he was an improbable choice to lead a company that aimed to become the software supplier of choice for the intelligence community. A biracial Jew raised in a staunchly left-wing household, Karp majored in philosophy at Haverford. He went on to earn a law degree from Stanford University and a doctorate in social theory from Germany's Goethe University Frankfurt, where for a time his mentor was Jürgen Habermas, perhaps Europe's most acclaimed living philosopher. That Karp was dyslexic made his scholarly achievements especially impressive.

But he had no desire to pursue a career in academia, and when Peter Thiel, a law school classmate who had cofounded PayPal, asked Karp in 2004 if he would be interested in joining a start-up that was building software to fight terrorism, he jumped at the opportunity. Not long thereafter, Karp became Palantir's CEO. His academic credentials, coupled with his distinctive appearance and manner, made him a compelling front man for a company like Palantir. So did his political views: for a time, he claimed to be a neo-socialist, which seemed unusual for someone working at the intersection of technology and national security. It also provided an intriguing contrast with Thiel, who was a libertarian (and who later would gravitate to the far right). And although some Silicon Valley venture capitalists initially snubbed Palantir, Karp turned out to be a convincing advocate for his company.

He pitched Palantir as if his life depended on it. In his mind, it did. From the time that he was a child, Karp had been consumed with a feeling of vulnerability—he was Jewish and black in a world that seemed implacably hostile to Jews and blacks. In addition, he had a learning disability. He believed that only in a society that afforded robust protections to minorities and other at-risk groups could someone like him survive and prosper. "My biggest fear is fascism," he said during one of our first conversations, in 2019. At that time, he unambiguously believed that defending liberal democracy was synonymous with defending the West, and for him, Palantir's mission was personal: Palantir was making the world safer for Alex Karp. And to an uncanny degree, the company was a reflection of him: of his habits and quirks, of the experiences that had shaped him, and above all, of his bleak worldview and the anxieties that weighed on him. His sense of foreboding, he said, "propels a lot of decisions for this company."

Karp's commitment to Palantir was absolute, a point he emphasized in a 2013 interview with *Forbes*. "The only time I'm not thinking about Palantir is when I'm swimming, practicing Qigong, or during sexual activity," he told the magazine. (Swimming was his main sport back then.) Karp rarely took a day off, and on most weeknights he ate dinner at his desk. He had no children but was in long-term, concurrent relationships with two women, an arrangement that worked in part because he was "geographically monogamous," as one colleague felicitously put it (this person also said that both women were "age-appropriate"). When Karp wasn't tending to business, he could often be found skiing. Most of his homes were in remote locations and were chosen for their proximity to cross-country skiing trails. If time permitted, he skied twelve to fifteen miles per day. But according to Karp, even his skiing was in service to Palantir: he believed that only someone conditioned like an elite athlete could maintain a schedule as grueling as his.

Under Karp, Palantir became a dominant force in data analytics, a multibillion-dollar enterprise with swank offices around the world and an aura of intrigue—meticulously cultivated—that set it apart even in the frenzied atmosphere of Silicon Valley. Validation—for Palantir, for Karp—came in 2020, when the company, after years of putting off an IPO, went public. The successful stock market listing affirmed Palantir's viability and officially made Karp a billionaire. Apart from buying additional homes (and, eventually, his own private jet), the wealth didn't change his lifestyle, and Karp professed to be indifferent to his net worth, although not everyone in his orbit was persuaded of that. "He's probably more financially motivated than he thinks, and I am less financially motivated than people think," Thiel said. But Karp did enjoy his enhanced stature. He was now a center of attention at events like the World Economic Forum, which was held each year in Davos, Switzerland. Heads of state were eager to hear his thoughts, and he was in ever-greater demand as a speaker. Except at Haverford.

The college's reluctance to embrace Karp was not surprising, though. Palantir was controversial. Its software could enable mass surveillance, and the company's ties to the intelligence community and law enforcement were a source of acute concern to civil libertarians and privacy advocates. The first Trump presidency had also made Palantir toxic in the eyes of many observers. The company was implicated in the Cambridge Analytica scandal, in which Facebook data was surreptitiously used to try to manipulate millions of Americans into voting for Donald Trump in 2016. An even bigger flash point was Palantir's work with U.S. Immigration and Customs Enforcement, or ICE. When Trump launched his immigration crackdown, Palantir was accused of abetting racist and inhumane policies. That Thiel had been one of Trump's most prominent supporters added to the furor.

Protests were held outside the company's offices, as well as in front of Karp's Palo Alto home, and Palantir found itself no longer welcome on some college campuses—including, apparently, our alma mater's. The Trump years, in addition to being a public relations fiasco for Palantir, exposed an uncomfortable truth: the company's technology would be a powerful weapon in the hands of an authoritarian regime.

But except for the Haverford part, all that was just an unpleasant memory when I visited Karp in New Hampshire in September 2021. I went there to discuss my interest in writing a book about him and Palantir. The previous year, I had published a story about Palantir in *The New York Times Magazine*. Karp and I didn't know each other until I was assigned the *Times Magazine* piece. We were in the same class at Haverford but somehow managed never to exchange a word, which seemed hard to believe given that the school had fewer than 1,500 students. We first met in April 2019, when I went to Palantir's New York office for an off-the-record conversation with him (perhaps hoping to rekindle the college spirit, or something approximating it, he drank a nonalcoholic beer while we talked). In the months that followed, we met again in New York, as well as in Washington, Paris, and Vermont. We developed a good rapport; Karp seemed comfortable talking to me and spoke candidly about Palantir and himself.

The article, which was published in October 2020, a few weeks after Palantir went public, was around nine thousand words. Even so, I felt that there was more to say. Karp was a sui generis figure on the business scene, and Palantir was arguably the most interesting company in the world—and possibly also one of the most dangerous. Its technology had the potential to help shape the balance of power in the twenty-first century and to alter the relationship between the individual and the state. Palantir was a window into the panoptic future that had now arrived, and one could not begin to understand the company without understanding the idiosyncratic person at its helm.

Karp was receptive to the book idea. He said that he figured a book would be written about Palantir and that it made sense to cooperate with an author he knew and liked. What he didn't say, but what was certainly true, was that he *wanted* to be the subject of a book. Although Karp was Palantir's CEO, the press often referred to the company as "Peter Thiel's Palantir." That was especially the case during the first Trump administration, when Thiel's name was clickbait. But while Thiel had conceived the idea for Palantir and served as its chairman of the board, he had never played a role in its day-to-day operations. In the wake of Palantir's public listing, Karp wanted to be recognized as the chief architect of the company's success, and this was his principal motive for agreeing to cooperate with me.

Karp was generous with his time and thoughts. Many of our conversations were in person, usually in New York or Washington. In addition, we spoke numerous times by video and phone. I had a standing offer to travel with him on his private jet, but I decided from the outset that it would be better not to. I feared it would undermine the integrity of the book. I also didn't want to fly with him because I worried that my presence on the plane would start to feel burdensome. It was hard to hold Karp's attention. Many of his colleagues assumed that he had ADHD. During meetings, he often played with a Rubik's Cube, and if not that, he would fidget with something else. If a conversation took place standing up, he would practice tai chi moves while listening or talking. Normally, he could give me thirty to forty-five minutes of productive conversation before he started to drift.

Although Karp was intensely private, he understood that it would be hard to write a book about him without input from those who know him best. His brother, Ben, who lives in Japan, spoke with me frequently and shared lots of memories and insights. I also interviewed Karp's mother. His father was in declining health and unavailable. There were some limits to Karp's cooperation: he refused, for instance, to put me in touch with the women with whom he is involved. I met one of them anyway, but only by chance. She is American. His other ongoing relationship is with a woman in Europe; he has been with her for more than two decades. Palantir is a complicated company, and Karp has a complicated existence.

When I started working on the book, Joe Biden was in the White House, demonstrators were no longer congregating outside Palantir's offices, the worst of the pandemic seemed over, and I did wonder if we were entering a period that would be uneventful for Karp and the company. But just weeks into my reporting, Russia invaded Ukraine, a conflict in which Palantir's technology would play a central role. Dramatic advances in machine-learning capabilities, underscored by the debut in November 2022 of ChatGPT, heralded the dawn of the AI revolution, and on both the military and commercial side, Palantir was at its vanguard. Then came October 7, the Hamas attack that left 1,200 Israelis dead. This tragedy was one of the defining events of Karp's career and an epochal moment for Palantir—it was the war on terrorism anew, in a world that now felt very unsafe for Jews, very unsafe for Alex Karp. All the major themes of Karp's life—his sense of vulnerability, his deep attachment to his Jewish heritage (in contrast to his seeming ambivalence about being part black), his disdain for the identarian left and for academia—converged around this one issue, and listening to him in the days and weeks following the massacre was especially revealing.

The slaughter in Israel also cemented his political metamorphosis. Although he had long ago stopped describing himself as a neo-socialist, he still claimed to be progressive when I first met him, and on certain issues, such as immigration, he expressed opinions that seemed consistent with a liberal worldview (at the same time, though, he opposed affirmative action and was a staunch supporter of the Second Amendment). But during Biden's presidency, it was hard not to notice that he seldom had a good word to say about the Democratic Party and was often contemptuous of it. By contrast, he went out of his way to praise Republicans—even Trump. For a time, I assumed this was just a contrarian reflex on his part, or a way of telegraphing an independent spirit. But at a certain point, it became clear that he was moving to the right, and the October 7 pogrom and the eruption of anti-Israel protests at colleges and universities led him to decisively break with the Democrats.

In the course of my reporting, I was also able to observe the transformation of Karp's public image. To the extent that he had attracted notice in the past, he was primarily regarded as an eccentric, an oddball. For a long time, he embraced that persona, proudly referring to himself as "the batshit-crazy CEO." But impressions of him began to change as a result of Ukraine, AI, and Israel. He was outspoken about all three issues and had interesting and often provocative things to say. He also demonstrated physical courage: in May 2022, three months into the war, he traveled to Kyiv to meet with Ukrainian President Volodymyr Zelensky. Karp now projected gravitas, a perception amplified by what seemed to be the unseriousness of other major figures in the tech world. While Karp was visiting conflict zones and talking about matters of war and peace, Mark Zuckerberg and Elon Musk were planning to face off in a cage match.

And yet, even as his stature and influence grew, Karp was incapable of casting aside his grievances. He was rarely more animated than when lashing out at Wall Street or Silicon Valley. I found this puzzling. His company was thriving, he was a billionaire; by any measure, he had "won." So why couldn't he just let it go? I eventually came to realize that he needed enemies. The doubters and the haters, real and imagined, gave him added motivation and were part of the larger narrative that Karp had constructed about himself and Palantir: that they were perennial outsiders, always the barbarians at the gate.

Karp and the company rode that rebellious image to great effect, but Palantir's success accelerated dramatically while I was working on the book. The company's struggle for profitability had been a source of exasperation for Palantir investors, not least Thiel. But in late 2022, after almost twenty years in business, the company finally notched a profit, and that proved to be an inflection point. Palantir was profitable every quarter thereafter, and on the back of the generative AI boom, its revenue growth surged. In September 2024, Palantir was added to the S&P 500, which Karp regarded as the company's most significant milestone yet. Its stock had more than doubled since the start of the year and was still rising. On November 4, Palantir released another stellar earnings report, and it gained almost $10 per share, closing above $50 for the first time.

Little more than twenty-four hours later, Donald Trump was elected president again. His signature issue was his promise of an even harsher immigration crackdown that would potentially see millions of people expelled from the United States. Trump's campaign was notable for its violent rhetoric, language that many scholars (and voters) regarded as fascistic. Two former generals who had served under Trump during his first administration, John Kelly and Mark Milley, publicly called Trump a fascist. Trump plainly had little regard for the rule of law and constitutional norms, a fact laid bare by his attempt to overturn the 2020 election. With Trump restored to power, it appeared that authoritarianism had triumphed in the United States and that Palantir, which Karp had always touted as a bulwark of the liberal international order, would henceforth be serving the agenda of a president who was contemptuous of America's political tradition, disdainful of the Western alliance, and strangely enamored of some of the world's most brutal tyrants.

ONE

THE SCHMATTES FACTORY

On April 14, 2021, President Joe Biden announced that he would withdraw the last remaining U.S. troops from Afghanistan no later than September 11 of that year, a date that would mark the twentieth anniversary of the terrorist attack that led to America's long military engagement there. Biden had been assured by the U.S. intelligence community that Afghan security forces would be able to hold off a resurgent Taliban long enough to allow for an orderly evacuation by the United States and its allies. Biden had campaigned for the presidency on a promise to end the "forever war" in Afghanistan, and now, barely four months after taking office, he had decided to make good on that pledge.

However, the intelligence assessments were too optimistic. By midsummer, Afghanistan's military had all but collapsed, its government was teetering, and the Taliban had captured large swaths of the country and were closing in on the capital, Kabul. In July, in response to the deteriorating situation, Biden moved up the date for the withdrawal of the last U.S. troops to August 31. Most of the 2,500 American servicemen who had been in Afghanistan when Biden initially announced the drawdown had already left the country, but several hundred remained. In addition, hundreds of Western diplomats and aid workers, as well as tens of thousands of Afghans who had assisted the United States and its coalition partners, were still trying to get out and were facing increasingly perilous circumstances. On August 13, Biden said that he was immediately dispatching three thousand additional American troops to Kabul to help with what would now be a very hasty and dangerous evacuation of noncombatants.

The operation was going to involve hundreds of aircraft and thousands of flights. The Pentagon also had to send additional Humvees and other support vehicles to Kabul, along with food and water for U.S. service members and the civilians being airlifted out of Afghanistan. At the same time, military bases in Europe and the Middle East had to be readied for the arrival of thousands of refugees, which meant ensuring that each location had adequate supplies of food, water, cots, porta potties, and other essentials. On top of that, every Afghan citizen seeking to resettle in the United States was going to have to be screened in order to prevent any known or suspected terrorists from being allowed into the country. Compounding the logistical challenge, a lot of information that American military planners needed to conduct the evacuation was siloed in different databases that they couldn't readily access. The mission was in jeopardy before it even started.

A day after Biden announced that he was sending additional troops to Afghanistan, the Pentagon reached out to Palantir for help. Since 2018, the Army had used Palantir's software to manage personnel and supplies; the system, which the military called Vantage, integrated more than 150 databases and over thirty thousand datasets, giving the Army a kaleidoscopic view of its own preparedness at any given moment. Now the Joint Chiefs of Staff wanted to use Vantage for the evacuation. The message from the Defense Department conveyed a sense of acute urgency. Mitchell Skiles, who oversaw Palantir's work with the Army, says that he and his colleagues were told that the goal was simply "to get the hell out while saving as many lives as possible." Within hours of receiving the call, Skiles and a team of Palantirians had embedded with the Joint Staff. Soon, around 150 Palantir engineers were contributing to the effort. Most were based in the United States, but some were overseas, and because of the different time zones, Palantir was able to provide round-the-clock support to the Pentagon.

Through Vantage, the company's engineers quickly pulled in and merged data from every branch of the military and every civilian agency that was involved in the evacuation, ranging from the United States Transportation Command, or Transcom, which oversees all American military transportation, to the State Department to Customs and Border Patrol, or CBP. In a matter of days, the Palantirians built a fully integrated data ecosystem for the Joint Staff, which could now see maintenance records to ensure that planes and support vehicles were actually operational; could easily locate supplies and match them with outbound flights; and could quickly verify how many evacuees were aboard every flight leaving Kabul. The Palantirians drew information from existing databases and also took in data from ad hoc sources: one data stream that they plugged into Vantage was a group chat among U.S. troops on the ground at Kabul's airport. Along the way, Palantir's software helped identify problems large and small. At one point, it flagged an issue with an American soldier who was about to leave for Afghanistan: he was only seventeen years old, and under U.S. law, a person had to be eighteen or older to serve in a conflict zone.

Palantir's technology also played a critical role in the effort to secure the airport in Kabul. That task fell to the Army's 82nd Airborne Division, under the command of Major General Chris Donahue. By the time the 82nd Airborne arrived in Kabul,

Afghanistan's president had fled the country, the government had collapsed, the Taliban had entered the capital, and thousands of desperate Afghans had converged on the airport. To help ensure that the evacuation could proceed unimpeded by the Taliban or by terrorist attacks, Donahue and his troops were equipped with several battlefield intelligence tools that ran on Palantir's software. The same software was also used on the other end, to help conduct background checks on refugees as they arrived in the United States. Palantir's technology became the nerve center for the entire operation.

The Pentagon's decision to enlist Palantir's help was testament to the quality of the company's products as well as the aptitude of its engineers. But it also spoke to a deeper truth: even organizations as well funded and seemingly sophisticated as the U.S. military often struggle to harness their own data. One of the axioms of this information-soaked age is that data can lead to better decision-making in almost every sphere of human activity—from the operating room to the assembly line to the battlefield to the baseball diamond. Fifteen years before the Afghan airlift, in 2006, a British mathematician and entrepreneur named Clive Humby gave a speech in London in which he boldly declared that "data is the new oil." By this, he meant that data would henceforth be the fuel driving economic growth and material progress. His clever formulation became the catchphrase of the Big Data revolution. But during that same speech, Humby extended the oil analogy to make another critical point: like crude oil, data needs refining in order to be of real value.

Raw data can be challenging to work with. It is often messy and riddled with mistakes—a misspelled name, an extra zero erroneously attached to a number, outdated or duplicate records. Data also comes in a wide variety of forms. It can be structured (charts, spreadsheets, phone logs) or unstructured (text messages, photographs, Instagram posts). Data can be coded in different languages, such as Python or Java. A further complication is that organizations routinely store data in multiple databases that aren't linked—and the larger the organization, the more data silos it is apt to have. Then there is the sheer volume of data that is generated now via phones, watches, trains, planes, satellites, automobiles, traffic lights, toasters, even toilets. It is estimated that the world will have produced 180 zettabytes of data in 2025, a tenfold increase from a decade earlier. A zettabyte is equivalent to one sextillion bytes, which is ... a lot.

Palantir's software helps create order out of all this chaos. It is a tool for merging, managing, and analyzing large quantities of data. Palantir does not collect data on behalf of its clients, nor does it store or sell data; its technology simply enables organizations to make better use of their own data. For a number of years, Palantir had two software platforms. One, called Gotham, was for the intelligence community and the military. The other, Metropolis, was mainly for financial institutions. But Palantir discontinued Metropolis in the mid-2010s and replaced it with a system called Foundry, which was geared to a broader spectrum of commercial users. Foundry proved to be so effective that the company soon began selling it to government agencies and the military, too. Now Foundry is Palantir's flagship offering, and Gotham is a suite of applications that sits on top of it. Foundry was used in the Afghan airlift and today anchors all of Palantir's work. There are rival products on the market, but most Palantir customers seem to think that the company's software is peerless (and worth the premium that it charges).

As Palantirians readily acknowledge, data integration is a vital but banal task. "It's plumbing work, basically," says Louis Mosley, who runs Palantir's London office. There is something to the analogy. Data is fed into Palantir's software through virtual pipelines (clients can build the pipelines themselves using Palantir's technology, or Palantir engineers can do it for them). The software cleans up and standardizes the data and turns it into a composite dataset. Customers run queries to obtain answers. They enter a name, a place, or an event, and they specify how they wish to see the results. It can be via tables, timelines, graphs, heat maps, histograms, spider diagrams, geospatial analysis, or artificial intelligence models. But the software then goes a step beyond and facilitates actual decision-making (something that distinguishes it from competitors): customers can use Palantir to run simulations, build new workflows, and otherwise act on the insights derived from their data.

Palantir's software is also known for its adaptability. It can be customized to reflect the particular needs and habits of mind that guide a corporation or a government agency, can easily absorb new sources of data, and can be applied to an astonishingly broad range of issues. Foundry has been used by the U.S. Centers for Disease Control and Prevention (CDC) to track foodborne illnesses; by the German pharmaceutical company Merck KGaA to accelerate the development of new drugs; by Airbus to troubleshoot production bottlenecks and to collate and analyze data generated by sensors on nearly every commercial Airbus plane in service; by the U.S. Securities and Exchange Commission (SEC) to combat insider trading; by Tampa General Hospital to optimize staffing levels and schedules; by the World Food Programme (WFP) to manage supplies and deliveries; and by the Italian automaker Ferrari to improve the performance of its Formula 1 race cars.

But counterterrorism and defense remain the cornerstone of Palantir's business. Much of this work necessarily takes place out of public view (it was never reported, for instance, that Palantir's software was used to help safeguard the 2024 Paris Olympics). Over the years, Karp has suggested that Palantir's impact in the war on terrorism was vast and occasionally decisive. During one of our conversations in 2019, he said Palantir had helped thwart several attacks in Europe that, had they succeeded, would have caused death and destruction on a scale that would inevitably have brought the far right to power in a number of places. Karp was given to dramatic proclamations, and he shared this nugget with typical brio. "I believe that Western civilization has rested on our somewhat small shoulders a couple of times in the last fifteen years," he said, adding that Palantir was the reason why people weren't "goose-stepping" through European capitals. But such claims, offered without proof, invited skepticism.

Even so, it is true that Palantir frequently operates in the background and often in fraught situations where unambiguously positive outcomes are not possible or cannot mask larger failures. That proved to be the case with the Afghanistan airlift. It ended up being the largest evacuation of noncombatants in U.S. history: over the course of seventeen days, some eight hundred aircraft were used to transport nearly 125,000 people. On average, 7,500 people were put on flights each day, and planes were taking off almost every half hour. By those measures, it was a formidable achievement, and especially impressive given the speed with which the mission was thrown together and the hurdles that the military faced in executing it. There was no way of knowing how many lives were saved, but the number was surely not a small one. At least three babies were born aboard flights out of Afghanistan; U.S. military personnel assisted with the deliveries.

However, the evacuation was ultimately marred by a pair of tragedies. On August 26, a suicide bomber killed more than 180 people at a section of Kabul's airport known as Abbey Gate, including thirteen American soldiers. Three days later, the U.S. military launched a drone strike that mistakenly claimed the lives of ten innocent Afghans, including seven children. These incidents, coupled with the scenes of chaos and desperation at the airport, created a widespread perception that the operation had been a fiasco. The success of the airlift was also overshadowed by the fact that many Afghans who had hoped to leave were unable to, and even more so by the harsh reality that the two-decade-long effort to establish stability and democratic rule in Afghanistan had failed. The war on terrorism had given rise to Palantir; it seemed somehow fitting that Palantir played a critical role in bringing one part of that war to an end, albeit with an ignominious conclusion. But as Karp once put it, "Palantir is the convergence of software and difficult positions."

"Welcome to the schmattes factory."

Karp was strolling down a corridor of Palantir's Washington office, wearing his usual work attire: a T-shirt, ski pants, and espadrilles. He also had on a baseball cap that bore the logo of an elite Norwegian cross-country skiing team called Team Veidekke Vest. Karp appeared to have an abundant supply of its gear, and was often photographed in it. The skiing apparel was his sartorial flourish—his answer to Steve Jobs's black turtleneck and Mark Zuckerberg's hoodie. However, his access to Team Veidekke Vest's clothing was a source of curiosity, and some consternation, in Norway. Karp wasn't a member of the team, nor did Palantir have any involvement with it. The Norwegian Broadcasting Corporation, or NRK, looked into the matter and discovered that a member of the team, whom it didn't identify, had supplied Karp with the clothes (what NRK didn't report was that this person had been training Karp on a freelance basis). A spokesman for Veidekke, the Scandinavian construction conglomerate that had sponsored the team, expressed displeasure with Karp. "It's just completely wrong when he appears to be an employee, a close associate, or someone sponsored by Veidekke," he said.

Karp's line about the schmattes factory was his way of greeting me, although he usually acknowledged my presence by declaiming, "Oh, my biographer is here. Be careful," a comment directed at whoever was within earshot. Karp walked like someone who spent a lot of time on skis: he had a kind of gliding gait and rolled his shoulders as if he were pushing through snow. As he made his way around, he stopped to chat with employees. Most of them were young, and a few looked like they were barely out of high school. But even though Karp was the boss, no necks stiffened as he approached. His colleagues addressed him as "Dr. Karp," and some would get a little starry-eyed when he spoke to them. However, they never seemed nervous in his presence. Karp would ask what they were working on and if they were getting adequate support from management. He sometimes broached other topics. He once decided to prove to me that Haverford was an institution in decline by asking two Palantirians if they had ever heard of our alma mater. Both confessed that they had not. Karp nodded glumly. "It won't even be a top-fifty school in a couple of years," he said.

Karp liked to entertain his colleagues and was often quite funny, though his jokes and quips could skirt the edge of propriety. Introducing me to one of his Norwegian bodyguards, he said loudly, "Do you know we are the first Jews he's ever seen?" He compared himself to Larry David and once suggested that his comic stylings might be called "Karp Your Enthusiasm." His desire to amuse the people around him was genuine, but he said that it also served a purpose: humor was a way of reaching the subconscious, and part of his job was to make sure that every employee's subconscious was aligned with Palantir's goals. "Freud's thesis is that the primary process, which is your subconscious, dictates to the secondary process, the conscious, how you see the world," Karp explained. "If you are dealing with a lot of people who have learned things that aren't true, like about how an organization should work, you need to change that so that your organization actually works, which means you have to get through to the primary process, and one thing that works pretty well is humor."

Karp tended to speak in an elliptical, discursive manner. Once, while hanging for a few minutes from a pull-up bar located outside his New York office, he gave an impromptu talk to a group of Palantirians about features and bugs. His basic point, to the extent it could be discerned, was that features were not always features but that bugs weren't always features, either, and that counterintuitive thinking was valuable except when it wasn't. However, it was hard to follow his train of thought because he quickly digressed into a discussion about his unhappily married friends, divorce lawyers, and prenuptial agreements. It was an orgy of free association but kind of entertaining, which was probably the real point. Karp was always energetic and upbeat around the office. He was trying to set a mood. Long hours were obligatory at Palantir, and while the perks were sweet (breakfast, lunch, and dinner Monday–Friday, beers in the fridge, snacks galore, dogs welcome), Karp also wanted it to be fun. He sometimes led tai chi classes for employees.

Like other Silicon Valley moguls, Karp seemed not quite of this world—there was an awkwardness to him, something a little off-center. I once sat with him in his office as he ate lunch. At the time, he had a cupcake infatuation, but he had an unusual way of consuming them: he would decapitate the cupcakes and eat only the tops—the icing was what he really wanted—leaving the cake part untouched. His lunch on that afternoon included two cupcakes. One was apparently meant for me, but Karp didn't know that and scarfed both of them. Not quite satiated, he stood up and started banging on the glass wall that looked out on the rest of the office. "Can I get more cupcakes?" he shouted, to no one in particular. An assistant quickly appeared at the door with several more cupcakes, which Karp proceeded to cut in half and eat.

But Karp also differed from his fellow tech barons in some important ways, and not just because of his background in the humanities. He appeared to have a high degree of emotional intelligence and was very attuned to the needs, interests, and desires of those around him. "Reading a room—that's Alex's superpower," says Ward Breeze, a classmate of ours at Haverford who was close to Karp and later became one of his attorneys. That was true when it came to winning over potential clients, and it was especially true in his dealings with Palantir employees. He had lieutenants who kept him apprised of personnel issues and office dramas, but he also had a keen ear for what was happening outside his door and seemed to genuinely care about the people who worked for him.

And he cared deeply about what they thought of him. At the World Economic Forum in Davos, Switzerland, in 2022, he was interviewed by CNBC's Andrew Ross Sorkin. CNBC loved having Karp as a guest; in contrast to most other CEOs, he was reliably unfiltered, thanks in part to his practice of getting hopped-up on Mexican Coke beforehand. Booking Karp almost always guaranteed headlines. I was with Karp in Davos, and as we walked to the CNBC set, he said he never got nervous before going on television but did feel a very specific kind of pressure: "I just don't ever want to say anything that would embarrass Palantirians." The interview with Sorkin was typical Karp—he was by turns funny, caustic (he teed off, as always, on Wall Street analysts), and apocalyptic about the state of the world (this was three months after Russia invaded Ukraine, and Karp suggested that there was a 20–30 percent chance that Moscow would use a nuclear weapon in the conflict). With the cameras still rolling, Sorkin had Karp teach him several tai chi moves. CNBC showed clips of the interview throughout the day. One aired while Karp and a number of Palantir employees were milling around the pavilion that the company had rented. Everyone turned to face the television except Karp: he was watching his colleagues watching him. As they laughed at his comments, he remained expressionless, just observing. It was clear that their verdict mattered a lot to him.

Karp often boasted of Palantir's meritocratic culture—he insisted that the company hired people strictly on the basis of qualifications. This wasn't entirely true: Palantir had its share of nepo hires, employees who had leveraged connections of one sort or another to get jobs there. Unsurprisingly, Ivy League universities and other comparably prestigious schools were overrepresented (except for Haverford: Karp insisted he wasn't blackballing our alma mater, but he was Palantir's lone Haverford grad). The company's payroll also included people with impressive achievements outside the classroom. A number of military veterans worked at Palantir. So did a former Olympian and a current astronaut.

Karp was good to those who worked for him. He was not one to scream or threaten, nor did he ever publicly upbraid or humiliate people. This was a reflection of his temperament, but also the fact that Palantirians were his de facto family, and he treated them as such (perhaps too much so: it occasionally felt as if he infantilized his colleagues, and some of them, in turn, seemed like needy children, constantly seeking his attention and approval). If anything, he was sometimes too loyal, a loyalty that could bleed into stubbornness. While Palantir was generally an agreeable place to work, there were a few employees who were not well-liked or trusted by others. But Karp resisted getting rid of them. He could be obstinate that way, although he also just really disliked firing people.

Karp often joked that his job was "managing unmanageable people." He was mainly referring to the nearly two thousand software engineers that the company employed, and he was convinced that he had an almost unique ability to lead them. "Once I stumbled on it, it turned out that I was built for certain things that are really valuable, like managing very complex, sometimes difficult—highly in many cases—technical software engineers. There are just very few people in the world built for that." While Karp was not lacking in self-regard, it was true that he had proven to be very adept at guiding the software engineers who worked at Palantir. One paradoxical reason for this was because he had no computer science training; he didn't try to micromanage them because he couldn't, and his respect for boundaries earned him their goodwill and trust.

This isn't to say that Karp refrained from offering input on technical matters. It was his idea to equip Palantir's software with robust privacy controls, a feature that became one of the company's major selling points. But whenever he shared his thoughts about the work the engineers were doing, he made clear that pushback was welcome.

In this way, too, he had won the confidence and allegiance of Palantir's engineers. Probably the biggest factor, though, was that he genuinely held the engineers in high regard, and not just because they were Palantir's lifeblood. Karp saw them as they saw themselves: as creatives. He recognized that a lot of ingenuity went into their work and that there was a certain beauty to the finished product. He gave the engineers their space and showed them respect. Karp liked to describe Palantir as "an artists' colony," and he really meant it.

In turn, Palantirians were intensely devoted to him. This partly reflected faith in his judgment—a belief, born of experience, that Karp's instincts, on subjects ranging from geopolitics to product development to project assignments, were almost unerring. But his colleagues were also loyal to Karp because working for him was a blast. One company executive, who had more than enough money to retire on, told me he couldn't bring himself to walk away because being around Karp was simply too much fun. "It's just a wild ride," he said with a satisfied smile. When Palantirians met for drinks or dinner, Karp was frequently the topic of conversation. It was often said that the company had a cultish vibe, and there was some truth to this. Certainly, there was a cult of personality around Karp. In the mid-2010s, several French employees hired a cartoonist to produce a graphic novel about Karp (it was never publicly released, but the cartoonist later got a job at Palantir).

Karp kept his private life walled off from even his closest associates at the company, which added to the fascination with him. (It wasn't until 2017 that he told his colleagues that his mother was black, and this was only because a reporter had learned that he was biracial.) He took pleasure in the aura that he enjoyed inside Palantir and was convinced that it helped make the company functional. In a workplace full of headstrong iconoclasts, he was the glue that held everything together. "You need a way you can bond, and my eccentric, nonstandard character is the bonding mechanism," he explained.

But Karp also believed that his managerial acumen was tied

to his dyslexia. From his point of view, the key variable in his life was not his racial or ethnic identity but, rather, dyslexia, which had turned out to be a burden and a blessing, although he liked to put it more colorfully: dyslexia, he said, "fucked me but also gave me wings to fly." Even though Karp ended up doing well in school, his formative years were marked by his struggle with dyslexia. But along the way, he developed certain attributes that would prove useful in business. He couldn't process as many details as other people, so he learned to get by on less information, which he believed gave him an advantage in situations that called for quick, decisive judgments. Dyslexia also taught him the power of collaboration; it is a disability, and those who have it need the help of others. In an environment that required team-building and delegating responsibility, Karp found that he had an intrinsic advantage. Dyslexics, he said, aren't raised on an ethos of self-reliance and tend to excel in situations in which it is important to get people to understand that "maybe if we work together it would be more powerful than if we don't."

As Karp later discovered, a number of well-known CEOs and entrepreneurs were dyslexic. In 2002, *Fortune* ran a cover story titled "The Dyslexic CEO," which drew attention to this phenomenon: the piece noted that Richard Branson, Charles Schwab, Cisco's John Chambers, the celebrated trial attorney David Boies (whose firm represented Palantir in a landmark lawsuit that it brought against the Army), and Paul Orfalea, the founder of the Kinko's chain, all suffered from dyslexia. A few years later, Julie Logan, a professor at the City University of London's Cass Business School, published a study in which she reported that 35 percent of the entrepreneurs she surveyed were dyslexic. "We found that dyslexics who succeed had overcome an awful lot in their lives by developing compensatory skills," Logan told *The New York*

Times. "If you tell your friends and acquaintances that you plan to start a business, you'll hear over and over again, 'It won't work. It can't be done.' But dyslexics are extraordinarily creative about maneuvering their way around problems." She also noted their collaborative skills: "The willingness to delegate authority gives them a significant advantage over nondyslexic entrepreneurs, who tend to view their business as their baby and like to be in total control."

All that said, Karp was hardly a pushover boss. His jocular manner belied a driven and demanding personality. While he understood that employees had lives outside Palantir, he got frustrated if he sensed they were not putting the company first. In the wake of the pandemic, he was often irritated by how it had changed attitudes and mores—the rise of remote work, the desire for greater work-life balance. There was some irony in this (perhaps some hypocrisy, too), in that the way he chose to work and live imposed unusual burdens on the people who answered to him. Employees often had to travel to various Karp homes to see him. During the summer, a steady flow of Palantirians would head to his place in New Hampshire. Sometimes they had to go to Alaska to meet with him at his house near Anchorage. A group once went to Northern Sweden with Karp because the first cross-country trails of the season had opened and he wanted to mix business with his own recreation (they stayed in heated huts while there). "It could be said that this is a company that works around the CEO's lifestyle," one Palantir executive drolly commented.

Karp took up cross-country skiing during his first trip to the World Economic Forum, in 2016. He didn't want to go to Davos—he generally avoided conferences and crowds. As an inducement, a colleague mentioned that Davos was renowned for its cross-country skiing trails. Karp gave it a try while there and was hooked.

According to Karp, as his skiing improved, members of his security detail had trouble keeping up. He also worried that they wouldn't be able to help him out if a heavy snowstorm struck while he was skiing; this was a particular risk if one went off-trail, as he sometimes did. A friend suggested that Karp try to recruit ex–Norwegian soldiers to serve as his skiing companions—they were often very accomplished skiers and were trained to operate in difficult winter weather. Karp was eventually introduced to a former member of the Norwegian special forces, a unit known as the FSK. He agreed to join Karp's security team and became his regular skiing partner. In time, Karp hired several other FSK veterans. He referred to them collectively as "the Norwegians" and also referred to them that way individually. "You should talk to the Norwegian," he would say to me, pointing to whichever handsome Nordic guy happened to be with him at that moment. The Norwegians took turns traveling with Karp; they would rotate in every two or three weeks, although sometimes two of them would overlap.

Karp claimed to have no interest in competing; he said his goal was simply to keep improving and to build a foundation that would allow him to ski into his later years. But he liked to boast of his Nordic skiing prowess. Maybe the happiest I ever saw him was after a Norwegian newspaper published an article that noted the impressive time he had logged on one of the country's most demanding cross-country skiing courses (he was, however, annoyed that the story included an unauthorized photo of the house he owned a few hours from Oslo). The only genuflecting that he seemed to expect from his colleagues was about his skiing: in my presence, he would periodically ask his assistants to attest to his aptitude, and they would dutifully oblige him. His videotaped messages to Palantir shareholders often opened with scenes of him skiing.

During the pandemic, the Norwegians introduced him to the so-called Norwegian method, which combines endurance, interval, and strength training. While Karp was already in good shape, he says that the conditioning program gave him even greater stamina. His VO_2 max—a measure of oxygen uptake during physical exertion and widely regarded as the premier gauge of cardiovascular fitness—became a source of particular pride for him: he now clocked in at around 65, a stellar number, particularly for someone his age. He supplemented his workouts with several dozen vitamins and antioxidants each day. He enjoyed wine but rarely drank. During the Covid lockdowns, he gave up the cupcakes and eliminated all sugar from his diet.

When I first met Karp, in 2019, he was spending most of his time in Europe. Living in Europe agreed with him (especially when snow was on the ground), and Palantir's business there was flourishing; indeed, London had become its largest office, with over five hundred employees. Unlike in the United States, Palantir was not weighed down by controversy in Europe. Its connection to the Cambridge Analytica scandal made headlines in the UK, but the ICE imbroglio didn't seem to register. The CIA link spooked some people, but even that wasn't usually a deterrent to winning business. On both the government and the commercial side, Palantir's European operations were thriving, helped in part by the European media, which found Karp very compelling.

But during the pandemic, Palantir's center of gravity shifted back to America. After winning a bruising legal fight with the Army over its procurement process, Palantir had landed a number of deals with the Pentagon and was becoming a major defense contractor. The critical role that the company played in helping the federal government track Covid-19 and distribute vaccines had burnished its reputation in Washington, and as war raged in Eastern Europe and conflict loomed in Asia, Karp was suddenly in wide demand on Capitol Hill and elsewhere. He was now in Washington so much of the time that he had recently purchased a home in the Maryland suburbs. He bought it for around $8.5 million, which was much more than he was normally willing to spend. For years, he had made it his policy to never pay more than $1 million for a home; he figured that was what the average Palantirian could afford, and he had made it his own limit as a way of affirming the company's democratic ethos. But while $1 million could get you a lot of house in Alaska, it wouldn't get you very far in the Washington area.

Palantir's Washington office was located in Georgetown, close to the Potomac waterfront. It occupied two floors, and on the morning that he greeted me with the "schmattes factory" quip, Karp visited both. On the lower floor, a team working on military projects showed him the latest version of the "augmented reality" glasses they were developing: on the "screen" was a meticulously detailed map of a Taiwanese island, along with real-time drone footage and live data streams. The glasses didn't completely cover your head—you could see your "real" surroundings. But they would give a soldier in the field a 360-degree view of the battlefield literally on the end of his nose. Nearby was the classified room, where top-secret U.S. government documents and other sensitive materials were held, accessible only to Palantirians who had security clearance. Karp was not one of them: he said that he never applied for security clearance because he feared that it would inhibit his ability to speak candidly in public and private.

Later that morning, Karp was meeting with former Secretary of State Mike Pompeo, who was stopping by the office to see him (Karp would change into business attire beforehand). Two decades after cofounding Palantir, Karp had become a Washington wise man, a sought-after figure in foreign policy and defense circles. It was another improbable twist in an unlikely career. Certainly, nothing about his upbringing suggested that he was destined for the business world, let alone at the helm of a company serving as an instrument of American power. Karp says that the idea would have horrified his parents and that even after all the success he has enjoyed, they still wish he had done something else with his life.

TWO

SPUN FROM A DIFFERENT ORBIT

Karp grew up in Philadelphia, and when he was a child, his parents regularly took him and his brother, Ben, to the Philadelphia Museum of Art. Ben says that Bob Karp, their father, liked to draw their attention to one particular work, a statue of Icarus. The myth of Icarus is perhaps humanity's most enduring cautionary tale, a warning about the perils of hubris. Years later, the brothers theorized that Bob kept returning to the statue because he sensed in Alex an overweening ambition that he found threatening and wanted to squelch. According to Ben, Bob was strangely competitive with his older son, and even after Alex had taken Palantir public and acquired a vast fortune, his father showed little inclination to acknowledge his success, let alone celebrate it.

It might seem as if the drive that propelled Karp to the pinnacle of the business world was a form of rebellion against his father's effort to lower his horizons. But he didn't think that was true, and given how deeply he lived inside his own head, I was inclined to take him at his word. He maintained instead that his achievements were rooted to some degree in what he regarded as the failure of both his parents to capitalize on their own abilities. His mother, Leah Jaynes Karp, was a talented artist who, in Karp's view, had never achieved the recognition she deserved.

Likewise, Bob was a gifted practitioner and scholar of pediatric medicine who had not gained the kind of stature within his field that Karp thought should have accrued to him. In Karp's estimation, both his parents lacked what he called "navigation skills"—a sense of how to make one's way in the world. For whatever reason, he had been blessed with those skills, and overachievement was his answer to their underachievement. As he once put it to Ben, "If our father had been an alpha, I never would have founded Palantir."

None of this became a source of resentment for Karp. His parents provided comfortably for him and his brother; when they divorced and Bob balked at paying for his college education, Karp felt stress and anger, but the anger didn't linger. In later years, as he became wealthy, he was financially generous with both of his parents, as well as his brother. For a long time, he was frustrated and puzzled by what he regarded as his parents' shortcomings—a frustration that extended (unfairly, I thought) to Ben, a bracingly intelligent man two years his junior who is a writer and college professor in Tokyo. Karp wasn't being judgmental; he just wanted to understand why his life had turned out so differently. A conversation with a friend and confidant helped him come to terms with the achievement gap in his own family. This person pointed out that qualities such as aptitude, ambition, and discipline were not evenly distributed and that Karp was the member of the household who had been endowed with all the *sechel*—a Yiddish term that loosely translates as savvy. He could fly close to the sun. They could not.

Bob Karp was born to a German-Jewish family in Philadelphia. His father, Manny, was a carpenter and later a school guidance counselor who also ran a Jewish summer camp in the Poconos.

Ben, who has done genealogical research into his family, believes that Karl Marx was a distant relation. Bob attended Muhlenberg College, in Allentown, Pennsylvania, and then Jefferson Medical College in Philadelphia. In 1963, while still in medical school, he met Leah Jaynes. She was moving into the same apartment building where he resided, and he offered to help carry her things up. At the time, Leah was working as a secretary at the University of Pennsylvania. She was originally from Pontiac, Illinois, and was the great-granddaughter of a former slave. Her father, Milo Jaynes, was a Baptist minister and a postal worker. He was also an abusive alcoholic, and Leah went to live with an aunt in Chicago when she was sixteen to escape her chaotic home.

In high school, Leah won a scholarship to travel to Israel. She spent three months there, was enthralled by the experience, and left enamored of Judaism. That Bob Karp was Jewish was a selling point for her. Likewise, part of the attraction for Bob was that Leah was black; he was politically liberal, and dating Leah was a powerful way of signaling his progressivism. "My father wanted to marry a black woman," says Ben. Still, a genuine romance developed, and Bob and Leah married in a civil ceremony in Philadelphia in 1964. (Leah eventually converted to Judaism, but only after she and Bob divorced.) Alex's realization, years later, that racial and ethnic identity had been foundational to his parents' relationship was part of the reason he developed a visceral dislike of identity politics. He felt as if he had been the product of virtue signaling, and it bothered him.

Alex was born in 1967 in New York City, where Bob was doing his residency at New York Hospital–Cornell Medical Center. Three years later, Bob was hired as a physician at Philadelphia's St. Christopher's Hospital for Children. Politically and socially, it was a fraught time in America, and race was at the forefront of the national conversation. There had been major progress in the form of the civil rights legislation enacted under President Lyndon B. Johnson. More pertinent, perhaps, to Bob and Leah, the U.S. Supreme Court, in *Loving v. Virginia*, had recently struck down anti-miscegenation laws. However, efforts to address racial discrimination had provoked a fierce backlash; Richard Nixon won the presidency in 1968 in part by stoking and exploiting white resentment and anxiety—the so-called Southern Strategy.

But the backlash wasn't confined to the South. Philadelphia was also a center of resistance to racial equity. In the late 1960s, under Commissioner Frank Rizzo, the Philadelphia Police Department was notorious for the brutality that it directed at the city's black community and other minorities. Rizzo, a proudly thuggish cop, didn't feel bound by new laws or changing mores; he was a northern version of the law-and-order sheriffs in the South who had terrorized blacks. (He and the police department were eventually charged by the U.S. Department of Justice with a pattern of abuse that in the words of prosecutors "shocks the conscience.") In 1971, Rizzo was elected Philadelphia's mayor, pitching himself as a champion of the city's white working-class population. In 1978, campaigning in support of a ballot measure that would have amended the city charter to enable him to seek a third term as mayor, Rizzo made his racist appeal explicit, urging Philadelphians to "vote white." (The proposal was rejected.)

In a city consumed by reactionary politics, the Mount Airy section of Philadelphia was an island of tolerance and enlightened thinking. Starting in the 1950s, local residents, along with religious leaders and civic groups, promoted racial integration in Mount Airy. They encouraged black families to move in and successfully pressured banks, many of which had discriminatory lending practices, to give them mortgages. In her book *Making Good Neighbors:*

Civil Rights, Liberalism, and Integration in Postwar Philadelphia, historian Abigail Perkiss says that "homeowners in Mt. Airy waged a community-wide battle toward intentional integration.... By replacing residential segregation with residential integration, they sought to disrupt a system of separation and infuse their day-to-day lives with the experience of interracial living."

Mount Airy was an ideal place for the Karps to establish roots. They initially lived in an apartment before purchasing a semi-detached house on Wellesley Road. The family later moved into a home on Lincoln Drive, a slightly more upscale street also in Mount Airy. They lived simply and frugally: For years, Leah outfitted Alex and Ben with clothes from consignment sales. The Karps had a television for a time, but after the boys got into an argument over a show, Leah deliberately broke it, and it wasn't replaced until they were in high school. Summer vacation was an annual trip to Vermont's Lake Ninevah, where the family owned a cabin that had neither electricity nor running water. They used a gas stove to cook and gas lamps for light, drew water from a well, and bathed in the lake.

Like others in Mount Airy, Bob and Leah were on the left politically. They were frustrated by what they regarded as America's failure to live up to its ideals and were also put off by its rampant consumerism. They took part in political protests, bringing their sons along. In 1979, the family attended an antinuclear rally and concert in New York. Bruce Springsteen was among the performers, and Leah introduced Alex and Ben to Noam Chomsky, who was also there.

According to Ben, misplaced idealism informed Bob and Leah's decision to have the boys attend Henry H. Houston School, the local K–8. They wanted to signal their support for public education and for school desegregation. But in doing so, they ignored how dysfunctional Henry Houston was. Ben recalls that there were "some really rough kids" who created a "bullying environment." He says that he and his brother often feared for their safety. At one point, Alex was bringing money to school to pay off another student who was menacing him. Yet even as other parents were pulling their children out and sending them to private schools, Bob and Leah insisted on keeping the boys at Henry Houston, which would become a source of lingering anger for Alex. "He still talks about it, the resentment is still there," says Ben.

Academically, Alex was curious and motivated, which led some kids to call him "Professor." Ben says they weren't taunting him; it was actually a playground compliment, an acknowledgment that he was really smart. But the nickname masked a cruel reality: Alex was struggling to learn to read. When he turned eight and was still having difficulty with written-word recognition, Bob decided to have him evaluated, and he was diagnosed with dyslexia. Henry Houston didn't have the resources to help him, so the Karps enrolled Alex in the Oliver P. Cornman School, which was for children with learning disabilities. At Cornman, there was a wide range of special needs; some kids were profoundly disabled. Alex attended Cornman from third grade through fifth, and working with the school's specialists, he got to the point where he could read fluently. He would later say that dyslexia was the greatest adversity he had ever faced (a point he often made in the service of another point—that he had never personally experienced racial discrimination). Leah Karp told me that her son was extremely diligent and organized when it came to homework, which she attributed to his dyslexia—he craved order.

Years later, Karp would say that dyslexia added to the sense of vulnerability that he felt as a child. He claims that he intuited from an early age that because he was a biracial Jew with a disability, he had some strikes against him. As he put it, "You're a racially amorphous, far-left Jewish kid who's also dyslexic—would you not come up with the idea that you're fucked?" He says that he also recognized that his parents, hamstrung by their own limitations, were not in a position to protect him. They loved him, of course, but couldn't shelter him from a world that seemed especially dangerous for someone with his particular identity. Long before he left for college, Karp felt that he could only truly depend on himself for survival.

After Cornman, Alex returned to Henry Houston, which he attended through eighth grade. From Houston, he went to Walter B. Saul High School, a magnet school that specialized in agriculture. There, he joined Future Farmers of America; Ben says that his brother seemed to especially enjoy working with the cows in the school's dairy barn. Alex spent two years at Saul before transferring to Central High School. Central was considered Philadelphia's finest public high school, and it had many notable graduates, among them Noam Chomsky. Bob Karp was also an alumnus. At Central, Alex blossomed academically, thanks in part to the influence of a guidance counselor who was struck by the gap between his high test scores and his solid if unremarkable grades and wanted to help him close it.

Karp's cousin, the novelist Mat Johnson, also grew up in Mount Airy and was close to Alex and Ben; he was essentially the third Karp brother. (Alex and Ben, denied a television of their own, would go to the apartment that Johnson and his mother, Pauline, shared to watch episodes of *Mork & Mindy*.) For a time, Johnson says, Alex was a moody adolescent. "He basically just growled and hid in his room reading comics," Johnson recalls. By then, it was clear to the family that Alex "lived in his own world," as Johnson puts it. Even so, he had plenty of friends. Almost all of them were black, and Karp seemed to identify strongly with black culture. "Alex in high school was a young black man," says Ben. During his senior year of high school, he got interested in girls and found that the interest was mutual. He cut his hair, grew a mustache, and began dressing more stylishly. He also turned heads with his dance moves. His brother and cousin started calling him "Al Smooth."

Johnson's mother worked until early evening, so he usually went to the Karps' after school and stayed through dinner. He says the house was always freezing—Bob kept the thermostat low to save on energy bills. At meals, the emphasis was on health foods and animated conversation. "It was a house that did a lot of arguing—not in a bad way, but in the highly opinionated Jewish way," says Johnson. "You really had to hold your own in that house." The discussions typically revolved around whatever issues were making the news that day. When Johnson would leave after dinner to walk back to his apartment, he could hear the Karps debating one another from outside. Bob and Leah wanted their sons to be intellectually curious and engaged, and they hoped that each would pursue a life of the mind. "My father said that he became a doctor so that his sons could become poets," says Ben.

By the fall of Alex's senior year at Central, it was clear that he was likely to have his pick of colleges. He was leaning to the Ivies when that same guidance counselor suggested that nearby Haverford College might be a better fit. It was smaller, had a very cerebral student body, and seemed as if it would be a more congenial place for him. Leah thought that her son ultimately chose Haverford in part because he had a fond memory of the school. When Alex was young, the family attended a dance recital at Haverford, which was followed by a dinner in the cafeteria.

The main course was steak, which was a treat for Alex and Ben ("We mostly ate vegetables, plus a little chicken," Leah told me). In Alex's memory, the steaks were not just delicious; they were huge slabs of meat, which gave him a favorable impression of Haverford. According to his mother, he was disappointed, upon matriculating at Haverford, to discover that steak was seldom on the menu and that when it was served, the portions were small.

For someone raised in the political milieu that Karp was, Haverford was a logical choice. Founded by Quakers in 1833, Haverford had a strong commitment to social justice and a history of political dissent. In the late 1960s and early 1970s, the college was a hotbed of opposition to the Vietnam War. In 1971, a group of activists led by a Haverford physics professor named William Davidon broke into a local FBI office and stole thousands of documents pertaining to the FBI's surveillance of antiwar protesters, as well as its monitoring of black civil rights leaders. Davidon and his coconspirators shared the documents with *The Washington Post* and *The New York Times*, and the media coverage ultimately helped prompt a congressional investigation. Davidon and the others were never identified by the police. Davidon died in 2013. Soon thereafter, three others who had participated in the break-in admitted to their roles. By then, the statute of limitations had expired and they were no longer at risk of prosecution.

Haverford was a more sedate place in the mid-1980s. The students mostly came from comfortable circumstances and were conventionally liberal. Many participated in protests against apartheid, but that was hardly a radical position. There were still some firebrands on the faculty. One professor, discussing the 1984 presidential election between President Ronald Reagan and former Vice President Walter Mondale, said it had been a choice between "a capitalist pig who's proud of it" and a "capitalist pig who feels a little guilty." Most faculty members, though, were like the students—mainstream progressives. But while the college's culture had mellowed, it retained its academic rigor. Haverford was a demanding school: lots of work was assigned, and professors resisted the grade inflation that was increasingly prevalent at other prestigious colleges and universities. A few of us tried, valiantly, to give Haverford a robust social life, but it was a never-ending struggle.

In the summer of 1985, just before Karp headed off to Haverford, Leah filed for divorce from Bob. She had been unhappy for some time. Bob had grown distant, lost in his own thoughts and frustrations. Leah had hoped to stay together until Ben left for college but decided that she could no longer stick it out. According to Ben, Bob was shocked when she told him she was ending their marriage, and then he got angry. He stopped paying the mortgage on the house and soon put it on the market. He forced Leah to move out but refused to cover the cost of an apartment for her and Ben; some family friends, the Weisbords, took them in. He also announced that he would not pay for Alex's college.

For Alex, the breakup of his parents' marriage was a crushing blow. He left for college feeling as if his world had been sundered. It was also unclear to him how he would be able to remain at Haverford if Bob was unwilling to pay for it. The first semester of freshman year was an exhilarating time for most of us at Haverford, but for Alex, it was a period of emotional upheaval and gnawing uncertainty. The divorce was bad enough; that Bob was taking out his anger on Alex and putting his future at risk was unconscionable. It was also, in Alex's mind, a betrayal of the Jewish values that his father had claimed were paramount and inviolable: the centrality of family and education.

Leah ended up paying for Haverford, taking out loans and tapping into her pension to cover the tuition charges and other costs. But her finances were sufficiently precarious that Karp was never certain he would be able to complete his degree. "Every semester was torture for Alex, just waiting to find out if his tuition had been paid and if he could stay," says Ben. It was the first time in Karp's life that he had experienced economic insecurity, and he came away from this period determined never to experience it again.

But while anxiety colored his experience there, Haverford became a kind of sanctuary for Karp, an escape from the turmoil engulfing his family. Despite his tenuous situation, he threw himself into college life. He ran, unsuccessfully, for student government and was a member of the cross-country and track teams. Tom Donnelly, who coached both teams and is a legendary figure in college track and field, says that Karp was never among the top runners but was "a real positive presence" who was "always loose and joking around." Looking back, Donnelly thinks that Karp's carefree attitude was "a cover for a very intense inner life that he probably balanced through the physical exertion of running and competing." He says that he and Karp bonded mainly over the fact that they were both Philly guys, but he admits that he "had no idea how smart this guy actually was."

Donnelly was not the only person at Haverford who found Karp a little hard to read. He wasn't aloof; there was just a part of him that seemed closed off to the rest of the world. That said, he was well-liked and had plenty of friends, and his inscrutability didn't seem to hurt him with women. He was in a relationship for two years with a classmate who was Jamaican. He later dated another classmate, a Latina woman. And as was true in high school, Karp embraced his black heritage. He was active in black student affairs, and his social life mainly revolved around Haverford's black community. "He was much more of a black man then than he is now," says Ward Breeze, who was one of Karp's closest friends at Haverford.

In the fall of senior year, Karp helped organize a conference at Yale University sponsored by a group called Campuses Against Racial Violence. A few months later, Karp was quoted in a *Detroit Free Press* story about racism at U.S. colleges and universities. "The most distressing thing was that finding someone to talk about racial violence was as simple as asking someone to speak," he told the paper. "It is that pervasive." Karp chided administrators for not doing more to combat bigotry at their institutions. "If your deans are unwilling to take action, it's a green light," he said. Karp also blamed Ronald Reagan for the pervasiveness of racial discrimination on campuses, saying the president had "set a mood" that signaled to bigots that racism was acceptable. Karp wore a kaffiyeh for his yearbook photo, which suggested a broader interest in fighting injustice.

Karp insists he didn't work all that hard at Haverford, but his grades suggested otherwise: in a school that had no shortage of grinds, he stood out as a particularly high achiever. He majored in philosophy, which was a strong department at Haverford. It included some eminent names in the field, notably Richard Bernstein, the famed scholar of American pragmatism. However, the professor to whom Karp was closest was Mark Gould, who taught sociology. Gould says that Karp had substance: he possessed a keen mind and could think deeply and insightfully about complex ideas. He believes that Karp could have made a significant mark as a scholar. "He had the capacity to do very, very interesting academic work if that's what he had chosen to do," says Gould.

But Karp opted instead to go to law school. He applied to Stanford, Harvard, Columbia, and Penn and got into all of them, which caused some envy and awe among other Haverfordians.

Karp decided on Stanford and matriculated at the end of the summer of 1989. He lived in Crothers Hall, a dorm for law students. Early on, he fell in with a group of fellow first-years who ate meals at Italian House, an undergraduate facility known to have good food and that allowed grad students to eat there. One member of the group, who preferred not to be cited by name, recalls that Karp was "wickedly funny" and that he also stood out for his intelligence. "There are people who you can immediately recognize are not just smarter, but who just see things differently, think about things differently—that was Alex," she says. Karp also didn't seem to have the self-doubt that plagued many of his classmates. Other first-years spent a lot of time fretting about whether they were worthy of Stanford Law and up to the challenge. Outwardly, at least, Karp displayed no such uncertainty. He didn't come across as cocky or entitled; he just projected a discernible assuredness.

That said, he quickly regretted going to law school. He says that he knew within a week of enrolling at Stanford that he had made a mistake and that it ended up being "the worst three years of my adult life." He found the classroom experience unsatisfying: in his view, Stanford Law was just a glorified trade school, the other students seemed mainly animated by a desire to land prestigious (and lucrative) jobs, and the intellectual discourse was "highly performative." What made Stanford bearable was the unlikely friendship that he formed with Peter Thiel, a fellow first-year. Thiel was already a figure of renown and some notoriety. As an undergraduate at Stanford, the self-declared libertarian had co-founded a right-wing newspaper called *The Stanford Review*, which challenged what he and his colleagues saw as a stifling liberal orthodoxy on campus.

Thiel also lived in Crothers Hall, and like Karp, he found Stanford Law disappointing. The two bonded over their shared dissatisfaction and spent a lot of time playing chess and debating politics with each other. "We argued like feral animals," Karp recalls. According to Thiel, their bull sessions generally took place late at night in the dorm. "It sounds too self-aggrandizing, but I think we were both genuinely interested in ideas," says Thiel. "He was more the socialist, I was more the capitalist. He was always talking about Marxist theories of alienated labor and how this was true of all the people around us." By Karp's account, the friendship he formed with Thiel, and the intellectual nourishment that it provided, sustained him at Stanford.

During the summer between his second and third years of law school, Karp traveled to Europe. At a café in Paris, he serendipitously ran into Ward Breeze, who was now doing graduate work at Goethe University Frankfurt. Karp went to visit him in Frankfurt a few weeks later. Impressed by the university and quite taken with the local scene, Karp soon decided that he wanted to pursue a doctorate in Germany. It was not an entirely random impulse: the thinkers who had engaged him the most during college—Kant, Hegel, Weber—were German. Studying in Germany was also of interest to Karp for another reason: the sense of vulnerability that he felt as a Jew was an outgrowth of the Holocaust, and he hoped to gain a deeper understanding of why Germany, a pillar of European civilization, had descended into barbarism.

Karp considered dropping out of Stanford and relocating to Germany immediately. But he knew that not completing his degree would anger his mother and disappoint his paternal grandfather, so he decided to return to Palo Alto for his third year. While his classmates, including Thiel, pursued federal clerkships and Big Law jobs, Karp made plans to move to Frankfurt, and within weeks of receiving his diploma, he left for Germany. (He and Breeze ultimately traded places: Breeze ended up earning a law degree from Stanford.)

Pursuing a doctorate in Germany was an ambitious undertaking, and especially so in Karp's case because he didn't speak German. After arriving in Frankfurt, he enrolled in an intensive German-language class. Within three months, he was speaking competent German. Isabelle Azoulay, a French-German graduate student who became a close friend of Karp's, refused to believe that he had only just learned the language when she heard him speak it for the first time; she figured he was just a typically boastful American. When she found out that he wasn't bullshitting, she was astonished. Over time, she came to believe that he had "a kind of photographic mind."

Karp also seemed to have a preternatural understanding of social dynamics—even in a country where he was a newcomer. Breeze spoke excellent German but found that his language skills did not gain him the kind of acceptance he sought. "I was doggedly trying to be seen as German, to conform," says Breeze. Karp told him the problem was that while his German was almost flawless, there were subtleties and "cultural cues" that he couldn't know as a non-native speaker, and because he was missing these, people assumed he was a "below-average German." He suggested that if Breeze deliberately mispronounced some words and threw in a grammatical error here and there, Germans would instead see him as a supersmart American whose near mastery of their language was indicative of his respect and affinity for their culture. Breeze says that Karp's strategy worked brilliantly: once he started mangling his German slightly, Germans embraced him in exactly the way Karp had predicted.

After completing the language course, Karp enrolled in Goethe University. At that point, he wasn't sure what he wanted to do his dissertation on, but he knew with whom he wanted to work. The philosopher Jürgen Habermas was arguably the preeminent European public intellectual of the postwar era, a remarkably prolific and wide-ranging scholar whose work focused on developing and sustaining democratic governance. He was a protégé of Theodor Adorno, one of the leading lights of the Frankfurt School, an intellectual movement that arose in the wake of World War II and that was known for its effort to understand the lure of fascism and its trenchant critique of modern capitalism—a mode of inquiry that came to be called Critical Theory. It grew out of the Institute for Social Research, a think tank affiliated with Goethe University. Adorno and most of the other major figures of the Frankfurt School were left-wing Jews who had fled the Nazis and who devoted their careers to reckoning, in one way or another, with the Holocaust. Habermas came from a different background: he was the son of a Nazi sympathizer and was himself a former member of the Hitler Youth. Later, appalled by the crimes of the Third Reich, Habermas moved sharply to the left and became an ardent champion of liberal democracy. He spent most of his career at the Institute for Social Research and was considered the second-generation standard-bearer of the Frankfurt School. As Karp jokingly put it, "If you can get Habermas to work with you for even two minutes, you can be a tenured professor at Columbia."

Habermas held a weekly colloquium for graduate students. Participants would discuss their research, and the group, including Habermas, would offer feedback. It was invitation only. Karp got in mainly on the strength of his academic record, although the Haverford connection helped: Richard Bernstein and Mark Gould, two of his former professors, were both close to Habermas. Karp has claimed that Habermas was his dissertation adviser for a time. The two did discuss his dissertation, but according to Habermas, it was never a formal relationship: he was nearing retirement when Karp arrived in Germany and was no longer advising doctoral candidates. He later turned down Karp's request to serve as the second reader of his dissertation. Karp had shared a draft with Habermas, and in a three-page letter explaining his decision, the famed scholar praised some aspects of Karp's work but was critical of others.

Habermas also expressed doubt about whether Karp's German comprehension was sufficient to allow him to grapple with some of the texts that he was drawing on. "Your topic would require a literary approach to a topic that often overwhelms the linguistic sensibility of us native speakers—and yours, you won't blame me, even more so," Habermas wrote. "For you, literary German must be as much a foreign language as literary English is for me. Moreover, it is not a reproach to remind oneself of the limits of the competencies that we expect from an educated sociologist." At the end, Habermas struck an apologetic note. "Please don't be angry with me, Mr. Karp, for my candid assessment," he wrote, adding, "I would be happy to see you again if the occasion arises." Not long thereafter, in what was apparently meant as a conciliatory gesture, Habermas wrote a generic letter of recommendation on Karp's behalf. "I appreciate Alexander Karp not only as an intellectual but as well as a sensitive person who is dedicated to the task he has set for himself," Habermas said. "He always impresses me by his moral sense, open-mindedness, and vitality." (Karp continues to maintain that Habermas was his doctoral adviser for a period. He says that Habermas, now in his late nineties, is downplaying their connection and that he is at a loss to understand why.)

Karola Brede, a professor at Goethe University who specialized in social psychology and who herself had studied under Habermas, ultimately served as Karp's doctoral adviser. She was an ideal mentor for the question that Karp wanted to explore—what turns ordinary citizens into perpetrators of genocide and accessories to mass murder? And Karp's timing was fortuitous, as this question was very much on the minds of Germans themselves in the mid-1990s. In 1996, while Karp was living in Frankfurt, Daniel Jonah Goldhagen, an assistant professor of government and social studies at Harvard, published a provocative book called *Hitler's Willing Executioners: Ordinary Germans and the Holocaust*, in which he alleged that tens of thousands of everyday Germans, acting on age-old "eliminationist" antisemitic impulses, had eagerly contributed to the Nazi effort to eradicate European Jewry. The book was a bestseller in Germany, where it sparked a ferocious debate about wartime guilt and whether there was something intrinsically malignant in the German character.

Perhaps the angriest response to Goldhagen came two years later, in October 1998, when the acclaimed German writer Martin Walser gave a speech in Frankfurt in which he challenged the notion that the Holocaust had been inevitable and decried what he saw as a relentless effort to tar his generation of Germans with the sins of their fathers and grandfathers. He expressed resentment over the "unceasing presentation of our disgrace," as he put it, and suggested that the Holocaust had become a cudgel that was being used to keep Germans in a perpetual state of shame—"a moral bludgeon," in his words. Walser's comments provoked an angry response from Jewish organizations and others who believed that he was deliberately stoking German resentment and inverting the roles of perpetrator and victim.

Walser's speech became a focal point of Karp's dissertation, which he wrote in German and completed in 2002. Its title, translated into English, was "Aggression in the Lifeworld: Expanding Parsons' Concepts of Aggression Through a Description of the Interrelationship Between Jargon, Aggression, and Culture."

("Lifeworld"—*Lebenswelt* in German—is a philosophical term that refers to everyday life.) Karola Brede says that it was essentially a study of what is known as "secondary antisemitism," a concept coined by the Frankfurt School and that referred to German bitterness over being held accountable for the Holocaust (an idea mordantly captured in the famous quip "The Germans will never forgive the Jews for Auschwitz"). Building on the work of the American sociologist Talcott Parsons, as well as Adorno's seminal study *The Jargon of Authenticity*—and drawing on Freud, too—Karp constructed a theoretical framework for assessing Walser's speech. He argued that the language Walser used was meant to establish a bond with his audience rooted in collective grievance over the inescapability of German guilt and that also tapped into a subconscious desire to commit violence against the perceived oppressor (in this case, Jewish groups and others who, as Walser saw it, were making the German people prisoners of their past). In essence, the dissertation was a study of in-groups, out-groups, and the rhetoric of fascism. Walser, Karp told me, had engaged in a "parochial form of fascism that occurs by purposely saying things that are incorrect in speech."

Many years later, after Karp had become a prominent figure, his dissertation would be a source of curiosity among journalists and scholars. In 2020, Moira Weigel, now an assistant professor of comparative literature at Harvard University, published a much-discussed critique of Karp's dissertation, "Palantir Goes to the Frankfurt School," in which she claimed to see in it a blueprint for turning big data into an instrument of oppression. But that seemed like a strained and implausible reading (and phrases like "this repressed insight of his dissertation" suggested some heavy lifting on her part). When Karp wrote his dissertation, he had no ambition to work in technology and no inkling of the turn his life would soon take. Given his improbable path to Silicon Valley, the desire to find a through line between his doctorate and Palantir was understandable, but this appeared to be a case of overinterpreting the data. For her part, Karola Brede sees no connection between Karp's scholarship and the career that he ended up pursuing.

Interestingly, even as Karp immersed himself in Germany's darkest chapter, he developed an unexpected affinity for the country, and for the German-speaking world more generally. "I went for intellectual reasons," he says. "The reason I stayed was emotional." Culturally and socially, Germany agreed with him in a way that no other place had; it felt like home. He assumed that this sense of belonging was rooted in his German heritage—that, in some sense, he *had* returned home. He seemed to connect with Germans, and they with him, in a way that suggested a degree of kinship. "I felt more naturally accepted in Germany than anywhere else," he says. German women apparently found him irresistible. To hear Karp tell it—and he was still telling it, proudly, thirty years later—he couldn't walk out his front door without being jumped by lustful German women. The sex wasn't just abundant; it was epiphanic. Personal experience had given him a dim view of marriage and parenthood and, by extension, monogamy. Germany—Europe, really—offered not just sybaritic pleasure, but also a sense of liberation. In Europe, there was no shame in sleeping with someone simply out of desire, nor was there any stigma to having a complex personal life. If one chose to remain single and found fulfillment in having multiple partners, that was perfectly fine. Karp abhorred American hypocrisy on the subject of sex; Americans screwed around just as much if not more than Europeans, but they maintained an outward Puritanism. Europeans, he thought, had a more evolved and honest view of human desire.

When not being dragged back to his bedroom, Karp socialized with a wide circle of people in Frankfurt—some associated with the university, some with the local Jewish community. One of his friends, a filmmaker named Hanna Laura Klar, asked him to serve as the narrator of a documentary that she was doing about Richard Plant, a writer and scholar best known for his 1986 book *The Pink Triangle: The Nazi War Against Homosexuals*. Plant was himself gay and a German-Jewish émigré who had settled in New York in the late 1930s. He was tangentially linked to the Frankfurt School—as a student, he had known Adorno, as well as the sociologist and critic Siegfried Kracauer.

The premise of the film was that Karp was intrigued by Plant and was traveling to New York to interview him. But Plant was in his late seventies and in poor health, and after initially agreeing to meet with Karp, he changed his mind. So Klar instead filmed Karp visiting places of significance to Plant, such as the City University of New York, where he taught for many years. The forty-three-minute documentary, *I Have Two Faces* (the title is a reference to the fact that Plant was both Jewish and gay and that his identity defined his life), culminates with Karp stopping by Plant's Greenwich Village apartment building to leave a gift for him. It is an odd film, but strangely watchable. With its moody shots of Manhattan and music to match, it is evocative of a Woody Allen movie, and the storyline—young American doctoral candidate on the trail of an obscure, reclusive German intellectual—seems right out of an Allen film, too. And Karp could have been playing a character conceived by the famed filmmaker—a cerebral Jewish guy with a thicket of curly dark hair and Coke-bottle glasses, walking around Manhattan in a trench coat and with a briefcase tucked under his arm, speaking mostly German. The only Allen touch that is missing is comedy: *I Have Two Faces* is defiantly humorless.

For Karp, part of Germany's appeal was the distance it offered from his family. Not long after his divorce from Leah, Bob started dating a woman named Linda Oppenheim, and they were soon engaged. Karp did not take the news well and refused to attend the wedding. Shortly after Bob and Linda got married, they adopted a son, a boy from the Dominican Republic. They then adopted another child, a girl from Ohio who, like Alex and Ben, was biracial. According to Ben, he and Alex sensed that Bob saw his new family as a fresh start and regarded them as relics of a first marriage that he very much wanted to forget. "We felt like castaways," says Ben. For several years, Alex didn't speak to his father.

Germany was an escape and a balm for Karp. Years later, he would say that "I only made two good decisions as an adult: going to Germany and starting Palantir. Everything else was, I wouldn't call it a mistake, but either preparation for these two decisions or a mistake." Still, while he adored Germany, he recognized that his racial and ethnic background would always set him apart—that no matter how long he lived there, he would always be an outsider. And even as he reveled in the pleasures that Germany afforded him, the shadow of the Holocaust was inescapable. During one summer weekend, he visited Isabelle Azoulay and her boyfriend in Berlin. To escape the heat, the three decided to go to nearby Lake Wannsee. It was there, in 1942, that Nazi leaders, meeting in a lakeside villa, committed themselves to the eradication of European Jewry. On the drive to the lake, Karp said to Azoulay and her boyfriend, "If I drown this afternoon, please don't tell my parents it was in Wannsee." Azoulay says that he was joking, making light of the location, but that there was an undercurrent of seriousness to his comment—the idea of swimming in that particular spot caused him discomfort.

By the time Karp earned his PhD, he had also concluded that

he had no desire to be an academic. Even though Habermas had played a limited role in his doctoral studies, Karp would later explain his decision by referring to the German philosopher. "Working with Habermas showed me that I couldn't be him and didn't want to be him," he said. But what *did* he want to be? He was now in his mid-thirties and had little practical experience to speak of—to that point, he had spent his entire adulthood as a student. He didn't have a wife or kids, so there was no pressure to become a provider. Even so, after two graduate degrees, he was still without a direction in life. But soon, he and Thiel reconnected.

THREE

THE SILICON VALLEY START-UP WITH A CHIP ON ITS SHOULDER

Nine days after Karp was born in New York City, Susanne Thiel gave birth to her first child, a son named Peter, in Frankfurt, Germany, where she and her husband, Klaus, lived. A year later, Klaus, a chemical engineer, took a job with a company in Cleveland. Eventually, the Thiels settled in Foster City, California, outside San Francisco. By then, Peter had a younger brother, Patrick. Like Bob and Leah Karp, Klaus and Susanne didn't permit their sons to watch television, although they relented when Peter was a teenager. Peter was a precocious student and a chess prodigy, too. And as was true of many socially awkward adolescent boys, he was entranced by *The Lord of the Rings* and also found his way to Ayn Rand, whose books *Atlas Shrugged* and *The Fountainhead* helped reinforce the libertarian views that would bring him to prominence.

Thiel enrolled at Stanford University in the fall of 1985, the same time that Karp started at Haverford, and also majored in philosophy. Their college experiences, however, were different. While Karp cherished Haverford, in part because of the refuge it afforded him from his warring parents, Thiel chafed against the ideological conformity and political correctness that he believed held sway at Stanford. *The Stanford Review*, the student newspaper that he cofounded, pushed back against those prevailing currents, often in ways intended to cause offense. The paper made light of date rape, expressed scorn for diversity initiatives, and seemed to take particular delight in gay-bashing (one headline read: "Homosexuality on Campus: Too Much of a Bad Thing"). In its early years, the *Review*'s staff was comprised almost entirely of young white men who felt that Stanford had turned its back on free inquiry and was hostile to conservatives. All were Thiel groupies who were mesmerized by his intelligence and ability to articulate the grievances that they shared, and some of them followed him into business. The *Review* was a journalistic enterprise, but it also became a major incubator of tech talent, and its alumni helped launch a number of start-ups, including Palantir.

Despite his frustrations with Stanford, Thiel excelled academically. He found an intellectual mentor in René Girard, a French literary critic, historian, and philosopher who had taught at Stanford since the early 1980s. Girard was best known for his theory of mimetic desire, which held that human desire was fundamentally imitative—we want things because other people want them, which inevitably leads to strife. Girard's work would strongly influence Thiel's approach to business and investing—notably, in his skepticism about the value of competition and his corresponding belief that the most compelling start-ups are those that aim to achieve monopolistic dominance in niche markets. In 2014, Thiel would lay out these principles in a book titled *Zero to One: Notes on Startups, or How to Build the Future*, an entrepreneurial guide that can be read as an ex post facto blueprint for Palantir.

After earning his undergraduate degree, Thiel attended Stanford Law School, which frustrated him for a different reason: he felt let down by what he perceived to be its shallow intellectual culture. In this, he found a kindred spirit in Karp. But Thiel wasn't as quick as Karp to give up on the idea of a legal career. After graduating in 1992, he applied for clerkships with two Supreme Court justices, Antonin Scalia and Anthony Kennedy. He was passed over by both and ended up clerking for U.S. appeals court judge James Larry Edmondson. Thiel was then hired as an associate at Sullivan & Cromwell, a leading New York law firm. But he quit after just seven months; he found the work unsatisfying and had finally come to the realization that he didn't want to be a practicing attorney.

A job as a derivatives trader for Credit Suisse, the investment bank, proved no more fulfilling, and in 1996 he left New York and returned to California with the aim of becoming an investor in the dot-com boom then sweeping Silicon Valley. To that end, he launched his own venture capital fund. Two years later, Thiel met Max Levchin, a twenty-three-year-old computer programmer originally from Ukraine who wanted to build an online payments system that could facilitate e-commerce. He and Thiel fleshed out the idea over a number of months, and their work gave rise to PayPal, a company they cofounded in 1998, although under a different name: it was originally called Confinity. They renamed it PayPal in 2000, after the company merged with X.com, an online payments start-up founded by Elon Musk. Eventually, Musk would be pushed out, and Thiel served as PayPal's CEO.

In time, PayPal would grow into an $80 billion business and acquire a mythic status because of the entrepreneurs who had been associated with it—the so-called PayPal Mafia, which included Thiel, Musk, and Reid Hoffman, among others—and the companies that it helped give rise to, such as LinkedIn, YouTube, Yelp, and Palantir. But PayPal was beset with problems in its early years, none bigger than fraud. Scammers were selling fake merchandise on eBay and pocketing the money via PayPal accounts.

Criminals in possession of stolen credit card numbers were using fake PayPal accounts to execute transactions; when victims reported the fraudulent charges, PayPal would be on the hook for the credit card charge-backs. By 2001, the company was losing millions of dollars a month due to illicit activity and facing the prospect of bankruptcy.

Levchin came up with two innovative solutions to combat fraud and save the business. Members of PayPal's security team, which grew to include dozens of analysts, had discovered that a lot of bogus accounts were being set up by computer programs. In response, Levchin and another PayPal engineer, David Gausebeck, developed software that required new PayPal users to correctly identify a series of images (traffic lights, oddly shaped letters) before allowing them to set up accounts. Computers were almost always incapable of performing this task, which was known internally as the Gausebeck-Levchin test and which became one of the first commercial uses of a concept known as CAPTCHA, the mercifully short acronym for "Completely Automatic Public Turing test to tell Computers and Humans Apart." The software proved to be so effective at shutting out bots that other tech companies adopted it, and it became a standard feature of e-commerce security.

But the Gausebeck-Levchin test was just a roadblock for fraudsters; to clean up PayPal, the company needed to identify and root them out. Through painstaking detective work, PayPal's head of security, an ex-Marine named John Kothanek, discovered a web of connections that he could trace back to a Ukrainian man who conducted transactions under the name "Igor" and who had allegedly pocketed $15 to $20 million via PayPal. Complicating matters, Kothanek found that Igor was a canny thief who had also done many legitimate transactions to create a smoke screen. If PayPal shut down every link to Igor, it would potentially be hurting lots of merchants who had unwittingly done business with him. Kothanek spent weeks poring over thousands of transactions and accounts to separate out the fraudulent ones and to cut off Igor's access to PayPal without causing unjust collateral damage.

Impressive as Kothanek's sleuthing was, it was clear to Thiel and others that PayPal couldn't rely on human analysts alone to stop fraud. It was a whack-a-mole problem; PayPal had over eight million users, and there weren't enough eyeballs or hours in the day for the security team to replicate Kothanek's effort on a sustained basis. The solution, Thiel says, had to be a "hybrid human-computer model." Humans alone couldn't solve the problem, but computing at that time wasn't advanced enough to solve it, either. "You'd have this AI-type person building this super-duper computer program that would figure out all the fraud but take twenty years to build," says Thiel, "and that wouldn't work, either, because we'd be out of business." But developing a software program that could analyze large data streams and find suspicious patterns of behavior seemed doable.

This was exactly the software that Levchin and several of his colleagues developed. They christened the program IGOR in honor of their biggest troublemaker, and it proved to be very effective; along with other, even more sophisticated anti-fraud tools that the company built, it kept PayPal from going under. After IGOR went live, PayPal experienced a 50 percent decline in fraud, and several individuals whose illicit activities had been detected by IGOR were later prosecuted by the U.S. government. The software was so good that FBI agents, at the invitation of Thiel and his colleagues, began visiting PayPal's Palo Alto office on a regular basis to test-drive the program and to learn more about the company's anti-fraud efforts. It was a mutually beneficial relationship: the FBI went after some of the criminals who had hurt PayPal's business, and the FBI got greater insight into the world of cyberthieves.

In August 2002, eBay acquired PayPal for $1.5 billion. Thiel walked away with $55 million, which he used to launch a hedge fund called Clarium Capital. He also tapped into his PayPal fortune to seed a variety of projects. He bankrolled a splashy restaurant/nightspot in San Francisco called Frisson (it didn't last very long) and launched a magazine about NASCAR called *American Thunder* (also short-lived). In addition, Thiel used some of his newfound wealth to invest in tech start-ups. He put $450,000 into Facebook, becoming the social media company's first outside investor (and gaining a board seat in the process). After a couple of lean years in Silicon Valley following the implosion of the dot-com bubble, the tech sector was booming again; Facebook, along with Amazon and Google, was one of the companies at the vanguard of what was known as Web 2.0.

But the tech industry's rebounding fortunes came against an ominous backdrop. The United States was still reeling from 9/11, and it was assumed that additional, possibly even deadlier attacks—involving dirty bombs or chemical or biological weapons—were inevitable. At some point—he can't recall exactly when—it occurred to Thiel that PayPal's anti-fraud algorithms could perhaps be repurposed to help the government thwart future acts of terrorism. It was an intriguing idea, not least because Thiel seemed to recognize that the intelligence failure that led to 9/11 was, at heart, a data integration failure: the CIA and FBI both had lots of evidence suggesting an attack was imminent, and if that information had been pooled, it was possible that analysts would have been able to piece together the plot in time to prevent the nineteen Al Qaeda hijackers from executing it. The 9/11 Commission, in the final report it issued in 2004, said government agencies had "failed to connect the dots" in part because of a "limited capacity to share information both internally and externally."

But the intelligence community didn't need a blue-ribbon panel or Peter Thiel to tell it that 9/11 happened in no small part because information that might have prevented the attack wasn't sufficiently disseminated. The Defense Advanced Research Projects Agency, or DARPA, which was effectively the R&D arm of the Pentagon, launched a program whose purpose was to use the most advanced technologies on the market to build what amounted to a massive dragnet that could help protect the country from terrorism. It was called Total Information Awareness, or TIA, an Orwellian title that signaled, in the view of some critics, its Big Brother ambitions. The appointment of retired rear admiral John Poindexter, who had been convicted in 1990 of lying to Congress and obstructing justice in the Iran-Contra scandal, to oversee the program only added to concerns that it would be implemented with little if any regard for civil liberties and privacy. Those fears, coupled with Poindexter's checkered reputation, ultimately doomed TIA; Congress stopped funding the program in late 2003. But the government was now looking for software that could integrate and analyze huge streams of data, and Thiel had identified his next big opportunity.

Thiel shared his idea about developing counterterrorism technology with two *Stanford Review* alums who were now working for Clarium Capital, Joe Lonsdale and Stephen Cohen. Lonsdale was twenty-one at the time and had joined the firm after graduating from Stanford with a degree in computer science. Cohen was then in his senior year at Stanford, finishing his degree in computer science and interning at Clarium. Lonsdale and Cohen had both grown up in Fremont, California, on the other side of San Francisco Bay from Silicon Valley. They didn't know each other as kids;

they met at Stanford. But they had traveled similar paths: they were enamored of computers, had taught themselves to code, and were intent on pursuing careers in technology even before matriculating at Stanford. As a teenager, Cohen often hung out at a local Barnes & Noble, where he would read books on computing. He got to know the inventory so well that he would offer free buying advice to other shoppers who were browsing in the computer section; one conversation landed him a coding job. For a time, he was also a Noam Chomsky devotee.

Thiel asked Cohen and a PayPal engineer named Nathan Gettings to begin working on a software program that could be pitched to the U.S. intelligence community. Although IGOR was the inspiration, it couldn't be used for counterterrorism: it was an internal product that analyzed PayPal's data to solve problems specific to PayPal. Cohen and Gettings, by contrast, were trying to build a commercial product that would help government intelligence analysts make use of their own data. It was a speculative undertaking, in that neither Thiel nor his associates had ever worked with the government, had no connections to the intelligence community, and had no clue as to how counterterrorism analysts wanted information presented. The project, which was called Palantir, seemed quixotic and hubristic. The federal government had vast quantities of data, exponentially more than PayPal collected, and while Thiel had significant engineering talent at his disposal, did he think that he and his associates could provide the corrective to the biggest intelligence failure in U.S. history? While the overarching ambition was supersized, the initial goal for Cohen and Gettings was modest: to build a simple prototype that might convince prospective users and investors that Palantir was plausible.

While Palantir was still in incubation, Karp moved back to the

Bay Area to take a job as a development officer with an organization called the Jewish Philanthropy Partnership. He had returned to the United States a few years earlier, sharing an apartment in New Haven with his brother, who was pursuing a doctorate in history and African American studies at Yale University. Karp completed his dissertation while residing in New Haven. He was also moonlighting as an investor, through a company he had started called the Caedmon Group (Caedmon is his middle name, after the first known English-language poet). Using $12,000 he had inherited from his paternal grandfather, he proved to be a shrewd stock-picker. Word got around that Karp had a knack for the markets, and some wealthy Europeans gave him money to manage on their behalf. (Karp says that his PhD was an added selling point for them, as it would later prove to be with European business leaders interested in working with Palantir.)

Karp had no interest in spending his career in finance and didn't aspire to become a superstar hedge fund manager. He later claimed that his goal was to amass a $250,000 nest egg, after which he planned to settle in Berlin and live as a highbrow dilettante, reading and writing and enjoying various "forms of debauchery," as he put it. Given his determination to compensate for what he saw as the professional shortcomings of his parents and to never experience economic hardship again, it is difficult to imagine that he would have been content with such a bohemian existence. It is possible the Berlin story was just a form of self-mythologizing, a way of underscoring how improbable his success with Palantir was.

Karp and Thiel had fallen out of touch after law school, but soon after Karp returned to the Bay Area, they reconnected. At one point, Karp invited Thiel to attend a meeting of major donors of the Jewish Philanthropy Partnership. "He thought it would be good to mix it up and have one non-Jewish person in the mix," Thiel recalls. "Alex had this crazy theory that it would be a better way for them all to be nicer to each other. They'd get way more done." It became clear to Thiel that Karp had "a terrific sense for people" and was "incredibly tenacious."

While doing his day job, Karp started raising money for Thiel's Clarium Capital. A few months later, Thiel asked Karp to join Palantir. He thought Karp could help market the company to potential customers and investors and also provide some adult supervision until they hired a CEO. Thiel's initial inclination was that Palantir would need a Washington insider or a retired senior military officer at its helm. He figured, not without reason, that Palantir was going to be a tough sell and that it would benefit from having a CEO with strong connections in the national security community and on Capitol Hill. Several people interviewed for the job, but none seemed like a good fit. Cohen, Lonsdale, and Gettings began to think that perhaps Karp was the right choice. Like Thiel, they were struck by his moxie, but they also saw something else in Karp. Although he didn't conceive the idea for Palantir, he spoke about it with the conviction of a true believer and exuded a spirit of entrepreneurship. "Alex was a founder; you could feel it," says Cohen. "The other people weren't." He, Lonsdale, and Gettings told Thiel that they thought Karp should be the CEO. Thiel didn't need much persuading and dispatched Cohen and Lonsdale to London, where Karp was meeting with investors, to offer him the position. He accepted.

On paper, at least, Karp wasn't a great fit himself. For one thing, he was thirty-four years old, which in the world of Silicon Valley start-ups made him a virtual geriatric. Start-ups were for kids, a point vividly illustrated in the memorable zip-line scene in the 2010 film *The Social Network*. The hope and goal of many young entrepreneurs was to hit it big early and then settle into a career backing the next generation of child-inventors. Marc Andreessen cofounded Netscape not long after graduating from college. When Andreessen was twenty-eight, Netscape was acquired by AOL for $4.3 billion, and by his mid-thirties, he had morphed into one of the Valley's most important venture capitalists. Thiel was following the same trajectory. In addition to his relatively advanced age, Karp lacked the baseline qualifications for the job: he had no managerial experience and no background in technology. (Thiel, during one of our conversations, noted that he had the same gaps in his résumé when he became PayPal's CEO.)

But although Karp couldn't write a line of code himself when he joined Palantir, the thinking that guided the company's software engineers wasn't entirely foreign to him. A key concept in data science is ontology, which, loosely defined, means how information is organized and structured. This mapping function is critical to drawing meaningful connections between disparate pieces of information. *Ontology* is a term that the tech world pilfered from philosophy. In the philosophical universe, ontology is a branch of metaphysics that deals with the nature of being and that creates categories of things (people, places, objects) to describe reality. For Karp, understanding ontology as it applied to data science wasn't much of a stretch—indeed, he would later say that Palantir's software was a philosophical system at heart. And in his view and that of his colleagues, the critical element in the software is its "dynamic ontology," which allows users to construct "digital twins" of their own operations that can be continuously updated and augmented to mirror the evolution of the organization.

And while Karp might not have been able to discuss the finer points of programming languages like Java and Python, in certain ways he was an ideal CEO for a company whose work was bound to arouse suspicion. He seemed genuinely passionate about privacy protection and could talk about issues related to civil liberties with a fluency that was rare in tech circles. It helped that he came out of academia, rather than the military or the intelligence community—having a trained philosopher at the company's helm signaled that Palantir took seriously the ethical and moral concerns that its work raised. It helped, too, that Karp was a self-described leftist; his political leanings would become a kind of shield for Palantir, especially when Thiel began moving even further to the right.

Thiel, Cohen, Lonsdale, and Gettings had started Palantir out of Clarium's office in San Francisco. But the company soon needed more space and relocated to 3000 Sand Hill Road in Palo Alto. That was where Thiel had launched Confinity. Initially, Karp wasn't in the office every day; he was residing in San Francisco and would come to Palo Alto several times a week. Because he didn't know how to drive, he hired a car to bring him back and forth. In the early days, Karp was something of a mystery to his colleagues. Some speculated, half-jokingly, that his German doctorate was a cover story and that he was actually a spy, possibly for the Mossad. (Years later, Karp hired an ex–Israeli intelligence officer to serve as a kind of fixer for him.) "We didn't know what to make of him," recalls Bob McGrew, a software engineer who joined Palantir in 2005. He describes it as an "impedance mismatch," an artful way of saying that they were on different wavelengths. To help Karp understand the people who now answered to him, McGrew and several others gave him a copy of Ray Kurzweil's *The Singularity Is Near*, a 2005 book that had instantly acquired canonical status in Silicon Valley. It was about artificial intelligence; Kurzweil, a computer scientist and futurist, predicted that the singularity—

the moment when computers surpass human intelligence—would occur by 2045. (Later, new hires at Palantir would be given several books to read, including Lawrence Wright's *The Looming Tower*, about Osama bin Laden, Al Qaeda, and the intelligence failures that led to 9/11, and *Impro*, a book ostensibly about improvisational theater but that acquired a cult following as a guide to creativity.)

While Karp was approachable and entertaining (then as now, he enjoyed regaling colleagues with stories about German women and their attraction to him), conversations with him could be difficult. He spit out thoughts and observations in a nonlinear fashion that sometimes left his colleagues befuddled. "I don't know that anyone would say he's easy to talk to," says Brian Schimpf, who was hired by Palantir in 2007 and eventually became its director of engineering. Joshua Goldenberg, who was Palantir's head of design, recalls that discussions with Karp were "unstructured" and sometimes seemed "a little bit incoherent." After all-hands meetings with Karp, staffers would congregate to try to make sense of what they'd heard. "We would debrief and see if anyone could divine the signal in the chaos of Karp's speech patterns," says one former employee. But he says that they all recognized that Karp had a kind of "crazy charisma" and was exceptionally intelligent.

They were also struck, and not a little freaked out, by his ability to get people to see things his way and to do things that he wanted. Karp insisted on a culture of unbridled discourse, in which employees were encouraged to express themselves with absolute candor. "Alex's attitude was that you should be able to tell even the CEO to fuck off," says Aki Jain, a software engineer who was another early hire. "We had open disagreement and debate about everything," recalls Schimpf. Even so, it felt to his colleagues as if Karp could almost burrow into people's minds and implant his ideas. Some Palantirians began referring to him as "Charles Xavier," aka Professor X, after the character in *X-Men* who possesses telepathic powers.

From the start, Karp said that Palantir's mission was to defend the West and liberal democracy. The company was a creation of 9/11 and of Karp's pessimistic worldview. Even before 9/11, Karp was skeptical that the end of the Cold War had ushered in an era of irreversible peace and prosperity; the terrorist attack on the United States showed that this had been a dangerous delusion and that there were still lots of people who meant to do us harm. Karp and his colleagues had no use for the techno-optimism that was so prevalent when Palantir started—the idea that the online world could somehow make the physical world a better, happier place. There was nothing utopian about Palantir; if anything, the company was founded on the conviction that we were facing a bleak future. Palantir's elevator pitch was that its technology could possibly make apocalyptic events a little less likely.

Palantir was also different from other tech start-ups in that it rejected the "fail fast, fail often" mantra that held sway in Silicon Valley—the idea that failure was not something to fear but was merely a setback that would lay the groundwork for future success. Karp, because of his relatively advanced age, didn't feel like he had the luxury of time; he was already in his mid-thirties, and failure was going to be much costlier for him than for some twenty-two-year-old just out of Stanford. Moreover, Karp wasn't a techie—if Palantir went bust, it wasn't as if he would be able to seamlessly move on to another start-up. From his point of view, failure really wasn't an option or something to be embraced. Karp had no use for the Beckettian "fail better next time" ethos because there was no guarantee that there would be a next time, and the urgency he felt permeated down the ranks at Palantir.

That's not to suggest that Palantir was a morose workplace filled with survivalists (although many years later, Karp would describe Palantir as "a prepper company"). In the early days, it looked like any other tech start-up: the office was full of enthusiastic, dweebish young men (it was a very male culture, something that has persisted). And although there was no zip line, the Palantirians did cut loose; a former employee sued Palantir in 2016 for what he claimed were injuries suffered during a raucous game of beer pong (the case was settled out of court). But there was a sense that Palantir was serving a higher purpose than other start-ups—that it was doing work that mattered. Aki Jain recalls that three of the brightest people in his cohort of Stanford computer science majors ended up working on Google's "Smart Ass" project—that was the in-house nickname given to the company's machine-learning ad targeting program (it directed ads at Google users based on their searches). Jain wasn't casting judgment or aspersions—he just knew that he preferred to be working on stuff that seemed more consequential.

Palantir was based in Silicon Valley, but in the minds of Karp and his colleagues, it was never truly part of the Valley. Karp had particular contempt for Google and Facebook. He recognized early on that harvesting and selling personal data was at the heart of what they did and that what he saw as their ethically dubious business models had the potential to hurt Palantir; if there were ever a backlash against Big Data, people wouldn't necessarily recognize that Palantir operated in a fundamentally different way from Google and Facebook (in that Palantir didn't collect, store, or sell data). In time, Karp became reluctant to hire people from either company. Exceptions were made, but in general he believed that Google and Facebook employees, no matter how talented they were, had internalized a predatory approach to data that was anathema to Palantir.

Karp especially loathed Facebook. Google, as a search engine, provided legitimate value. He saw zero value in Facebook; he regarded it as frivolous and destructive—"a carcinogen," as he put it. Palantir and Facebook were founded at around the same time, and although they were not competitors, Facebook in some ways became the company that Palantir defined itself against. That Thiel was a major investor in Facebook and sat on its board suggested that there was perhaps also a kind of sibling rivalry at play. Moreover, the two companies always seemed to be in one another's shadow. Both were headquartered for a time in the same Palo Alto office park, and when Palantir later expanded in Palo Alto, it took over a building that had previously been occupied by Facebook. (The Facebook office there became famous because its walls had been painted by a local graffiti artist who was paid in Facebook stock; when the company went public in 2012, his shares were worth around $200 million. After Palantir moved in, it painted over the walls.) Years later, Facebook and Palantir would each be ensnared in the Cambridge Analytica scandal.

Palantir did much of its early recruiting by word of mouth. In 2005, a group of Stanford alums, among them Bob McGrew, were living in a house in Los Altos Hills that was known informally as Phi Psi South, after a fraternity popular with computer science majors. Aki Jain attended a party there one night and had a long conversation with McGrew, who encouraged him to seek a job with Palantir. Soon thereafter, Jain joined the company. Stanford's proximity and abundance of engineering talent made it an obvious place for Palantir to seek new hires. Lonsdale and Cohen put up posters in the computer science building that said, "Are you part Bill Gates and part James Bond? Palantir is the place for you." Whether it was personal connections or those flyers or both, a number of Stanford grads ended up at Palantir.

Thiel seldom visited the office after Palantir moved to Palo Alto (on those rare occasions when he did drop by, a bowl of pistachios would be put out for him—he had a taste for them). But he did help with recruiting. In 2004, he tried to get a young engineer named Garry Tan to leave Microsoft and join Palantir. He flew Tan to San Francisco, took him to dinner at Frisson, and encouraged him to come work for his new start-up. Thiel promised him a sizable equity stake if he joined. At one point, Thiel asked Tan how much he was being paid at Microsoft. Tan told him $72,000, whereupon Thiel pulled out his checkbook and wrote him a check in that amount, which was meant as an added inducement. But Tan declined the money and the offer—he wanted to stay with Microsoft. Many years later, Tan recounted this story in a short video he made called "My $200 Million Mistake." The kicker is that not long after he rebuffed Thiel's overture, he took a job with Palantir, becoming its tenth hire. He even ended up designing Palantir's logo and would go on to a successful career as a venture capitalist and as the CEO of Y Combinator, a company that incubates start-ups. But he would have been hundreds of millions of dollars richer had he joined Palantir sooner.

To land a position at Palantir, you needed to show enthusiasm for the company's mission—if a candidate didn't seem gung ho about using technology to kill terrorists, or appeared squeamish about working with the U.S. government, he or she had no chance of being hired. Another dealbreaker was any hint of get-rich-quick ambitions. Thanks to the dot-com frenzy of the late 1990s, the Valley was seen as a place where one could become fantastically wealthy in a relatively brief time span: you'd spend a few years slaving away at a start-up, being paid partly or largely in equity, and when the company went public, you'd cash in. But if a potential hire at Palantir gave off even the faintest whiff of interest in IPOs and exit strategies, he or she wasn't getting the job. Shyam Sankar, who was the thirteenth person hired at Palantir and is now its chief technology officer, says it was a question of "mercenaries versus missionaries"—of people who were interested in potential windfalls versus those who were attracted to Palantir because of the work it did. Palantir wanted the latter and went to lengths to avoid hiring the former.

Palantir didn't pay all that well relative to other tech firms, which helped weed out the mercenaries. New employees had three compensation options: low cash/high equity, mid-cash/mid-equity, or high cash/low equity. But "high cash" wasn't all that high. Salaries were capped at what Karp was paid, and he took a modest salary: for most of Palantir's first decade, he was paid only around $125,000 per year. This was true even through the mid-aughts, when the company had a $20 billion valuation. "I only make money when you make money," Karp told his colleagues, and he meant it. He also liked to say that his goal with Palantir wasn't to build the world's most valuable company but, rather, its most important one. Although Karp wasn't shy about flaunting his American Express Black Card, he otherwise frowned on displays of wealth or excessive materialism. One of the few times he expressed anger was when he noticed a new Porsche in Palantir's parking lot (it belonged to a company executive).

According to Nathan Gettings, the comparatively low pay, coupled with the fact that Palantir was an unknown company doing arcane work, initially made it hard to attract promising job candidates. "It was difficult to hire people, because why wouldn't you go work at Facebook or some other company that is going to pay well now and that you can explain to your friends?" says Gettings. He and the other cofounders would eventually conclude that people who joined Palantir straight out of college had the best chance of succeeding at the company. Money wasn't as much of an issue for them, and they generally had an easier time adapting to Palantir's distinctive culture.

During the early years, Karp, Gettings, Cohen, and Lonsdale all interviewed prospective hires, and each of them had to sign off on every job offer. Interviews with Karp were challenging—not because he asked hard questions, but because he hardly asked any and had neither the interest nor the ability to engage in small talk. Almost no one ever left the room thinking that he or she had nailed the interview. Quite the opposite: they would walk out resigned to not getting the job. But in his odd way, Karp proved to be adept at sizing up software engineers. Bob McGrew and Aki Jain became sufficiently intrigued by his nose for technical talent that they began sending him job candidates whom they had already decided they didn't want, just to see if Karp would also veto them. Karp had an unerring ability to sniff out the rejects.

But what was perhaps Karp's most notorious interview was with someone who got the job. Louis Mosley was an Oxford graduate who had hoped to pursue a political career in Britain. But his family history made that an impossibility: his grandfather was Oswald Mosley, the British fascist leader during World War II, and his grandmother was Diana Mitford, one of the famous Mitford sisters and who is best remembered for her close friendship with Hitler. A group of historians once named Oswald Mosley the worst Briton of the twentieth century, and while Louis had rejected his grandparents' views, his surname proved to be an insurmountable liability—Conservative Party insiders ultimately made clear that they would never be able to put him up for office because he was tainted by association.

Through a friend, he was introduced to Palantir, and after several rounds of interviews, he flew to Palo Alto to meet with Karp.

As soon as Mosley took a seat, Karp began reciting a fiery speech that Oswald Mosley gave in 1939 demanding that Britain seek peace with Nazi Germany. ("Our generation shall not die like rats in Polish holes. They shall not die but shall live to see above their heads the English sky, to feel beneath their feet the English soil, and to enjoy the fair English countryside. . . .") Karp didn't just repeat a few sentences; he went on for minutes, reproducing the speech from memory. Mosley sat in stunned silence. When Karp finished, he executed a few tai chi moves and walked out of the room without saying goodbye. A shaken Mosley figured that his family's dark past had torpedoed him again. But it hadn't: he was hired and ended up running Palantir's UK business. (A few years after the interview, Karp was in London, where he met with Mosley and a retired British military officer who was consulting for Palantir. Karp asked this person if he was aware of Mosley's background. He said that he was but added, "Well, we all have skeletons in our closet." Karp looked at him with disgust. "A skeleton?" he said incredulously. "That's fucking Godzilla in the closet.")

From its inception, Palantir had a policy of not hiring salespeople. According to Lonsdale, he and the other founders decided that a sales team would have a corrosive effect on innovation. "When you hire really strong alpha salespeople, they take over the culture," Lonsdale says. "They say, 'We're delivering the revenue, we're bringing the food home, and in order for us to feed you, we need X, Y, and Z.' The culture becomes really oriented around serving the alpha salespeople." The Palantirians believed that they could develop truly transformative technology and wanted to avoid a situation in which there would be pressure to push products out the door too quickly, and eschewing a sales force was a way of making sure that short-termism didn't prevail. Plus, Palantir already had an ace salesman in Karp, who would prove to be as persuasive with potential customers as he was with his colleagues. The irony was that no one at Palantir was more disdainful of salespeople than Karp. He once said that the only way he would ever hire a sales team was if he were "hit by a bus." He finally relented in 2019, the year before Palantir went public, but even then, he made clear that he took a dim view of salespeople. It was hard to tell if his antipathy to them sprang from a (well-founded) belief that they could never sell Palantir as capably as he could, or if it was an expression of self-loathing. Maybe it was a little of both.

However, Karp's initial effort to sell Palantir failed. Thiel had put up $100,000 to start the company and subsequently kicked in another $543,000. A venture capital firm that Thiel started in 2005, the Founders Fund, also made an early $856,000 investment in Palantir. But the company needed additional capital to continue to grow, and Thiel wanted to see if it could attract other investors. In 2005, Karp met with several leading VC firms. He was able to get meetings mainly on account of Thiel, whose involvement with Palantir opened doors that might otherwise have been closed. However, Karp quickly discovered that along Sand Hill Road, which traversed Palo Alto and Menlo Park and where nearly all the major VCs were clustered, there was little interest in the concept that Palantir was selling. The VCs were fixated instead on what Karp would later disparagingly refer to as "the commercial Internet"—basically, start-ups that sold things to consumers. They wanted to find the next Amazon.com. There was also a lot of buzz building around social networks such as Facebook and Myspace.

Skepticism about Palantir ran deep. For one thing, data analytics was as sexy as it sounded—which is to say, it wasn't at all. The so-called Big Data revolution was just taking off (and would be driven in no small part by the advent of those same social networks), and Silicon Valley investors just couldn't muster much enthusiasm for a data integration business. An additional stumbling block for Palantir was its focus on government work. While the VCs admired Palantir's patriotic spirit and agreed that technology being developed in the Valley could probably help combat terrorism, government contracts were hard to come by and often didn't pay all that well. From a national security standpoint, Palantir might have been a worthy, even noble endeavor. But as an investment proposition, it was unappealing.

The nadir came during a pitch meeting that Karp and some colleagues had with Sequoia Capital, which was arguably the most influential Silicon Valley VC. Sequoia had been an early investor in PayPal; its best-known partner, Michael Moritz, sat on the company's board and was close to Thiel. But Sequoia proved no more receptive to Palantir than any of the other VCs that Karp and his team visited; according to Karp, Moritz spent most of the meeting absentmindedly doodling in his notepad. Karp didn't say anything at the time, but later wished that he had. "I should have told him to go fuck himself," he says, referring to Moritz. But it wasn't just Moritz who provoked Karp's ire: the VC community's lack of enthusiasm for Palantir made Karp contemptuous of professional investors in general. It became a grudge that he nurtured for years after.

But the meetings on Sand Hill Road weren't entirely fruitless. After listening to Karp's pitch and politely declining to put any money into Palantir, a partner with one venture capital firm had a suggestion: if Palantir was really intent on working with the government, it could reach out to In-Q-Tel, the CIA's venture capital arm. In-Q-Tel had been started a few years earlier, in 1999 (the name was a playful reference to "Q," the technology guru in James Bond films). CIA Director George Tenet believed that establishing a quasi-public venture capital fund through which the agency could incubate start-ups would help ensure that the U.S. intelligence community retained a technological edge. The CIA had been created in 1947 for the purpose of preventing another Pearl Harbor, and a half century on, its primary mission was still to prevent attacks on American soil. Two years after In-Q-Tel was founded, the country experienced another Pearl Harbor, the 9/11 terrorist attacks, a humiliating intelligence failure for the CIA and Tenet. At the time, In-Q-Tel was working out of a Virginia office complex known, ironically, as the Rosslyn Twin Towers, and from the twenty-ninth-floor office, employees had an unobstructed view of the burning Pentagon.

In-Q-Tel's CEO was Gilman Louie, who had worked as a video game designer before being recruited by Tenet (Louie specialized in flight simulators; his were so realistic that they were used to help train Air National Guard pilots). Ordinarily, Louie did not take part in pitch meetings; he let his deputies do the initial screening. But because Thiel was involved, he made an exception for Palantir and sat in on its first meeting with In-Q-Tel. What Karp and the other Palantirians didn't know when they visited In-Q-Tel was that the CIA was in the market for new data analytics technology. At the time, the agency was mainly using a program called Analyst's Notebook, which was manufactured by i2, a British company. According to Louie, Analyst's Notebook had a good interface but had certain deficiencies when it came to data processing that limited its utility. "We didn't think their architecture would allow us to build next-generation capabilities," Louie says.

Louie found Karp's pitch impressive. "Alex presented well," he recalls. "He was very articulate and very passionate." As the conversation went on, Karp and his colleagues talked about IGOR and how it had basically saved PayPal's business, and it became apparent to Louie that they might just have the technical aptitude to deliver what he was looking for. But he told them that the interface was vital—the software would need to organize and present information in a way that made sense for the analysts using it, and he described some of the features they would expect. Louie says that as soon as he brought this up, the Palantir crew "got out of sales mode and immediately switched into engineering solving mode" and began brainstorming in front of the In-Q-Tel team. "That was what I wanted to see," says Louie.

He sent them away with a homework assignment: he asked them to design an interface that could possibly appeal to intelligence analysts. On returning to Palo Alto, Cohen and Gettings sequestered themselves in a room and built a demo that included the elements that Louie had highlighted. A few weeks later, the Palantirians returned to In-Q-Tel to show Louie and his colleagues what they had come up with. Louie was impressed by its intuitive logic and elegance. "If Palantir doesn't work, you guys have a bright future designing video games," he joked. In-Q-Tel ended up investing $1.25 million in exchange for equity; with that vote of confidence, Thiel put up another $2.84 million. (In-Q-Tel did not get a board seat in return for its investment; even after Palantir began attracting significant outside money, the company never gave up a board seat, which was unusual, and to its great advantage.)

Karp says the most beneficial aspect of In-Q-Tel's investment was not the money but the access that it gave Palantir to the CIA analysts who were its intended customers. Louie believed that the only way to determine whether Palantir could really help the CIA was to embed Palantir engineers in the agency; to build software that was actually useful, the Palantirians needed to see for themselves how the analysts operated. "A machine is not going to understand your workflows," Louie says. "That's a human function, not a machine function." The other reason for embedding the engineers was that it would expedite the process of figuring out whether Palantir could, in fact, be helpful. If the CIA analysts didn't think Palantir was capable of giving them what they needed, they were going to quickly let their superiors know. "We were at war," says Louie, "and people did not have time to waste."

Louie had the Palantir team assigned to the CIA's terrorism finance desk. There they would be exposed to large data sets, and also to data collected by financial institutions as well as the CIA. This would be a good test of whether Karp and his colleagues could deliver: tracking the flow of money was going to be critical to disrupting future terrorist plots, and it was exactly the kind of task that the software would have to perform in order to be of use to the intelligence community. But Louie also had another motive: although Karp and Thiel were focused on working with the government, Louie thought that Palantir's technology, if it proved viable, could have applications outside the realm of national security, and if the company hoped to attract future investors, it would ultimately need to develop a strong commercial business. In-Q-Tel's mission was to fund start-ups whose products could help safeguard the United States but that "wouldn't be captured by the government," as Louie puts it. For Palantir, terrorism finance could be a springboard to opportunities in the financial sector.

Stephen Cohen and Aki Jain worked directly with the CIA analysts. Both had to obtain security clearance, and over time, numerous other Palantirians would do the same. Some, however, refused—they worried about Big Brother, or they didn't want the FBI combing through their financial records, or they enjoyed smoking pot and didn't want to give it up. Karp was one of the refuseniks, as was Joshua Goldenberg, the head of design. Goldenberg says there were times when engineers working on classified projects needed his help. But because they couldn't share certain information with him, they would resort to hypotheticals. As Goldenberg recalls, "Someone might say, 'Imagine there's a jewel thief and he's stolen a diamond, and he's now in a city and we have people following him—what would that look like? What tools would you need to be able to do that?'" Goldenberg says that some of his colleagues became very adept at conjuring imaginary scenarios that would tell him what he needed without giving away what they were really working on.

Starting in 2005, Cohen and Jain traveled on a biweekly basis from Palo Alto to the CIA's headquarters in Langley, Virginia. In all, they made the trip roughly two hundred times. They became so familiar at the CIA that analysts there nicknamed Cohen "Two Weeks." The Palantir duo would bring with them the latest version of the software, the analysts would test it out and offer feedback, and Cohen and Jain would return to California, where they and the rest of the team would address whatever problems had been identified and make other tweaks. In working side by side with the analysts, Cohen and Jain were pioneering a role that would become one of Palantir's signatures. It turned out that dispatching software engineers to job sites was a shrewd strategy—it was a way of discovering what clients really needed in the way of technological help, of developing new features that could possibly be of use to other customers, and of building relationships that might lead to additional business within an organization. The forward-deployed engineers, as they came to be called, proved to be almost as essential to Palantir's eventual success as the software itself. But it was that original deployment to the CIA, and the iterative process that it spawned, that enabled Palantir to successfully build Gotham, its first software platform.

However, all that makes the story sound tidier than it was. Ari Gesher, an engineer who was hired in 2005, says that from a technology standpoint, Palantir was pursuing a very ambitious goal. Some software companies specialized in front-end products—the stuff you see on your screen. Others focused on the back-end, the processing functions. Palantir, says Gesher, "understood that you needed to do deep investments in both to generate outcomes for users." According to Gesher, Palantir also stood apart in that it aimed to be both a product company as well as a service company. Most software makers were one or the other: they either custom-built software, or they sold off-the-shelf products that could not be tailored to the specific needs of a client. Palantir was building an off-the-shelf product that could also be customized.

In the end, it took Palantir around three years, lots of setbacks, and a couple of near-death experiences to develop a marketable software platform that met these parameters. One early challenge: the Palantirians had assumed, incorrectly, that CIA analysts mainly used structured data—formatted information such as spreadsheets and charts. What they discovered instead was that intelligence analysts made heavy use of memos, reports, diplomatic cables, and other written materials. The engineers were able to solve that problem, but others quickly arose, and even the most resilient employees experienced doubts. "There were moments where we were like, 'Is this ever going to see the light of day?'" Gesher says. The work was arduous, and there were times when the money ran short. A few key people grew frustrated and talked of quitting.

Palantir also struggled to win converts at the CIA. Even though In-Q-Tel was backing Palantir, analysts were not obliged to switch to the company's software, and some who tried it were underwhelmed. Rosa Smothers, who worked as a CIA counterterrorism and cyberthreat analyst from 2006 to 2017, says that neither she nor any of her colleagues ever used Palantir. At one point, Smothers says, she and other analysts were given a weeklong Palantir tutorial. While the interface was impressive, the program was just too complicated to operate. "It was such a cumbersome piece of software," she says. "Maybe it was great if you really knew how to use it, but who had time to get a PhD in Palantir?"

The CIA has at least twenty thousand employees—for security reasons, it doesn't give a precise figure—and while Palantir met resistance in some corners, it found a more receptive audience in others. In what would become another pattern in Palantir's rise, one analyst was not just won over by the technology; she turned into a kind of in-house evangelist on Palantir's behalf. Sarah Adams discovered Palantir not at Langley, but rather on a visit to Silicon Valley in late 2006. Adams worked on counterterrorism, as well, but in a different section. She joined a group of CIA analysts at a conference in the Bay Area devoted to emerging technologies. Palantir was one of the vendors, and Stephen Cohen demoed its software. Adams was intrigued by what she saw, exchanged contact information with Cohen, and upon returning to Langley asked her boss if her unit could do a pilot program with Palantir. He signed off on it, and a few months later, Adams and her colleagues were using Palantir's software.

Adams says that the first thing that jumped out at her was the speed with which Palantir churned data. "We were a fast-moving shop; we were kind of the point of the spear, and we needed faster analytics," she says. She and her colleagues found that Palantir yielded quicker results than Analyst's Notebook. That wasn't all. According to Adams, Palantir's software had a "smartness" that Analyst's Notebook lacked. It wasn't just better at unearthing connections; even its basic search function was superior. Often, names would be misspelled in reports, or phone numbers would be written in different formats (dashes between numbers, no dashes between numbers). If Adams typed in "David Petraeus," Palantir's search engine would bring up all the available references to him, including ones where his name had been incorrectly spelled. This ensured that she wasn't deprived of possibly important information simply because another analyst or a source in the field didn't know that it was "Petraeus." Beyond that, Palantir's software just seemed to reflect an understanding of how Adams and other analysts did their jobs—the kind of questions they were seeking to answer, and how they wanted the answers presented. She says that Palantir "made my job a thousand times easier. It made a huge difference."

Her advocacy was instrumental in Palantir securing a contract with the CIA. Similar stories would play out in later deployments— one employee would end up championing Palantir, and that person's proselytizing would eventually lead to a deal. But the CIA was the breakthrough: it was proof that Palantir had developed software that really worked, and also the realization of the ambition that had brought the company into being. Palantir had been founded for the purpose of assisting the U.S. government in the war on terrorism, and now the CIA had formally enlisted its help in that battle.

FOUR

SEEING STONES AND PRYING EYES

In 2013, *Forbes* published a feature about Karp and Palantir. The story opened with Karp taking a hike near Stanford University's campus, trailed by a bodyguard. Karp told the magazine that having full-time protection was a drag. "It puts a massive cramp on your life," he said. "There's nothing worse for reducing your ability to flirt with someone." He spoke wistfully of his student days in Germany, when he "would walk around, go into skanky places in Berlin all night. I'd talk to whoever would talk to me, occasionally go home with people, as often as I could. I went to places where people were doing things, smoking things. I just loved it." He stressed the importance that he attached to his own privacy: "I didn't sign up for the government to know when I smoke a joint or have an affair." The article cited a talk that he had given to Palantir employees, in which he said that part of Palantir's mission and challenge was to ensure that civil liberties and personal privacy enjoyed strong protection amid the rise of surveillance technology. "We have to find places that we protect away from government so that we can all be the unique and interesting and, in my case, somewhat deviant people we'd like to be."

For Karp, the *Forbes* piece was an opportunity to try to assuage concerns about Palantir. In emphasizing how much he valued his own privacy, he was conveying the message that he valued everyone else's privacy, too, and that Palantir could be trusted to respect civil liberties. It was clever marketing, but it wasn't just lip service. From the outset, Karp recognized the danger inherent in the kind of technology that Palantir was building. Inevitably, a lot of the data that intelligence analysts waded through was personal—phone records, credit card bills, and so forth—and any software program that made their work easier could contribute to the erosion of privacy and civil liberties. The early engineers at Palantir were generally too young and besotted with coding to consider the broader implications of their work. But Karp was alert to the risks.

Despite his lack of technical training—or, perhaps, because of it—Karp came up with a novel idea for addressing worries about civil liberties: he asked the engineers to build privacy controls into the software. Gotham was ultimately equipped with two guardrails—users were able to access only information that they were authorized to view, and the platform generated an audit trail that indicated if someone tried to obtain material off-limits to them. Karp liked to call it a "Hegelian" remedy to the challenge of balancing public safety and civil liberties, a synthesis of seemingly unreconcilable objectives. As he told Charlie Rose during an interview in 2009, "It is the ultimate Silicon Valley solution: you remove the contradiction, and we all march forward."

According to Max Chafkin, who wrote an unauthorized biography of Peter Thiel called *The Contrarian*, Thiel was initially skeptical of the privacy controls—even though he was an avowed libertarian. But when I interviewed Thiel at his office in Los Angeles in December 2019, he touted Palantir's commitment to privacy and civil liberties. We met in an airy conference room with a wide view of the Hollywood Hills, and Thiel used a whiteboard to illustrate the privacy concerns that helped give rise to Palantir. With a black marker, Thiel drew a graph. At the end of one axis he wrote "Dick Cheney," and at the other end he wrote "ACLU." Cheney was vice president of the United States when 9/11 occurred and was known for his hawkishness. Thiel explained to me that Cheney represented "lots of security and no privacy," while the American Civil Liberties Union, or ACLU, was "lots of privacy but little security." After 9/11, Thiel said, it seemed likely that the Cheney view would prevail. He drew another axis, this one with "low-tech" at one end and "high-tech" at the other. "Low-tech" was a catchall for crude, highly intrusive technology that might be used by the government in its effort to combat terrorism. "High-tech," he said, was technology that was far more effective but also less invasive. Thiel's fear was that we would end up with a combination of low-tech and Cheney, in which case civil liberties would probably be crushed. He and Karp wanted to build software that could help the government keep the country safe while protecting privacy rights. "Maybe there were still trade-offs, but they were at a very different level," he said.

Legislation enacted by Congress six weeks after 9/11 reflected the Cheney view. The United and Strengthening America by Providing Appropriate Tools Required to Intercept and Obstruct Terrorism Act of 2001, otherwise known as the USA PATRIOT Act, vastly expanded the government's power in the realm of national security, an increased mandate that extended to electronic surveillance conducted overseas and domestically. And the Cheney view could also be seen in the advent a few months later of Total Information Awareness, or TIA, John Poindexter's controversial (and quickly shelved) program that was supposed to use sophisticated data analysis tools and predictive behavior modeling to help the government identify likely terrorists.

In 2005, on a trip to Washington to try to drum up interest in Palantir, Karp and Thiel met with Poindexter. Richard Perle, a prominent neoconservative who was serving as an adviser to Palantir, set the meeting up. Poindexter expressed interest in working with Karp and Thiel, but the feeling was not mutual. Poindexter seemed unchastened by the blowback that TIA had received; Thiel says that he was still pushing "harebrained ideas." Plus, he had made a lot of enemies in Washington and might have been more of a liability for Palantir than an asset. (According to Thiel, Poindexter wasn't angry about being snubbed but was unhappy when he later learned that Perle had been given a generous allotment of Palantir shares while he had received none.)

Ari Gesher, who was one of the first engineers at Palantir to work on privacy safeguards, says that apart from the justifiable concerns about civil liberties, it was apparent to him and others that mass surveillance was just not going to be an effective way of combating terrorism. The needle-in-the-haystack metaphor—the idea that you would have to go through mountains of information, most of it extraneous, to find a potential terrorist, was not correct. It was relatively easy to narrow searches down to potential bad actors; the real challenge was sorting out the people who truly posed a threat—who were either likely to commit acts of terrorism themselves or who were the masterminds behind future attacks. "It was a needle in a stack of needles" problem, as Gesher puts it, and as such, it required finely calibrated technology to sift through the data being collected by the CIA and other intelligence services.

Privacy engineering at Palantir was ultimately overseen by Courtney Bowman. He joined the company in 2010 from Google. Ordinarily, Karp was loath to hire people from the search giant, but Bowman shared his contempt for Google's business model.

A Stanford graduate who had double-majored in philosophy and physics, Bowman had worked in data analytics and quantitative analysis at Google and had come to believe that the company was an advertising firm "masquerading as a cuddly start-up." Google's technology, he says, "existed for the purpose of selling advertising and getting people to buy things."

Even more troubling, in Bowman's view, was that Google was stoking political division. The company was collecting massive quantities of personal data, and like Facebook, it was sorting people according to their political views and directing them to content that reinforced their biases and that was often inflammatory and misleading. This was six years before the 2016 election, in which disinformation on social media sites played such a critical role, but Bowman already recognized the potential danger. "There were all these externalities—the erosion of the political and social fabric, the Balkanization of society," says Bowman. "It was clear that we were tearing at the fabric of something that was really important, and this caused me a lot of discomfort. I had a lot of frustration on a philosophical level—what am I contributing to?" Adding to the frustration was the sense that most of his colleagues were either blind or indifferent to the damage Google's algorithms were doing. "I was in this world of really smart people who were mostly oblivious to this stuff, who were just happy to be on the Mountain View campus drinking smoothies all day."

Bowman had a friend at Palantir who had tried for several years to interest him in joining the company. Finally, in 2010, Bowman agreed to interview with Palantir, and after meetings with Karp, Stephen Cohen, Joe Lonsdale, Nathan Gettings, and others, he was offered a job. Bowman was not hired for a specific role, but Karp soon decided that he would lead Palantir's privacy engineering group. Bowman didn't have any obvious qualifications—he was neither an attorney nor a software engineer. But Karp was struck by the thoughtfulness that he brought to the issue of technology and civil liberties and saw him as someone who could lead a spirited internal conversation and also make a compelling case for Palantir externally. Under the wiry, intense Bowman, the privacy engineering group would grow to include not just engineers, but also lawyers, social scientists, and even philosophers. He also spearheaded the creation of an outside advisory panel on privacy and civil liberties, comprised mostly of academics. He came to serve as a kind of resident ethicist and ombudsman, making sure that Palantir's technology and employees adhered to legal requirements across a range of jurisdictions, as well as to the company's own standards for data protection.

And a moral sensibility did drive a lot of the decision-making at Palantir. At one point, a cigarette manufacturer sought Palantir's help with marketing and distribution. As Karp and Bowman considered the offer, it became clear to them that the company was looking to target poor, predominantly minority communities, and they opted to pass. In 2012, the U.S. State Department gently pressured Palantir to sell its software to Saudi Arabia. With the Arab Spring threatening governments throughout the Middle East and North Africa, American officials were worried about the stability of the Saudi regime and wanted to furnish it with technology that could help stave off a potential uprising. The deal would have been lucrative: the Saudis were willing to pay $100 million. But Karp balked; Saudi Arabia had an abysmal human rights record, and he did not want Palantir contributing to the abusive treatment of protesters or dissidents.

But that spurned deal highlighted what was perhaps the greatest risk with Palantir: that the values that supposedly guided its work wouldn't necessarily be shared by those who were buying its software. From Palantir's inception, there was always a question of whether clients would have the same commitment to privacy and civil liberties. Moreover, Palantir did not police the use of its software, nor were the controls foolproof; the client decided who within the organization had access to data and how energetically it wished to enforce those restrictions. The potential for abuse seemed vast. Lots of personal data would flow through Palantir's digital pipelines, and that information could be put to improper use. Karp didn't deny that possibility when I asked him about it. "Every technology is dangerous, including ours," he said.

When I asked Thiel about the risk of misconduct with Palantir, he answered by referring to the company's literary inspiration. "The Palantir device in the Tolkien books was a very ambiguous device in some ways," he told me. "There were a lot of people who looked into it and saw more than they should see, and things went badly wrong when they did." But that didn't mean the Palantir itself was flawed. "The Tolkien point I always make is that at the end of the day, it was actually a good device that was critical to the plot of the whole story. The way it worked was that Aragorn looked into the Palantir, and he showed Sauron the sword with which the One Ring had been cut off Sauron's finger at the end of the Second Age. This convinced Sauron that Aragorn had the One Ring and caused Sauron to launch a premature attack that emptied out Mordor and enabled the hobbits to sneak in and destroy the One Ring. The plot action was driven by the Palantir being used for good, not for evil. This reflected Tolkien's cosmology that something that was made by the good elves would ultimately be used for good."

Bowman, however, couldn't rely on good elves to ensure that Palantir's software was deployed responsibly. With customers, he tried a combination of moral suasion and appeals to self-interest to encourage rigorous use of the privacy controls. He said it was imperative to stress these points at the outset of the relationship. "There is a limited window of opportunity in which you can get organizations to contemplate self-regulation," Bowman explained. "The argument that you can make that we've found to be reasonably compelling is that if you self-regulate and talk about the ways that you've chosen to self-regulate, it positions you much better to use that data responsibly and avoid a backlash that can result in much more expansive regulation."

But Palantir's work with the investment bank JPMorganChase exposed the danger inherent in its technology. The bank became a client in 2009, enlisting Palantir's help for cybersecurity. Soon, though, the software was being used to surveil the bank's own staff, a story recounted in a *Bloomberg Businessweek* article in 2018, published under a misleading headline: "Palantir Knows Everything About You." The title suggested that Palantir had access to all the data filtering through its software—even sensitive personal information. But that wasn't true. The only time that Palantir engineers would see that data was when they were working directly with a client, and that was usually only temporary. The headline reflected a misconception about Palantir's work and ended up overshadowing the article, an excellent piece of reporting that highlighted the risks of Palantir's software, which were alarming enough.

According to *Bloomberg Businessweek*, the official at JPMorganChase who oversaw its use of Palantir's software was a former Secret Service agent. He allegedly went rogue, ignoring internal restrictions on data use to snoop on scores of employees, including senior figures at the bank. He became a "one-man National Security Agency," as the magazine put it. The bank discovered his misconduct after launching an investigation into a leak to *The New York Times*; he had apparently used Palantir's technology to unearth the information given to the *Times*. A former JPMorganChase cyber expert told *Bloomberg Businessweek* that Palantir's software had created a dystopian atmosphere inside the bank. "The world changed when it became clear everyone could be targeted using Palantir," this person said. "Nefarious ideas became trivial to implement; everyone's a suspect, so we monitored everything. It was a pretty terrible feeling."

The episode illustrated the potential pitfalls with Palantir's software: no matter how well-intentioned Karp and his colleagues were, it was the end users who ultimately determined whether the software was employed ethically. And there were some scandals involving Palantir itself that called into question just how well-intentioned the company really was. When Palantir first began working with the CIA, most analysts there were using i2's Analyst's Notebook. Information sitting in Palantir's software couldn't be exported to Analyst's Notebook, and vice versa, and the lack of interoperability was impeding Palantir's effort to gain new users at Langley. Analyst's Notebook was also used by others in the intelligence community, as well as by the U.S. military. If Palantir hoped to make inroads across the national security landscape, it was going to have to solve the interoperability problem.

In 2010, i2 sued Palantir for fraud and industrial espionage. It alleged that in 2006, Shyam Sankar, Palantir's head of business development at the time, had established a bogus company called SRS Enterprises for the purpose of obtaining i2's software. According to i2, Palantir used its access to that technology to "develop new Palantir software products and capabilities designed to enable Palantir to compete unfairly against i2." Specifically, i2 charged that Palantir stole trade secrets in order to build tools that would allow users to migrate their data from Analyst's Notebook to Palantir's software. The complaint cited other acts of theft and deceit. It claimed, for instance, that Palantir had copied a number of interface icons from i2. Palantir denied the allegations, but a year after i2 filed suit, it agreed to settle the case for a reported $10 million.

Other incidents also stoked concerns about Palantir's trustworthiness. In the late 2000s, while Karp and his colleagues were focused on deepening their ties to the intelligence community, the company did pro bono work in the hope of raising its profile.

It gave its software to the Combating Terrorism Center at West Point to help analysts there sift through material captured from Al Qaeda fighters in Iraq. Similarly, the company granted the International Consortium of Investigative Journalists free use of its technology to try to piece together the network of individuals responsible for the 2002 kidnapping and murder in Pakistan of *Wall Street Journal* reporter Daniel Pearl.

In 2008, Palantir provided its software free of charge to Citizen Lab, a research group associated with the University of Toronto's Munk School of Global Affairs and Public Policy. Founded in 2001 by Ron Deibert, a political scientist, Citizen Lab specialized in what he described as "counterintelligence for civil society"—it was a watchdog that aimed to put a spotlight on digital threats to NGOs and other entities. It first drew recognition for its study of how Russia used cyberattacks as a precursor to its invasion of the republic of Georgia in 2008. Soon thereafter, Palantir reached out and offered Citizen Lab the use of Palantir Gotham. It was an open-ended arrangement; there was no time limit, nor any obligation to become a paying customer after a certain period. The Palantirians told Deibert that he and his team could use the software however they wished. Citizen Lab was a small unit with a limited budget, and Deibert was happy to give Palantir's technology a try. He and his colleagues decided to use it for their next major investigation: representatives of the Dalai Lama, concerned that the computer systems of various Tibetan organizations had been infiltrated, had asked Citizen Lab for help trying to determine who the perpetrators were. Two researchers traveled to the Dalai Lama's office in Dharamshala, India, to gather evidence. They also visited Tibetan consulates in Europe and the United States.

They discovered that the cyber espionage directed at Tibetan interests was part of a much larger spying network that they traced back to China. Over 1,200 computers in more than one hundred countries had been targeted. The case was cracked when Nart Villeneuve, an analyst for Citizen Lab, found some odd coding that appeared in multiple files that he was examining. Via a Google search, he figured out that the malware behind GhostNet, as investigators dubbed the espionage campaign, had originated in a group of servers on China's Hainan Island. Deibert and his colleagues could not establish whether the Chinese government itself was behind the attacks, but that seemed like a reasonable assumption.

In March 2009, Citizen Lab published a fifty-three-page report detailing its findings. The report included screenshots of several spidergrams that had been generated using Palantir's software. But according to Deibert, Palantir's contribution to the project was minimal. While its software helped identify connections between some domains and IP addresses, the Citizen Lab team would have found those links with or without Palantir. And apart from that, says Deibert, Palantir "didn't play much of a role in the investigation." It wasn't that the software was deficient; it was simply geared to a different kind of challenge. Palantir's technology was for big datasets; with GhostNet, Citizen Lab was painstakingly assessing a limited amount of data, and Palantir just wasn't all that helpful. "It was the wrong tool for us," says Deibert.

A few months after Citizen Lab released its report, someone sent Deibert a picture of an ad that Palantir had placed in the Washington, D.C., Metro's Pentagon City station touting the role that it had supposedly played in solving the GhostNet case. It was a strategic choice of location: with Palantir trying to win business from the U.S. military, the ad was a direct pitch to Pentagon personnel. Deibert was dismayed to discover that Palantir had "appropriated our report for marketing purposes," as he puts it. And it wasn't just that the company was claiming credit that it didn't deserve; Deibert believed that he and his colleagues had been played. "We thought, 'So that's how it works,'" Deibert says. "We felt used, for sure." (During the interview with Charlie Rose, Karp cited Palantir's work on the Dalai Lama case.)

In 2011, at the same time that it was tied up in litigation with i2, Palantir became embroiled in a bigger scandal. In February of that year, the hacktivist group known as Anonymous released thousands of emails from a California-based company called HBGary Federal, which specialized in corporate intelligence. Anonymous had obtained the emails after an HBGary Federal executive claimed that he would publicly unmask members of the group. The messages implicated Palantir in a plot to wage a disinformation campaign on behalf of Bank of America. The bank, fearing that it would be targeted by WikiLeaks, the shadowy online organization that published classified U.S. military documents as well as internal communications from governments and corporations, had enlisted the help of the law firm Hunton & Williams to launch a preemptive strike. The law firm invited HBGary Federal to develop a proposed plan of action. HBGary Federal recruited Palantir and another software company, Berico Technologies, to assist in this effort.

The emails revealed an elaborate scheme to undermine the credibility of WikiLeaks. One idea was to submit falsified information to WikiLeaks, which would then be revealed as fake to damage the group's credibility. Another was to target WikiLeaks supporters, notably the lawyer and activist Glenn Greenwald. The emails showed that HBGary Federal, Palantir, and Berico Technologies, whose collaborative efforts were referred to internally as Team Themis, were also involved in a plot against critics of the U.S. Chamber of Commerce. The Chamber allegedly wanted to dig up information that could be used to discredit its detractors—by finding evidence, for instance, that they were being financed by unions. Here, too, one solution proposed by Team Themis was to use fake documents.

When Anonymous announced that it had the HBGary Federal emails, Palantir quickly sought to distance itself from the controversy. The company released a statement saying that it "never has and never will condone the sort of activities that HBGary recommended" and that Palantir had played no part in conceiving the planned subterfuge. However, the emails suggested otherwise. For instance, one Palantir employee who was a member of Team Themis expressed enthusiasm for the idea of trying to damage Greenwald's credibility. Palantir suspended that employee, and Karp ultimately issued a statement expressing regret for Palantir's role in the scandal. "We do not provide—nor do we have any plans to develop—cyber offensive capabilities," he wrote. "Personally and on behalf of the entire company, I want to publicly apologize to progressive organizations in general, and Mr. Greenwald in particular, for any involvement that we may have had in these matters." Karp later told me that he had no knowledge of the plots to target WikiLeaks and the Chamber's critics, and he attributed Palantir's involvement to "growing pains."

Two years after that scandal, in May 2013, Greenwald was at the center of one of the biggest intelligence leaks of the postwar era. He helped the whistleblower Edward Snowden disseminate thousands of classified documents that he had illegally taken from the National Security Agency, or NSA. The purloined files showed that the NSA had conducted mass surveillance programs that monitored the phone calls and electronic communications of Americans and other private citizens around the world. As the investigative reporter Shane Harris noted at the time, it was the realization of John Poindexter's TIA program, but with two important differences. Poindexter had wanted to anonymize all personal information and to include an audit trail to guard against potential abuses, but the NSA spurned both recommendations.

One of the NSA surveillance programs, called PRISM, allowed the agency to pull data from the servers of Google, Apple, Yahoo!, and other major tech firms. The companies were adamant that they did not give the government access to their servers, which raised an obvious question: If they weren't willingly sharing that data, how did the NSA obtain it? As it happened, Palantir had a tool called Prism, and not surprisingly, this prompted speculation that Palantir had somehow helped the NSA hack the databases of its fellow tech companies. Palantir denied that its Prism program had anything to do with the NSA's spying. In a statement it released in early June 2013, the company said that Prism was a data integration tool that it had developed for hedge funds and other financial institutions.

But what Palantir did not acknowledge at the time was that it had a relationship with the NSA. While the NSA already had its own data visualization software, a system called Renoir, it had used Gotham on a trial basis. A former NSA analyst said Renoir was a flop—"probably the worst piece of software I've ever used in my life," as he put it. He explained the difficulties he encountered with Renoir: "I would run twelve different searches in twelve different databases, and then I would export all of the search results into CSV files. And then I pull up Excel and run CONCAT functions to connect all of the spreadsheets together, and then I would run an import into Renoir. But Renoir would break constantly because I think its max was like ten thousand rows, but in practice, based on how many columns there were, the memory might overload at two thousand rows, but you didn't know until you started it. So you'd kick it off, it would run for two hours, and then it would crash. You would lose all your work, and you'd have to reboot and start again. And I would do this for a whole day every week on every targeting package that I was working." He said that Palantir's software "wasn't magical" but didn't crash or require the bootstrapping that Renoir did. However, his request to switch to Palantir was denied; he was told that if his needs were not being satisfied by the software that was already available to him, he could try to have something new built in-house.

Apart from the statement that it released regarding PRISM, Palantir never publicly commented on its work with the NSA. In a town hall meeting with Palantir employees in 2015—a recording of which was obtained by *BuzzFeed*—Karp said that the NSA had ended its relationship with Palantir but didn't elaborate. He and Thiel both suggested to me that the decision was made by senior officials who rejected Palantir in part because the software automatically produced audit logs, and they did not want to leave a trail of evidence that might indicate illegal conduct. The former NSA analyst believed that there was a simpler explanation: the NSA had sunk a lot of money into Renoir and just didn't want to own up to the fact that it was an expensive bust. "Don't attribute to malice things that can be much more easily explained as incompetence," he said. Regardless, it was possible that Palantir's software had contributed in some way to the NSA's dragnet—and the spy agency was under no obligation to let Palantir know that.

Palantir's foray into domestic law enforcement was an extension of its counterterrorism work. In 2007, the New York City Police Department's intelligence unit began a pilot program using Palantir's software. Before 9/11, the intelligence division had primarily focused on crime syndicates and narcotics. But its mandate changed after the terrorist attacks. The city tapped David Cohen, a CIA veteran who had served as the agency's deputy director of operations, to run the unit, and with the city's blessing, he turned it into a full-fledged intelligence service employing some one thousand officers and analysts. Several dozen members of the team were posted overseas, in cities including Tel Aviv, Amman, Abu Dhabi, Singapore, London, and Paris. "The rationale for the N.Y.P.D.'s transformation after September 11th had two distinct facets," *The New Yorker*'s William Finnegan wrote in 2005. "On the one hand, expanding its mission to include terrorism prevention made obvious sense. On the other, there was a strong feeling that federal agencies had let down New York City, and that the city should no longer count on the Feds for its protection." Finnegan noted that the NYPD was encroaching on areas normally reserved for the FBI and the CIA but that the federal agencies had "silently acknowledged New York's right to take extraordinary defensive measures."

Cohen became familiar with Palantir while he was still with the CIA, and he decided that the company's software could be of help to the intelligence unit. In what was becoming a familiar refrain, there was internal resistance. "For the average cops, it was just too complicated," says Brian Schimpf, one of the first forward-deployed engineers assigned to the NYPD. "They'd be like, 'I just need to look up license plates, bro; I don't need to be doing these crazy analytical processes.'" IBM's technology was the de facto incumbent at the NYPD, which also made it hard to convert people. Another stumbling block was price: Palantir was expensive, and while the NYPD had an ample budget, not everyone thought it was worth the investment. But the software caught on with some analysts, and over time, what began as a counterterrorism deployment moved into other areas, such as gang violence.

This mission creep was something that privacy advocates and civil libertarians anticipated. Their foremost worry, in the aftermath of 9/11, was that innocent people would be ensnared as the government turned to mass surveillance to prevent future attacks, and the NSA scandal proved that these concerns were warranted. But another fear was that tools and tactics used to prosecute the war on terrorism would eventually be turned on Americans themselves. The increased militarization of police departments showed that "defending the homeland" had indeed morphed into something more than just an effort to thwart jihadis. Likewise, police departments also began to use advanced surveillance technology. Andrew Guthrie Ferguson, a professor of law at George Washington University who has written extensively about policing and technology, says that capabilities that had been developed to meet the terrorism threat were now "being redirected on the domestic population."

Palantir was part of this trend. In addition to its work with the NYPD, it provided its software to the Cook County Sheriff's Office, the Virginia State Police, and the New Orleans Police Department (a relationship that was part of a broader engagement with the city and that would dissolve in controversy). However, it attracted much of its police business in its own backyard, California. The Long Beach and Burbank Police Departments used Palantir, as did sheriff departments in Los Angeles and Sacramento counties. The company's technology was also used by several Fusion Centers in California—these were regional intelligence bureaus established after 9/11 to foster closer collaboration between federal agencies and state and local law enforcement. The focus was on countering terrorism and other criminal activities.

But Palantir's most extensive and longest-lasting law enforcement contract was with the Los Angeles Police Department. It was a relationship that began in 2009. The LAPD was looking for software that could improve situational awareness for officers in the field—that could allow them to quickly access information about, say, a suspect or about previous criminal activity on a particular street. Palantir's technology soon became a general investigative tool for the LAPD. The department also started using Palantir for a crime-prevention initiative called LASER. The goal was to identify "hot spots"—streets and neighborhoods that experienced a lot of gun violence and other crimes. The police would then put more patrols in those places. As part of the stepped-up policing, officers would submit information about people they had stopped in high-crime districts to a Chronic Offenders Bulletin, which flagged individuals whom the LAPD thought were likely to be repeat offenders.

This was predictive policing, a controversial practice in which quantitative analysis is used to pinpoint areas prone to crime and individuals who are likely to commit or fall victim to crimes. To critics, predictive policing is something straight out of the Tom Cruise thriller *Minority Report*, in which psychics identify murderers before they kill, but even more insidious. They believe that data-driven policing reinforces biases that have long plagued America's criminal justice system and inevitably leads to racial profiling.

Karp was unmoved by that argument. In his judgment, crime was crime, and if it could be prevented or reduced through the use of data, that was a net plus for society. Blacks and Latinos, no less than whites, wanted to live in safe communities. And for Karp, the same logic that guided Palantir's counterterrorism work applied to its efforts in law enforcement—people needed to feel safe in their homes and on their streets, and if they didn't, they would embrace hard-line politicians who would have no qualms about trampling on civil liberties to give the public the security it demanded. Palantir's software, at least as Karp saw it, was a mechanism for delivering that security without sacrificing privacy and other personal freedoms.

However, community activists in Los Angeles took a different view of Palantir and the kind of police work that the company was enabling. An organization called the Stop LAPD Spying Coalition organized protests and also published studies highlighting what it claimed was algorithmic-driven harassment of predominantly black and Latino neighborhoods and of people of color. LASER, it said, amounted to a "racist feedback loop." In the face of criticism, the LAPD grew increasingly sensitive about its predictive policing efforts and its ties to Palantir. In 2019, when I was working on my story about Palantir for *The New York Times Magazine*, I tried to meet with LAPD officials to talk about Palantir, but they declined.

Six years earlier, however, a Princeton doctoral candidate named Sarah Brayne, who was researching the use of new technologies by police departments, was given remarkable access to the LAPD. Over the course of many months, Brayne went on ride-alongs in patrol cars and helicopters, interviewed dozens of officers, and saw up close how Palantir's technology was being employed. She found that it was used extensively—more than one thousand LAPD employees had access to the software—and was taking in and merging a wide range of data, from phone numbers to field interview cards (filed by police every time they made a stop) to images culled from automatic license plate readers, or ALPRs. Through Palantir, the LAPD could also tap into databases of police departments in other jurisdictions, as well as those of the California state police. In addition, they could pull up material that was completely unrelated to criminal justice—social media posts, foreclosure notices, utility bills.

Via Palantir, the LAPD could obtain a trove of personal information. Not only that: through the network analysis that the software performed, the police could identify a person of interest's family members, friends, colleagues, associates, and other relations, putting all of them in the LAPD's purview. It was a virtual dragnet, a point made clear by one detective who spoke to Brayne. "Let's say I have something going on with the medical marijuana clinics where they're getting robbed," he said. "I can put in an alert to Palantir that says anything that has to do with medical marijuana plus robbery plus male, black, six foot." He readily acknowledged that these searches could just be fishing expeditions and even used a fishing metaphor. "I like throwing the net out there, you know?" he said.

Brayne's research showed the potential for abuse. It was easy, for instance, to conjure nightmare scenarios involving ALPR data. A detective could discover that a reluctant witness was having an affair and use that information to coerce his testimony. There was also the risk of misconduct outside the line of duty—an unscrupulous analyst could conceivably use Palantir's software to keep tabs on his ex-wife's comings and goings. Beyond that, millions of innocent people were unknowingly being pulled "into the system" simply by driving their cars. When I spoke to Brayne, she told me that what most troubled her about the LAPD's work with Palantir was the opaqueness. "Digital surveillance is invisible," she said. "How are you supposed to hold an institution accountable when you don't know what they are doing?"

FIVE

THE COMMERCIAL BREAK

In 2012, journalist Mark Bowden published a book about the U.S. military raid that killed Osama bin Laden. It was titled *The Finish* and included a reference to Palantir. Bowden wrote, "The hunt for bin Laden and others drew on an unfathomably rich database, accessible to anyone in the world with the proper security clearance, whether a Marine officer at an outpost in Afghanistan or a team of analysts working in Langley. Sifting through it required software capable of ranging deep and fast and with keen discernment—a problem the government itself proved less effective at solving than were teams of young software engineers in Silicon Valley. A start-up called Palantir, for instance, came up with a program that elegantly accomplished what TIA [Total Information Awareness] had set out to do. Founded . . . by Alex Karp and Peter Thiel—the latter the billionaire cocreator of PayPal and an early Facebook investor—Palantir developed a product that actually deserves the popular designation Killer App."

Bowden, who was best known for the book *Black Hawk Down*, did not say that Palantir had contributed to the daring operation that resulted in bin Laden's death the year before; he merely cited Palantir as a company producing the kind of technology that could help America prosecute the war on terrorism. But some readers inferred that the company's software had been used to track down the Al Qaeda leader. Soon after *The Finish* was released, Palantir was being hailed as the Silicon Valley start-up that helped take out the terrorist mastermind responsible for 9/11.

When bin Laden was killed, there were murmurings in Palantir's Palo Alto office that the company had somehow been involved. It was not unreasonable conjecture: the CIA used Palantir's software, as did the United States Special Operations Command, or SOCOM, which oversaw the units that conducted the assault on bin Laden's compound in Pakistan. But neither the military nor the CIA has ever commented publicly. (The son of Admiral William McRaven, who was in charge of the raid, ended up working at Palantir, but that didn't prove anything.) In 2020, I spoke—separately—to two former CIA analysts who had been part of the hunt for bin Laden, and both insisted that Palantir had played no part in their work.

But when Bowden's book was published, Karp and Palantir were handed a PR bonanza. Karp became very adept at answering questions about Palantir's possible role in a cryptic way that was meant to suggest that it was true. In 2019, during one of my interviews with him for *The New York Times Magazine*, I asked about the bin Laden claim. "People say that," he replied. "I'm very proud of what people think." Several years later, I raised the topic again and pressed Karp for proof. He conceded that he had no way of knowing whether Palantir's technology was used but had come to believe that it had been. By that point, though, the story was part of Palantir lore.

Karp and his colleagues naturally hoped that the bin Laden rumors would generate new business, not only in the area of national security and defense but also in the commercial sphere, where Palantir was having difficulty gaining traction. What flag-waving company wouldn't want the same technology that had snagged America's most-hated enemy? Melody Hildebrandt, a forward-deployed engineer, says that she and her colleagues were not shy about mentioning the bin Laden link to potential clients. "We dropped it in every meeting, though sometimes they brought it up themselves," she recalls.

However, Palantir's sudden cachet didn't yield much in the way of new corporate business. For people in government, Palantir's software was a revelation—even in its earliest iterations, Gotham was usually better than what was otherwise available to them. When it came to technology, the government was a notoriously slow adopter, and much of its hardware and software was, by Silicon Valley standards, archaic. In the private sector, by contrast, the technology was more current, and Palantir's software didn't have the same novelty or wow factor. Moreover, companies tended to believe that they could meet most if not all of their technology needs through their own IT departments. But a bigger problem for Palantir was that it didn't yet have a product that could help corporate users on a sustained basis.

The company's first push into the commercial space was with a software platform tailored to financial institutions. Joe Lonsdale oversaw the project, which started in 2006. At the time, he was still employed by Clarium Capital, and he thought the pattern-recognition technology that Palantir was developing could be of value to people who traded stocks and bonds for a living. In-Q-Tel's Gilman Louie had foreseen that possibility when he seeded Palantir; it was with an eye toward developing a business line on Wall Street that he had the company assigned to the CIA's terrorism finance unit.

However, at a time when it still wasn't clear that Gotham was even going to work, some at the company thought it was ill-advised to divert resources and attention to a second, completely unrelated project. It ran counter to the prevailing wisdom about tech startups: that the likeliest path to success was a laser-like focus on one product. You didn't spread your bets: you staked it all on one big thing. But Palantir was not likely to survive on government contracts alone, and given that it didn't *have* any government contracts in 2006, it needed to cultivate a commercial business. Besides, Karp was predisposed to defying conventional wisdom; he was a contrarian by nature, inclined to go left if everyone else was going right.

Lonsdale and the team that he assembled—they called themselves the Hedgehogs—had an ambitious goal: they wanted to build a product that could rival and supplant the Bloomberg terminal. Named after its creator, former New York City Mayor Mike Bloomberg, the Bloomberg was a staple of trading desks around the world, essentially functioning as a one-stop shop for financial institutions—among its key features, it provided real-time data for global markets, served as a platform for electronic trading, and allowed users to message one another directly. The working name for the alternative that Palantirians hoped to produce was the Thiel Tool. It was a name chosen mainly as a way to get Thiel interested in the project; Lonsdale and his colleagues thought that his buy-in would be crucial to their prospects.

However, it was soon apparent that trying to take on Bloomberg was a bad idea—there was no way that Palantir, with its limited resources, was going to be able to challenge such an entrenched incumbent. So the Thiel Tool was abandoned in favor of something more modest: software that could collate market data in order to identify arbitrage opportunities and that could also help traders price alternative or distressed assets. But even as the project was scaled back, the finance team grew in size—at its peak, it had around one hundred employees—and attracted some notable talent, including Garry Tan, Kevin Simler, and Andy Aymeloglu. And the Hedgehogs had one advantage when it came to recruiting: the work didn't require government security clearance. Unless they were naturalized citizens, foreign-born engineers couldn't be hired for Gotham, so they were instead steered to the finance side.

But the Palantirians working on the investment software suffered from a sense of inferiority relative to their Gotham colleagues. "They were saving the world while we were building something to help rich people get richer," says one former engineer. He and others also felt that Karp was not as committed to the finance project as they might have hoped. He developed a deep affection for some of the people involved with it but showed little interest in what they were actually building, and while the engineers appreciated his hands-off approach, they found his detachment unsettling—they took it as an indication that Gotham mattered more to him (and it did).

Physical separation reinforced the status anxiety they felt. As Palantir continued to hire new employees, there wasn't sufficient space in the office to accommodate both teams. Fortunately, there was a solution right outside the front door. Palantir had relocated to Stanford Research Park, a complex that was jointly owned by Stanford University and the City of Palo Alto and that had been home to a number of notable tech companies. The development, located in a slightly remote part of town, was a fifteen-minute walk to the university and to the center of Palo Alto. Karp and his colleagues didn't mind being somewhat out of sight: they were building software for the intelligence community and thought it best to be working sub rosa. In the courtyard of the complex, there was a small, eight-sided building known, appropriately, as the Octagon, and the finance crew moved there from the main office. It gave them the added room they needed, but they now felt even more alienated from the rest of the company. "We called ourselves the redheaded unwanted stepchild," says the former engineer.

Even though the Hedgehogs felt like outcasts, the software platform that they built, called Metropolis, turned out to be quite good. However, timing had become an issue: the software was ready to go in 2008, but by then, the global financial crisis had started, an inopportune moment to be flogging a new product to banks and hedge funds. It didn't help that Palantir was expensive. Karp set pricing strategy, and his edict was that Palantir would compete on quality, not price. In his view, Palantir made the best data analytics software and was entitled to charge accordingly. But Metropolis was an unproven new entrant in what was already a competitive market, and its cost deterred some potential customers. However, Palantir did land a few notable clients. Bridgewater Associates, the secretive Connecticut-based hedge fund, bought Metropolis, as did Thomson Reuters, the financial data provider and news service. Credit Suisse signed on for help tracking insider trading and money laundering.

JPMorganChase also became a customer. Its relationship with Palantir began in 2009. Bank executives had learned that the New York City Police Department had recently hired Palantir to assist with counterterrorism; intrigued, they reached out seeking help in combating fraudsters who were trying to hack customer accounts and ATMs. Not long thereafter, the bank asked for Palantir's assistance with another problem: around 10 percent of the mortgages it had issued were in default at that time, a hangover from the Great Recession. But to dispose of those toxic assets, the bank had to be able to accurately value them, which required pulling in and analyzing huge data streams. For this task, Palantir supplied the bank with Metropolis. As the relationship with JPMorganChase deepened, Palantir opened a New York office—initially, it was an apartment in Tribeca that Lonsdale had rented—and a number of forward-deployed engineers essentially worked full-time at the bank's headquarters.

Although Palantir was not a cybersecurity firm, helping companies defend themselves against online fraud became a gateway into the corporate sector. Karp would be brought in to close deals, and by all accounts, he excelled at it. He seemed to perform the same mind tricks on fellow CEOs that he performed on his Palantir colleagues—he was offbeat and entertaining and very convincing without ever lapsing into sales jargon. Melody Hildebrandt sat in on a number of meetings in which Karp clinched contracts with new Palantir customers. "It was amazing to watch," Hildebrandt recalls. "We'd be there supposedly to talk about data and how to get it integrated, and he'd get on a whiteboard and just draw these circles and smiley faces, and people would be like, 'Yes.' I'd be thinking, *What is happening here?* But people were just in awe."

But while Karp was masterful at sealing deals, Palantir often struggled to keep those deals. In 2014, Home Depot enlisted Palantir's help after its payments systems were hacked and more than fifty million credit card numbers were stolen. Soon, the company was paying Palantir $5 million per year to use its software across a range of activities. But Home Depot ended the relationship in 2017. According to William Alden, a reporter for *BuzzFeed*, it dropped Palantir mostly on account of cost—it didn't think it was getting enough benefit from the technology to justify the relatively high price, and Home Depot's own IT department had come to believe that it could do the same job for less money. But some Home Depot executives had also become uncomfortable with how the Palantir team operated. They were put off by its efforts to solicit business from different parts of the company. This was standard practice for

Palantir—in the absence of a sales team, the forward-deployed engineers served as salespeople. As one former employee told Alden, "They try to find a specific problem the customer is trying to solve, and use that as a fishing expedition to leverage that into a bigger scope of work." There was nothing inherently shady about this—it was a smart strategy—but it did seem as if the Palantirians were especially aggressive with Home Depot—attending a company retreat, for instance.

Price and attitude became consistent complaints. In 2014, Hershey began using Palantir's software to help it analyze consumer trends at a granular level; it wanted to know not just how its products were faring in different markets, but the breakdown in sales between small grocery stores and supermarkets. Hershey was also deploying Palantir to try to derive greater insight into its supplier network—to learn more, for instance, about cacao-farming productivity in West Africa. But Hershey and Palantir also had greater ambitions: they wanted to establish a consortium of major consumer product companies that would use Palantir's software to pool and analyze data in order to make all their businesses more efficient. Karp cast the partnership in lofty terms, suggesting that it had the potential to transform the global economy. "I think capitalism is flawed," he told *Fortune* magazine. "We focus on big problems and finding the best partners to solve those problems."

Several companies signed on, including Coca-Cola and Kimberly-Clark, the paper goods manufacturer. Both agreed to do pilot projects with Palantir, with an eye to signing longer-term contracts. But the relationships quickly foundered. Kimberly-Clark, which was paying Palantir around $1 million per month, decided it could develop its own analytic tools for a fraction of that price. Cost was also an issue for Coca-Cola, but the company had additional complaints. According to internal Palantir documents that were obtained by *BuzzFeed,* Coca-Cola executives found it hard to work with the Palantirians, who were quite young and too casual for their taste. In addition, they felt that Palantir didn't have enough understanding of the soft drinks market to make it an effective partner.

All these concerns—cost, culture clashes, lack of industry-specific knowledge—were arguably just teething pains, the kinds of problems that were to be expected for a tech start-up trying to win business from Fortune 500 companies. The initial thrust into the commercial market did yield some successes, and the setbacks were valuable learning experiences—Palantir was being paid a lot of money to figure out what worked and what didn't. "It was a really significant applied R&D exercise," says Ted Mabrey, who now heads Palantir's commercial business. And in Palantir's defense, he says that while companies were eager to embrace Big Data, they sometimes had unrealistic expectations. "There was this idea that Big Data equals magic, in the same way that generative AI is now seen as magic," Mabrey recalls. "A lot of customers were just looking for buttons to make their problems go away—basically, give me the 'find terrorist' button."

Mark Elliot, who led the forward-deployed engineering team, says it was a "discovery phase," and what he and his colleagues discovered was that, as challenging as the data integration problems were at government agencies, they were even more acute on the commercial side. Palantir had one client, a multinational insurer, whose biggest customer was an international restaurant chain. It was a lucrative relationship, but astonishingly, the insurer had no idea if it was actually profitable. "They had a hundred different databases," Elliot recalls. "They mapped the customer's name a hundred different ways. The contracts were in many different languages. Their business was fine, they were getting paid. They just didn't know if they were making a profit on the relationship. And we were thinking, *Man, how can that be?*" It was clear to him and others that even major corporations, despite all the data and resources that they had at their disposal, sometimes lacked even the most basic information about their own businesses.

The frustration for Elliot and his colleagues was that Palantir didn't have software that could solve that problem. Neither alone nor in combination were Gotham and Metropolis capable of meeting the day-to-day operational needs of corporations. Gotham was a digital detective board, facilitating investigative workflows; it was useful for cybersecurity, but it was not software for the entire enterprise. Metropolis was even more limited in scope; it was a niche product, tailored to the financial industry. And as Mabrey puts it, the two platforms could be "tortured" only so much to make them useful for commercial clients.

To the forward-deployed engineers, the work felt like a prolonged exercise in bootstrapping—they were constantly having to build out new functions because they would encounter problems that couldn't be solved using the tools available in Gotham or Metropolis. There was value in that, and the engineers took satisfaction in devising those fixes. Too often, though, they were spending their days working around the limitations of Gotham and Metropolis and fashioning solutions for individual clients. "So much of the product work was just customized, which is fine, but that just helps you with one customer," recalls a former employee. It was this bespoke service that led some analysts to suggest that Palantir was a consulting firm as much as it was a tech company, and to question whether it could ever scale its business.

The way that Palantir operated—sending teams of software engineers all over the world, for projects that often took months—was also expensive. Karp had been promising a turn to profitability since the late 2000s, but by the mid-2010s, Palantir was nowhere near achieving that goal. True, it was a relatively young company and was still developing its products and reinvesting for growth. It took Amazon seven years to book its first quarterly profit, and it was an online retailer, not a company trying to sell esoteric software to the government. Even so, Palantir was hemorrhaging money; as late as 2018, it had a net loss of almost $600 million.

Oddly, despite its financial struggles, Palantir was suddenly finding it much easier to raise money. A decade after the company was shunned by the venture capital community, private investors were now eager to back it. Rupert Murdoch was one of them. The change in sentiment was driven in large part by recognition that the Big Data revolution was real. No doubt, the bin Laden story was an added selling point with some investors, giving Palantir a patriotic sheen or an appealing edginess. After a successful fundraising round in 2015, Palantir was valued at around $20 billion, which made it one of Silicon Valley's biggest so-called unicorns (companies with a valuation in excess of $1 billion).

The gap between Palantir's lofty valuation and its fundamentals was significant, and Thiel, who was exasperated by the slow growth of the business, saw it as a possible opportunity. In 2016, his friend Michael Ovitz, the famed Hollywood agent, tried to broker the sale of Palantir to Oracle. Thiel took a meeting with Oracle cofounder Larry Ellison to talk about the idea. It never went beyond that—Thiel and Ellison agreed that the two companies were not a great match. But Thiel told me later that Palantir was wildly overvalued at that time, and had Oracle been willing to pay $20 billion, the deal would have been a no-brainer. "We would have taken it," Thiel said. When he sat down with Ellison, he asked, "Has Oracle ever bought a company for anything like our price that was losing money?" The answer was no, and that was the end of the negotiation, such as it was.

As Palantir entered its second decade, there was also growing dissatisfaction inside the company. Some employees were frustrated by the ad hoc way in which the business operated—yes, Palantir had a mission, yet it often seemed to lack a sense of direction. That perception was amplified by the absence of an organizational structure, which made it hard to discern and pursue career paths. But while Palantir didn't have a formal hierarchy, a shadow one had emerged, which added to the unhappiness. According to one former employee, there was an in-crowd that received preferential treatment—more access to high-level conversations, more generous equity grants. The lack of transparency when it came to compensation was also a source of irritation for employees. Amid the internal discontent, Palantir found itself accused of racially biased hiring practices: in 2016, it was sued by the Justice Department for allegedly discriminating against job applicants of Asian descent. Palantir disputed the claim but ultimately paid $1.7 million to settle the case.

The company couldn't make its problems in the commercial market go away quite so easily. By the mid-2010s, it was obvious to many Palantirians that their work in the corporate sector was being handcuffed by the inadequacies of Gotham and Metropolis. That was Mark Elliot's view. He says the two software platforms were not going to make Palantir competitive in that space. As he puts it, "They weren't going to generate enough value for organizations that they'd want to pay us enough to make it worthwhile for us." While on a deployment, it occurred to Elliot that some of the data integration and analytical tools that Palantir had built to compensate for the shortcomings of Gotham and Metropolis could serve as the foundation for an entirely new system.

Elliot's insight touched off an intense debate within the company. No one disputed that Gotham and Metropolis were too limited to carry the corporate business forward. But there were pockets of resistance to change. One was the finance team, which recognized that if the company developed a commercial product with broader applications, Metropolis would almost certainly be taken off the market, which was obviously not an outcome that they wanted. Others, like Mabrey, were dubious about making such a dramatic shift because, even with the deficiencies of Gotham and Metropolis, Palantir's commercial side was booking sales. "My goal was to win, not to be pristine about how I won," says Mabrey.

But Karp concluded that a new product was needed. He had soured on Metropolis, and not just because of its limitations: he felt that it was too narrowly focused, and it catered to a clientele—hedge funds and other professional investors—that he wasn't really interested in serving. "We didn't get into this to build things that would make rich guys richer," he says, echoing the comment of the former Palantir employee. Still, terminating Metropolis was painful; most of the key figures in the finance group left Palantir as a result of Karp's decision. "It was like amputating your hand," says Shyam Sankar. "These people were legitimate geniuses and engineering titans."

Mark Elliot and several colleagues developed the new software in about eight weeks. It was called Foundry, and it quickly caught on with clients. BP, which hired Palantir to assist it with well management following the Deepwater Horizon disaster, began utilizing Foundry as soon as it was available, and it eventually became the company's operational software, used by thousands of employees around the world. Something similar happened with Airbus. In 2016, Airbus brought in Palantir to help solve production problems with a new commercial jet, the A350.

The A350 was being assembled by hundreds of workers spread across eight plants and four countries, and the plane consisted of around five million components. In other words, there was much that could go wrong. Even something as seemingly trivial as a shipment of defective screws could have a ripple effect. Faulty parts, missing parts, communications lapses—all these could cause bottlenecks. But with an operation of that scale, pinpointing exactly where delays were occurring was not easy. It stood to reason that the answer could be found in the profusion of data being generated on the assembly line, which was why Airbus turned to Palantir. The company dispatched five software engineers to Airbus's headquarters in Toulouse, France. They merged twenty-five data silos and integrated some four hundred datasets, and the results were almost immediate. Before, it took Airbus an average of twenty-four days to fix production glitches. After the company began using Palantir's software, it cut the turnaround time by a week, which translated into millions of dollars in savings.

From that initial engagement, a more extensive relationship evolved. Palantir opened an office in Toulouse, and in time, more than forty thousand Airbus employees were using Foundry. It ended up wiring the entire Airbus ecosystem: through a joint venture between Airbus and Palantir called Skywise, around 120 airlines worldwide began funneling data from their Airbus jets into Foundry. This information was used for everything from improving on-time performance to preventive maintenance. As with BP, Foundry became Airbus's operational software. "It had unique capability," said Marc Fontaine, who oversaw digital operations for Airbus at the time. He added that the company looked at alternatives to Palantir but had found nothing remotely equivalent. His boss, Airbus CEO Tom Enders, was even more enthusiastic; he said that bringing in Palantir was "one of the best decisions of my career."

With Foundry, Palantir finally had a product that could broaden its appeal to corporate users. However, there was no software solution to the challenge it was facing in trying to build its defense business. That would require an audacious lawsuit against the Army, litigation that exposed deep flaws in the Pentagon's procurement process and that ultimately enabled Palantir to become a major military contractor itself.

SIX

THE WAR AGAINST THE ARMY

In June 2024, an organization called Business Executives for National Security honored Karp at a dinner in Washington, D.C. He was one of two recipients that night of the group's annual Eisenhower Award, given to public servants and private citizens who help advance America's interests; the other honoree was U.S. Commerce Secretary Gina Raimondo. Karp was suffering from a cold and wasn't his usual animated self. But he also seemed humbled to be receiving an award named for President Dwight Eisenhower, especially as the United States and its allies had just marked the eightieth anniversary of D-Day, the invasion of Normandy that he led. Karp told the audience, gathered in a ballroom of the Ritz-Carlton Hotel, that he didn't feel entirely worthy of the award. "I'm a civilian and have never served in the military and have not put myself in harm's way," he said. He talked about Eisenhower's life, then turned his attention to the soldiers who had been under his command. "Why did young men from Iowa and Kansas risk their lives knowing that they could die to free Europe and to free people like me?" Karp asked. He tried to continue, but his voice cracked. "So moving," he said. The audience, touched by his sentiments, erupted in applause. Seeing him choke up was a first for most of his colleagues.

His comments that night expressed gratitude, but they also highlighted his respect for the military, which he saw as a repository of American strength and decency. Karp liked to point out that it had been at the forefront of desegregation, and he regarded it as the ultimate guarantor of the American-led international order. True, the Pentagon was a Palantir customer, and he had an incentive to lavish praise on the military. But he really did view it as a force for good. He had grown up with a different perspective. His parents, like many people of their generation, had protested against the Vietnam War and were generally opposed to the projection of American military power. At Haverford, Quaker pacifism remained an animating force on campus, even though the college was a nonsectarian institution by the time Karp arrived there. His speech in Washington that evening underscored the distance that he had traveled from Mount Airy as well as from our alma mater.

But if Karp's reverence for the military was surprising in light of his upbringing, it might also have seemed surprising for another reason: winning business from the Pentagon was the hardest fight that Palantir ever waged. It took years to resolve and was a particularly lurid tale of Washington bureaucratic scheming, made all the more scandalous by the fact that the United States was engaged in two wars at the time and that many soldiers had been killed or injured owing in part to the inadequate technology at their disposal. Palantir ended up suing the Army over its refusal to allow the company to bid on a contract for a new battlefield intelligence system, the final twist in a saga that cost Palantir millions of dollars in lobbying and legal fees and that drew the involvement of senior military figures and some of Congress's most influential voices, among them Senator John McCain. The skirmish created ill will in the Pentagon that lingered long after the dispute was resolved.

When Karp and his cofounders started Palantir, they knew that working with the military was high on their list of aspirations. As if declaring that ambition, they salted Palantir's culture with military lingo. *Forward-deployed* was a term that had its roots in warfighting. Internally, Palantir referred to forward-deployed engineers as *deltas*, after one of the military's most elite special operations units. Palantir came into being at a time when the tech industry had little interest in collaborating with the Pentagon, and with its defiantly casual dress codes, enthusiasm for recreational drugs, and do-no-evil pretensions, Silicon Valley seemed a world removed from the military and its warrior ethos. In this way, too, the Palantirians were outliers. But they were also throwbacks, because in many ways America's tech sector owed its existence to the military.

What had been a sleepy, pastoral corner of Northern California transformed in the 1950s and '60s into the world's most fertile technology hub, mainly as an outgrowth of the Cold War and America's determination to keep ahead of the Soviet Union on land, at sea, and in space. Fairchild Semiconductor, the San Jose–based company that gave rise to the tech industry as we know it, invented the silicon microchip in the late 1950s; the first buyer was the Pentagon, which used Fairchild's microchips for the B-70 bomber and the Minuteman missile program. Stanford University became the leading incubator of tech talent due to Pentagon research grants. The Internet began as a defense project: in the 1970s, the military needed a wireless computer network that troops could access even in remote locations, and this technology spawned the commercial Internet. Through the 1980s, defense spending was the lubricant for Silicon Valley innovation. As historian Margaret O'Mara puts it in her book *The Code: Silicon Valley and the Remaking of America*, the Pentagon budget "remained the big-government engine hidden under the hood of the

Valley's shiny new entrepreneurial sports car, flying largely under the radar screen of the saturation media coverage of hackers and capitalists."

The end of the Cold War saw a sharp reduction in America's defense outlays. The Pentagon's procurement budget was cut by more than half following the collapse of the Soviet Union. In 1993, Deputy Defense Secretary William Perry hosted a dinner at the Pentagon for the CEOs of the nation's leading defense contractors and delivered a bracing message: there was no longer enough business to support all of them, and the industry needed to consolidate. The gathering became known in military circles as "the last supper," and the companies did as advised: what had been a core group of around fifty aerospace and defense companies shrank, through mergers and acquisitions, to just five. With the United States now firmly established as the global hegemon and enjoying a so-called peace dividend, the long, mutually beneficial relationship between Silicon Valley and the Pentagon withered. The consumer Internet was where the real action was now, thanks to the emergence of companies like Amazon, which Jeff Bezos started in his garage in 1994.

9/11 shattered the post–Cold War tranquility. But while the terrorist attack drew comparisons to Pearl Harbor, there was little sense in Silicon Valley that the Pentagon's money spigot was going to be turned on again; in general, the tech industry didn't see much opportunity in the war on terrorism and remained fixated on e-businesses. Palantir may have been a start-up working at the leading edge of software, but its focus on national security and defense did not match the times. The frigid reception that Karp got from the venture capital community reflected a belief that Palantir had meager prospects.

In 2008, Karp hired a former Army Ranger named Doug Philippone to build Palantir's defense business. Philippone was a West Point graduate with a math degree who had served tours of duty in Iraq, Afghanistan, and Pakistan. He had distinguished himself in war, winning three Bronze Stars, two with citations for valor. General Stanley McChrystal, who led U.S. troops in Afghanistan, wrote that Philippone was "the single most aggressive and effective combat CDR [commander] I command." Multiple back surgeries forced Philippone to retire from the Army, and as he was considering his options, a friend told him that Palantir was in the market for someone who could help it win business from the military. Philippone was unfamiliar with Palantir but thought that being a "terrorist-hunting mathematician" could be interesting. For his part, Karp believed that a decorated veteran who had won the admiration of senior military figures could help Palantir make inroads at the Pentagon. He also thought that Philippone's battlefield skills might translate well to bureaucratic tussles. As he put it, "Doug is a killer, and he knows it's a zero-sum game."

Philippone was thirty-seven when he joined Palantir. Like Karp, he was an adult in a company that was otherwise full of kids, and he was the first person hired at Palantir whose personal experience could inform product development. From his multiple deployments, he knew what kind of information soldiers in the field needed and how they wanted it delivered, and although he had no background in technology (another similarity with Karp), he wasn't shy about asserting himself.

He saw that his colleagues were unfamiliar with battlefield intelligence and seemed to assume that the military operated the same way that the CIA did. "All the founders were thinking about the workflow around 9/11, where you're trying to connect the dots with all these intelligence agencies and police forces, and that's not how the military works," he says.

But there was an even more basic problem: the software did not include mapping capabilities. "In the intelligence world, you read a lot and then you write cables," says Philippone. "But in the military, everything starts and finishes with a map. You're always looking at a map, searching and discovering from the map, planning from the map, and running your battle from the map. You definitely go into other applications, but the centerpiece is the map." Among Palantir's engineers, there was some resistance to the idea of maps. It wasn't that they thought that Philippone was wrong; they just didn't want to add another wrinkle to the enormous technological challenge of trying to build software that could make a difference in the war on terrorism.

Philippone prevailed, and the engineers added a map application to Gotham. But the internal fight turned out to be a prelude to a much bigger battle. Palantir recorded some early successes in its effort to win military contracts. In 2008, a Special Missions Unit, or SMU, a designation given to the most elite and secretive fighting squads (the Navy's SEAL Team 6 is an SMU), began using Gotham. Shortly thereafter, so did a similar unit, the Army's 10th Special Forces Group (Airborne). Both the SMU and the 10th Special Forces Group had ample budgets and enjoyed discretion over how they spent their money. But other, larger units didn't have the same leeway, and the Army was already supplying troops in Afghanistan and Iraq with a battlefield intelligence platform.

Distributed Common Ground System-Army, or DCGS-A, known informally as "D-sigs," had been developed by Lockheed Martin, Raytheon, and Northrop Grumman, three of the survivors of the Last Supper. Introduced in 2007, it was supposed to give soldiers in theater the same data-collection and data-sharing capabilities that the intelligence community sought after 9/11. In an ironic twist, the software component was Analyst's Notebook, which was now owned by IBM.

But D-sigs had proven to be a clunker. It required hours of training, was cumbersome to operate even for those who were fully versed in it, frequently crashed, and was inaccessible in remote locations. Above all, it was failing at its most critical function: protecting soldiers. Roadside bombs and other improvised explosive devices, or IEDs, were killing large numbers of American and allied troops. An article in *Fortune* quoted one unnamed officer who served in Afghanistan. "D-sigs was a piece of shit, totally hopeless," he said. "You had to toggle from one thing to the next. You couldn't see anything as a whole. It was completely nonintuitive. If you misspelled a name, it would not match up with the other intel on the same guy or the same place." He went on. "You couldn't download anything onto a thumb drive, so whatever information you recorded, no one else had, unless you happened to have a secure broadband connection, which you rarely did. It was all on your laptop, and if you left the field, the person who replaced you had none of it. Plus, it pretty much always crashed at some point when you did get a connection."

That wonkiness contributed to one of the biggest breaches of classified information in U.S. history. Bradley Manning, an Army intelligence officer based in Iraq, had been trained to back up all his work, but as he testified during his 2013 court-martial trial, "The need to create backups was particularly acute given the relative instability and reliability of the computer systems we used in the field during deployment." Over time, Manning grew disenchanted with the U.S. wars in Iraq and Afghanistan, and because the inadequacies of D-sigs had forced him to make copies of everything to which he had access, he had a vast quantity of damaging material at his disposal when he decided to become a whistleblower. Manning ultimately shared over seven hundred thousand documents with WikiLeaks. The files included intelligence reports that revealed battlefield setbacks and human rights violations, as well as embarrassing cables sent by American diplomats.

Dissatisfaction with D-sigs was widespread, and in 2008 the Army's 5th Stryker Combat Brigade, Infantry 2nd Division, expressed interest in Palantir's software. Colonel Harry Tunnell led the unit. He was a colorful and controversial figure, considered brilliant by many of his colleagues but also someone with a habit of going rogue. He had been wounded in Iraq in 2003, sustaining a severe leg injury. On his desk, he kept the metal rod implanted in his leg during rehabilitation; a fellow colonel later alleged that Tunnell was determined to avenge his injury and kept the rod as "an illustration" of what the U.S. military was up against. According to a *New York Times Magazine* article, he had been reprimanded several times by other senior officers for what they regarded as overly aggressive tactics.

Most notably, he refused to embrace the counterinsurgency strategy that had become U.S. policy under General David Petraeus's leadership in 2007. Petraeus believed that effective counterinsurgency involved more than just killing enemy combatants; it required winning the favor of locals, in part by ensuring their security and helping promote economic development. Tunnell maintained that the Army was ill-equipped to handle such a broad mandate and that Americans were not "culturally suited" to take on the role of nation-building. In his view, the military's job was to eradicate the enemy, even if that required measures that "political correctness dictates that we cannot talk about," as he put it. Despite his open dissent from the Pentagon's established doctrine, he remained in command of his 3,800-troop brigade.

A few weeks after the 5th Stryker Brigade reached out to Palantir, Doug Philippone went to Fort Lewis, Washington, where the unit was based, to demonstrate Gotham for Tunnell. Impressed by what he saw, Tunnell invited Palantir to take part in a field training exercise with his brigade. Philippone dispatched two Palantir engineers to represent the company. Both were in their early twenties, had no combat experience, and were kind of ungainly. "You wouldn't have put a gun in their hands," Philippone jokes. The Palantirians, equipped with their own software, were pitted against the 5th Stryker's intelligence analysts, who were using D-sigs. The goal was to see who could pinpoint with greater speed and accuracy enemy locations and areas where U.S. troops had been attacked with IEDs. Despite their greenness, the Palantir duo easily outperformed the Army analysts—another in what would become a string of *Moneyball* moments as Palantir tried to win over the military. At the end of the exercise, Tunnell turned to his colleagues and said of Palantir's technology, "Does anyone *not* want this?"

In February 2009, Tunnell's brigade traveled to the National Training Center in Fort Irwin, California. Located in the Mojave Desert, the NTC was where U.S. troops went for final preparations before deploying overseas. The 5th Stryker's intelligence analysts were now using Gotham for their work. The software had also been updated to solve two of the biggest problems that the military was encountering in Afghanistan and Iraq (and some core flaws with D-sigs). Through Gotham, information collected in areas with little or no connectivity could now be uploaded and synchronized with other data as soon as a connection was reestablished. Gotham also now included a feature that Palantir called Nexus Peering that allowed analysts to merge and harmonize data across different servers, giving everyone in the field the same view. "This was absolutely the hardest technological work we ever did," says Bob McGrew. It was a breakthrough, he says, that became "foundational" to Palantir's defense business.

The 5th Stryker Brigade had been scheduled to go to Iraq, but at the last minute, it was reassigned to Afghanistan. Just before shipping out, the Pentagon informed Tunnell that his brigade would not be allowed to use Palantir. Tunnell was incensed, and after deploying to Afghanistan, he continued to lobby for it. In 2010, his persistence helped land Karp and Philippone a meeting with the Army's head of intelligence, Lieutenant General Richard Zahner. McGrew joined them for the meeting, where the Palantir group showed the latest version of Gotham. According to Philippone, Zahner responded enthusiastically and indicated that the Army was ready to award Palantir a contract to provide its software to a nine-brigade combat team that included Tunnell's unit. But the contract never materialized: higher-ups in the Pentagon, still committed to D-sigs, blocked it. It was a devastating setback for Palantir, which at that point had spent roughly $1.5 million to develop tools for the battlefield. "That's the kind of thing that can put a start-up out of business," says Philippone. "We had leveraged the whole company around this."

In the meantime, Tunnell's brigade was taking heavy casualties; in its first year in Afghanistan, it lost more than thirty soldiers. The Army finally relented and allowed Tunnell to have Palantir's software. Philippone dispatched several forward-deployed engineers to Kandahar Airfield, where the 5th Stryker Brigade was stationed, to help Tunnell's intelligence analysts merge their data and provide other technical support. There were also Palantirians on the ground in Iraq. Matt Grimm, who would later cofound Anduril, the multibillion-dollar start-up specializing in autonomous and semi-autonomous weapons, was a forward-deployed engineer in both Iraq and Afghanistan. He says he and his colleagues traveled with containers full of servers and laptops. Grimm typically spent two or three days at an outpost, working with analysts to solve whatever needs they had—targeting enemy combatants, identifying where roadside bombs were likely to be located. "I'd hop around between these bases and say, 'Hey, I'm the Palantir guy here to help you out—what are you working on?' And they'd say, 'I think there's a bomb-making financing network near here, but I can't quite figure it out, can you help me?' So I'd be like almost an augmented intelligence analyst sitting next to the intel person, helping find the bad guys." Getting from one base to another was not easy. Grimm had to hitch rides in military convoys and helicopters and learned that bartering was the key to getting a lift. "The currency of war zones is nicotine," Grimm recalls with a laugh.

The forward-deployed engineers in Iraq and Afghanistan also served a marketing function: as word spread about Palantir's software, they could visit troops who wanted to try out the technology. In 2011, an Army officer stationed in Afghanistan sent an email to Palantir's general mailbox. He wrote:

"The last 72 hours has been rough for the 2-shop here, as we had six catastrophic IED attacks, including the first three fatalities from IEDs in two attacks against the new dual-v-hull Strykers, in one week. Our CIED cell was over a barrel to dig through a lot of data and come up with some answers, and we barely slept for a couple days doing queries to external data sources, going through spreadsheets of data, filtering and re-filtering shapefiles in ArcGIS, and trying to sift out a pattern of what was happening. Total serendipity, we had made an inquiry about Palantir and their engineer showed up in the middle of our crisis to do a demo. We gave him a piece of the problem to solve, and what he was able to turn around in a couple hours compared to what we had spent days on made our jaws drop. Now that we've seen it, we have to have it."

For Palantir, the backdoor approach yielded some success: individual battalions that had the budgets and the authorization to make purchases on their own were able to acquire the software. But these piecemeal gains couldn't solve the problem that Palantir was encountering at the Pentagon. In 2010, the Center for a New American Security, a Washington think tank, published a paper called "Fixing Intel: A Blueprint for Making Intelligence Relevant in Afghanistan." Its authors were the soon-to-be-infamous Army Lieutenant General Michael Flynn, who at the time was an intelligence officer on General McChrystal's staff; Matt Pottinger, a former *Wall Street Journal* reporter who had joined the Marines after 9/11; and Paul Batchelor, a senior adviser to coalition forces in Afghanistan. The gist of the article, which was widely discussed in military circles, was that the U.S. and its allies were not gathering and disseminating nearly enough information about the environment in which they were operating—the political, cultural, and economic factors at play in various parts of Afghanistan—to wage a successful counterinsurgency. The authors also acknowledged "severe technological hurdles" to developing that fuller picture, such as "the lack of a common database and digital network available to all partners."

Philippone read the paper and decided that Flynn needed to become familiar with Palantir. Flynn would later gain notoriety as a supporter of Donald Trump and for his brief, scandal-plagued stint as Trump's national security adviser, after which he became a QAnon-influenced Christian nationalist. (Years later, when recounting Palantir's interactions with Flynn, Philippone would preface his comments by saying, "The old Mike Flynn.") Two Palantir employees who were in Afghanistan visited Flynn and showed him Gotham. Instantly sold on it, he wrote to the Pentagon requesting that it supply all the troops under McChrystal's command with Palantir. "Intelligence analysts in the field do not have the tools required to fully analyze the tremendous amounts of information currently available in the theater," Flynn wrote. "This shortfall translates into operational opportunities missed and lives lost." But the Army rejected Flynn's request, telling him that D-sigs was sufficient for troops on the ground. Flynn wasn't alone in requesting Palantir and being denied it. Between 2010 and 2014, the Army received almost thirty urgent appeals for Palantir from soldiers and units in Afghanistan and Iraq and turned down all of them.

While Army units were begging for Palantir, the Marines had an easier time obtaining the software. That was because they weren't stuck with D-sigs; that was a system only for the Army, and a version being developed for the Marines wasn't going to be ready until 2013. Peter Dixon, a commander with the 2nd Battalion, 7th Marine Regiment, had a pivotal role in getting Palantir in the hands of the Marines. The 2/7, as it was known, was deployed in a volatile part of southern Afghanistan and suffered heavy casualties. It lost forty men and saw dozens of others injured. It became known as the "Forgotten Battalion" because it was often cut off from supply lines and frequently ran low on ammunition and other essentials. Thirteen members of the unit later committed suicide.

On top of its supply problems, the 2/7 was fighting blind because it didn't have a common, easily accessible database of battlefield intelligence. "We had turnover files, and they were very poor quality," Dixon says. "They were cobbled-together Word documents and PowerPoint presentations, and that depended on whether some overtaxed platoon commander had found the time to try and put something together." In the absence of good information, Dixon and his colleagues had no idea where enemy combatants had attacked in the past. "We'd be knocking on compound doors, not knowing if previous deployments had been met with gunfire or tea," he says. "We were paying to relearn the same lessons over and over, and were paying in blood. Counterinsurgency is a big dirty data problem, and we had no battle tracking software."

In 2010 Dixon was reassigned to a job at the Pentagon. He was determined to try to get the Marines who were on combat duty the help that he had so conspicuously lacked. At one point he led a Pentagon delegation to a conference hosted by In-Q-Tel in Silicon Valley, where start-ups that it had funded were demoing their products. Dixon was struck by Palantir's software. He later visited the company's Palo Alto office and came away even more impressed. "There was a light-bulb moment when they started mapping a bunch of diverse datasets and laying them into a heat map," Dixon says. "Being able to see Afghanistan, with all this information laid into it, what was actually happening on the ground—we had no collective situational awareness, and this was the tool that could give it to us."

Dixon returned to Washington and wrote an urgent need request asking that Palantir be made available to Marines in Afghanistan. The only resistance he encountered was from an Army colonel who berated him for trying to obtain Palantir. In all, some thirty Marine units ended up using Gotham. "I believe that I saved more lives by getting Palantir into Afghanistan than I did leading infantry and sniper Marines outside the wire," says Dixon. Palantir's impact did not go unnoticed by senior leadership. One Palantir booster was Marine Corps General James Mattis, who at the time was the head of the United States Central Command, which was responsible for American military operations in the Middle East, North Africa, and South Asia and included representatives of all six uniformed services. (Mattis, like Flynn, would go on to serve in the Trump administration; he was secretary of defense from 2017 to 2019. Mattis resigned over policy disagreements with Trump and issued a blistering denunciation of his former boss during the George Floyd protests in 2020.)

But of course, it was easier for the Marines to embrace Palantir because, unlike the Army, they did not have an incumbent system that Palantir might displace. Jonathan Wong, a former Marine who became a policy researcher at the RAND Corporation, says Army officials weren't necessarily acting out of malice toward Palantir—at least not at first. They wanted a more comprehensive battlefield intelligence system than Palantir was offering at the time, one that could be used against "what we are fighting today and what we will be facing tomorrow," as he puts it. But Wong, whose dissertation focused in part on the early relationship between Palantir and the Pentagon, says that Palantir's software was better for the counterinsurgency and counterterrorism challenges that the military was then confronting.

And Doug Philippone concedes that there were missteps on the Palantir side. The one that still haunts him was a sartorial mistake. He and a colleague had a meeting at the Pentagon with an acquisitions officer, and, seeking to strike a balance between Washington decorousness and Silicon Valley informality, they wore suits but no ties. The decision to forgo ties infuriated their host. "I don't think he heard a word that we said," Philippone recalls. Not only that: news of the fashion faux pas spread and caused outrage elsewhere at the Pentagon. "I heard through the grapevine for years how offended they were that we didn't wear ties," he says.

The clothing blunder reinforced the hostility that some senior officers already had toward Palantir. In early 2012, the Army surveyed one hundred soldiers and contractors to see what they thought of Palantir; ninety-six responded positively and recommended that the military make wider use of its software. But a few months later, the Army allegedly spiked a report that cited these results and issued a new one that omitted much of the praise for Palantir. Representative Duncan Hunter, a former Marine who was a member of the House Armed Services Committee and who had become one of Palantir's staunchest advocates on Capitol Hill, learned of the discarded report and demanded an explanation from the Pentagon. "The system is broken when your war fighters on the ground are taking casualties every day and can't get a cheap piece of software that works wonders," Hunter said at the time. In April 2013, Army Chief of Staff Ray Odierno, testifying before the Armed Services Committee, got into a shouting match with Hunter over Palantir. "I'm tired of somebody telling me I don't care about our soldiers and don't respond," Odierno angrily told Hunter, adding that D-sigs had given the Army "twenty times" more intelligence capability than it had a decade earlier.

Hunter, who would be forced to resign from Congress in 2020 after pleading guilty to misusing campaign funds (President Trump would later pardon him), was not Palantir's only ally on Capitol Hill. Senator John McCain also expressed frustration with D-sigs and demanded that the Army make Palantir available to more units in Iraq and Afghanistan. While Karp and his colleagues would portray the fight with the Army as a classic David-versus-Goliath tale, with Palantir in the role of David, the truth was more complicated. Palantir was a plucky outsider, but the company also spent millions of dollars on powerful lobbyists who could plead its case with members of Congress. The headline on a *Politico* story in 2016—"How Palantir Wired Washington"—reflected the lengths the company had gone to cultivate support.

Its growing visibility in Washington did pay dividends—during this period, Palantir landed contracts with a number of federal agencies, including the FBI, the IRS, the SEC, the Department of Homeland Security, the National Institutes of Health (NIH), and the Centers for Disease Control and Prevention (CDC). Palantir was indeed wiring much of official Washington now. It just couldn't break down the Army's resistance. In December 2015, the Army announced that it was shelving the initial version of D-sigs and invited bids to build a second, presumably better version, which it referred to as Increment 2. However, it indicated that it would only accept proposals to build a new system from scratch—it was not willing to consider off-the-shelf products, which meant Palantir could not compete for the contract. A few weeks later, Palantir filed a complaint with the U.S. Government Accountability Office, or GAO, which evaluates federal programs. Palantir alleged that the Army, in refusing to allow it to even take part in the bidding, had violated a law enacted by Congress in 1994 that required federal agencies to consider off-the-shelf products to meet their needs.

By that point, the Pentagon was no longer denying that D-sigs was a bust. In April 2016, General Mark Milley, the chairman of the Joint Chiefs of Staff, acknowledged to the Senate Armed Services Committee that D-sigs had failed soldiers in Afghanistan and Iraq. Milley was diplomatic; he said the system was "performing reasonably well at, kind of, echelons above brigade" and that his own experience with it was "very, very good." But at the tactical level, he said, it was "more difficult to work with, not quite as fast, and difficult to jump from location to location on the whole battlefield." He said he had taken "a hard look" at the issues surrounding D-sigs, was "keenly aware of the various controversies," and conceded that "there may be some other options out there," which seemed like a reference to Palantir.

But a few weeks later, the GAO rejected Palantir's complaint;

it said that Congress had given federal agencies broad discretion when it came to deciding between commercial products and custom-built ones. At that point, Karp decided that litigation was Palantir's only recourse. Suing the Army might have seemed a counterintuitive way to cultivate business with the Army, but there was a recent precedent, and it involved another company backed by Peter Thiel: in 2014, Elon Musk's SpaceX had sued the Air Force for awarding a no-bid contract to a rival company, United Launch Alliance, a joint venture between Lockheed Martin and Boeing, to provide thirty-six rocket booster cores to help launch national security satellites. The suit was settled the following year when the Air Force agreed to open up the bidding process for future launches. Palantir retained Boies Schiller Flexner LLP, the law firm that had represented SpaceX, to bring its case against the Army.

Karp says he would have pursued litigation even without the SpaceX precedent. He was appalled by the Army's conduct and couldn't fathom why officials seemed more interested in protecting a failed program than protecting warfighters. He met soldiers who had used Palantir's technology in Iraq and Afghanistan and who considered it a lifesaver, and although the lawsuit against the Army was a business decision, in Karp's mind it was also a moral imperative. Beyond that, he said it was not in his nature to walk away from a fight; if punched, he punched back. When he told me that, I jokingly remarked that it didn't sound very Haverford-like. "Well, Haverford didn't teach us how to fight," he replied sharply, a comment meant as an indictment.

In late June 2016, Palantir sued the Army in the U.S. Court of Federal Claims, which handles disputes over government contracts. Its complaint was blunt, at times caustic. Palantir accused Army officials of sacrificing the lives of soldiers in order to avoid having to admit that D-sigs had been a failure. The suit said that the bidding requirements for D-sigs Increment 2 had "committed the Army to a failed procurement approach that is unlawful, that benefits no one but the incumbent defense contracting industry, that irrationally resists innovation from Silicon Valley, that wastes billions in taxpayer dollars, and that even risks the lives and effectiveness of our Soldiers in uniform."

Four months after Palantir filed suit, the court handed it a resounding victory. In her ruling, Judge Marian Blank Horn said the Army had acted "arbitrarily and capriciously" in setting up a bidding process that effectively excluded Palantir and had, in fact, violated the law by not giving fair consideration to an off-the-shelf alternative. She issued a permanent injunction and said the Army could award the contract only after fulfilling its legal obligation to entertain commercial options.

Her decision was made public on October 31. Eight days later, Donald Trump was elected president.

SEVEN

THE PETER PROBLEM

In 2009, Peter Thiel published an essay titled "The Education of a Libertarian." It ran in a journal called *Cato Unbound*, published by the Cato Institute, a Washington think tank. Sounding more chastened than frustrated, Thiel declared that his dream of seeing America become a libertarian Valhalla was dead. The problem was participatory democracy. "I no longer believe that freedom"—by which he meant economic freedom—"and democracy are compatible," he wrote. He went on to say that "the 1920s were the last decade in American history during which one could be genuinely optimistic about politics. Since 1920, the vast increase in welfare beneficiaries and the extension of the franchise to women—two constituencies that are notoriously tough for libertarians—have rendered the notion of 'capitalist democracy' into an oxymoron." Thiel urged his fellow travelers to join him in withdrawing from the political arena. "In our time, the great task for libertarians is to find an escape from politics in all its forms—from the totalitarian and fundamentalist catastrophes to the unthinking demos that guides so-called 'social democracy.'" He suggested three possible escape routes: cyberspace, outer space, and seasteading.

Not surprisingly, the essay sparked controversy, especially the line about women's suffrage. The backlash was sufficiently intense that Thiel felt compelled to write an addendum. He didn't apologize—he said that his point about women was based on a "commonplace statistical observation about voting patterns that is often called the gender gap." However, he insisted that he wasn't advocating disenfranchisement but was simply arguing that democracy would not lead to the libertarian future that he had hoped for. He concluded by saying that "politics is way too intense.... Politics gets people angry, destroys relationships, and polarizes peoples' [sic] vision; the world is us versus them; good people versus the other. Politics is about interfering with other people's lives without their consent. That's probably why, in the past, libertarians have made little progress in the political sphere. Thus, I advocate focusing energy elsewhere, onto peaceful projects that some consider utopian."

But Thiel did not step away from politics. In 2012, he donated $2.6 million to the presidential campaign of Ron Paul, a Republican congressman from Texas who was known for his libertarian views and who had published newsletters in the 1980s and '90s that included virulently racist and antisemitic content. Paul finished fourth in the delegate count for the Republican nomination. Four years later, Thiel switched his allegiance to another Texan, Republican Senator Ted Cruz. When Cruz entered the 2016 presidential race, Thiel was one of his main supporters. But after winning the Iowa caucuses, Cruz's campaign sputtered. Most of his colleagues in Congress reviled him (former House Speaker John Boehner once described him as "Lucifer in the flesh," and in a 2016 speech, South Carolina Republican Senator Lindsey Graham joked, "If you killed Ted Cruz on the floor of the Senate, and the trial was in the Senate, nobody would convict you"), and it turned out that GOP voters were also put off by his smarminess and general unlikability. At the same time, Donald Trump was proving to be a more viable candidate than most people had imagined, and as Thiel recounted during one of our conversations in the spring of 2023, he found himself increasingly drawn to Trump's message—that America had lost its way and that elites had betrayed the country's working class.

For some time, Thiel had been arguing that the United States had become stagnant—that even Silicon Valley, supposedly a wellspring of world-changing innovation, was failing to deliver on the promise of the digital revolution. In his judgment, the output of transformative technologies was declining, not accelerating. As he famously put it, "We wanted flying cars, instead we got 140 characters," which was a swipe not just at Twitter but at Silicon Valley writ large. Thiel had come to believe that the political system needed a shock, an upheaval that would force America to reckon with its shortcomings and spark the inventiveness that he longed to see. Why he thought that a serially bankrupt reality TV star who probably wouldn't have known a silicon chip from a silicone implant could shake America out of this supposed torpor seemed puzzling, and Thiel would later admit that it had been a miscalculation on his part.

While keeping close watch on the battle for the GOP nomination, Thiel also had something else on his mind in early 2016: the lawsuit that the wrestler Hulk Hogan had brought against the website Gawker after it posted a video of Hogan having sex with the wife of a friend. The case, filed in Florida, went to trial in March of that year. What was not known at the time—it was revealed only after the jury delivered its verdict—was that Thiel had bankrolled Hogan's litigation to exact revenge against Gawker for outing him as gay several years earlier. After a two-week trial, the jury ruled in Hogan's favor and awarded him $100 million, the maximum allowed under Florida law. A few months later,

Gawker declared bankruptcy and went dark. Thiel told me that he hadn't expected Hogan to prevail, and the size of the jury's award shocked him. He said the Hogan verdict was the moment he realized that Trump could win the presidency—he saw the court case as auguring a revolt at the polls that November. In his words, "Hogan was Trump, Gawker was the media, and the jury was the voters."

Cruz dropped out of the race in early May. A week later, the Trump campaign released its list of delegates for the Republican National Convention, which was being held in Cleveland in mid-July. Among the Trump delegates from California was Thiel. This was the first indication that he was getting behind Trump, and for the ragtag Trump operation, winning Thiel's backing was a coup, especially since most business leaders, stunned by Trump's rise, were publicly keeping their distance from the presumptive Republican nominee. The Trump campaign rewarded Thiel with a prime-time speaking slot at the convention. He spoke on the last night, prior to Trump's own speech. Thiel, smiling awkwardly and looking uncomfortable, said that Trump was "a builder" who was going to "lead us back to that bright future."

Up until then, Thiel's political activities had never been a source of concern at Palantir; employees rarely ever encountered him, and even people who were troubled by some of the views he had expressed regarded Thiel's ideological predilections more as a curiosity than a public relations problem. However, he was now supporting arguably the most demagogic presidential candidate the country had ever seen, and it was hard to imagine that this wasn't going to have implications for Palantir. One former Palantir employee who was personally fond of Thiel said that it was jarring to observe his trajectory from "being an unhappy libertarian to being an enthusiastic fascist." In October, four weeks before the election, the *Access Hollywood* controversy erupted. Trump had been caught on tape bragging about how his celebrity enabled him to assault women; he could, as he put it, "grab them by the pussy." For several days, it was not clear that Trump would survive the scandal; many Republicans expressed disgust with his comments, and there were calls for him to quit the race. But then Thiel stepped forward and announced that he was making his first financial contribution to the Trump campaign, and it was a substantial one: $1.25 million. His donation outraged many Palantirians (in a subsequent speech to the National Press Club in Washington, Thiel said that Trump's remarks had been "clearly offensive and inappropriate").

Karp, for his part, was a Hillary Clinton supporter, and he had made clear to employees that he was personally repulsed by Trump. In a town hall meeting in 2015, the video of which was later obtained by *BuzzFeed*, Karp told his colleagues, "I've had the rare opportunity to meet Trump, which I turned down. I mean, this is off the record, but I like respect—I respect nothing about the dude. It would be hard to make up someone I find less appealing." He mocked Trump's business acumen, pointing out that he would be richer if he had just invested the money he inherited from his father in the stock market, and he scoffed at Trump's claim of being a billionaire. Karp called it "fictitious wealth" and speculated that Trump was worth only around $500 million. He said that "purely on the vulgar metric" of moneymaking prowess, Trump was a failure. He also called him a bully.

But Karp says that he took Trump much more seriously than most observers and was convinced by the fall of 2016 that he would win. He thought that Trump was skillfully channeling the anger, resentment, and sense of betrayal that many Americans felt. Karp says he warned the Clinton campaign and Democratic officials that Trump was heading for victory. He said the same thing in a private conversation with FBI Director James Comey, who insisted that Karp was wrong. (In his memoir, Comey acknowledged that he didn't believe Trump would prevail.) On election night, as it became clear that Trump was the winner, a Palantir board member said to Karp that the outcome would be a boon for the company thanks to the Thiel-Trump connection. Karp vehemently disagreed. "This is all downside for us," he said.

He anticipated, correctly, that any government contracts that Palantir won with Trump in the White House would be seen as rewarding Thiel for the support he had given the campaign. The Trump-Thiel-Palantir nexus was in the spotlight a few weeks after the election, when Trump held a meeting with leaders of the tech industry. Thiel organized the gathering, held in a twenty-fifth-floor conference room at Trump Tower in New York. The attendees included most of tech's biggest names: Jeff Bezos, Elon Musk, Tim Cook, Sheryl Sandberg, Larry Page, Eric Schmidt, and Satya Nadella. Thiel sat to Trump's left; Vice President–elect Mike Pence was to his right. Three of Trump's children—Don Jr., Eric, and Ivanka—were also at the table. Karp was there, too. Thiel had asked him to attend, and although Karp recognized that the optics would not be good—it would raise obvious concerns about conflicts of interest—he agreed to go.

The meeting was one of the fruits of victory for Trump, but it was also significant for another reason: it highlighted the profound transformation of the American economy. A half century earlier, a president-elect might have met with the CEOs of the Big Three automakers. Twenty-five years earlier, Wall Street executives would probably have been at that table. Now, though, it was the leaders of the tech industry. For better and worse, Silicon Valley had become the main driver of the U.S. economy (and, really, the global economy), a point symbolized by the Trump Tower gathering.

Trump started the meeting by profusely thanking Thiel for arranging it and for backing his campaign. "You're a very special guy," he told Thiel. He then reached over and awkwardly clasped Thiel's hands in a way that called to mind a boxing referee declaring the winner of a fight. Thiel looked mortified, and his hands fell limp as Trump clutched them. The president-elect then turned his attention to his other guests. "This is a truly amazing group of people," he gushed. "There's nobody like you in the world. In the world!" Trump had campaigned as a business maven, a dealmaker of unparalleled skill. In truth, he was such a bad credit risk that he had been cut off by all the major U.S. banks. Now, surrounded by some of the most successful entrepreneurs and business leaders in history, Trump seemed to recognize that he was out of his depth—that the boasting he had done on the campaign trail wasn't going to work with this crowd. His tone was solicitous, even supplicatory. In his opening remarks, he said, "I'm here to help you folks do well," adding, "We're going to be there for you."

Trump asked everyone to identify themselves, a request that elicited some nervous coughs and pained smiles—did Jeff Bezos really need to play the Name Game? Karp was seated across the table from Trump; Eric Schmidt, the CEO of Alphabet, was to his right, the Trump kids to his left. When it was his turn to speak, Karp said, "Alex Karp, CEO of Palantir, hoping to help bolster our national security and reduce waste," a comment that drew an approving nod from Trump. It was all that Karp said during the meeting, which lasted around ninety minutes.

As Karp had anticipated, his participation aroused concern. Palantir was the only privately held company represented there, and it was a minnow compared to the likes of Amazon and

Apple. Purely on a market-capitalization basis, there was no justification for Palantir, which was valued at around $20 billion, to be at the same table with companies that were worth hundreds of billions, and many observers took it as a sign that the firm was going to benefit unduly from Trump's presidency. CNBC's website ran a story about Karp's presence at the meeting under the headline "Palantir CEO at Trump-tech Summit Raises Red Flags." The article quoted government ethics expert Norman Eisen: "I don't like the way it looks having Karp in that room. Even if [Palantir] had a much larger market cap or he had a much bigger personality, it still looks as if [Thiel] is using the transition for personal advancement."

The negative reaction was a foretaste of what lay ahead. Palantir prospered during the Trump years; after prevailing in the lawsuit that it brought against the Army, it was awarded a number of Pentagon contracts. But those wins were regarded with suspicion. To Karp's fury, many observers assumed that they were the result of political favoritism. Palantir was also embroiled in major controversies during Trump's first presidency, scandals that caused fissures within the company, that cast fresh doubt on its ethical and moral standards, and that put a bright light on the relationship between Karp and Thiel.

From the moment, in June 2015, that Trump descended the golden escalator at Trump Tower and attacked Mexicans as rapists and criminals, his campaign was steeped in racism and xenophobia (and long before he announced his candidacy, the former Democrat had endeared himself to many Republican voters with the birther smear against President Barack Obama). In December of that year, following a deadly terrorist attack in San Bernardino,

California, Trump called for a "complete and total shutdown of Muslims entering the United States." He also made comments suggesting he favored creating a database to track Muslim Americans. It wasn't a new idea: the Bush administration had created a de facto Muslim registry after 9/11. But coming from Trump, it seemed especially sinister and alarming. Facebook, Google, and Apple all issued statements saying that they would not cooperate with any effort to establish a Muslim database. Karp didn't address the issue during the campaign but chimed in just prior to Trump's inauguration, telling *Forbes* that "if we were asked, we wouldn't do it." But his words didn't reassure everyone: a few days later, some fifty tech workers picketed outside Palantir's Palo Alto office, in what amounted to a preemptive protest.

In the end, the Trump administration didn't create a Muslim registry. But just a week into his presidency, Trump signed a series of executive orders that barred people from a handful of Muslim-majority countries from entering the United States. Trump's so-called Muslim ban (which the U.S. Supreme Court upheld in 2018 but the Biden administration later rescinded) presaged a broader assault on immigration. While Trump never delivered on his promise to build a wall along the southern border and force Mexico to pay for it, he instituted a "zero tolerance" policy for illegal immigration that included separating children from their parents. In all, four to five thousand children were taken from their mothers and fathers. U.S. authorities failed to track the whereabouts of the children and their parents, and years later, many families had still not been reunited. Under Trump, there were also mass worksite raids aimed at finding and deporting undocumented people.

U.S. Immigration and Customs Enforcement, or ICE, was one of the agencies involved in implementing Trump's crackdown. Palantir had a long-standing relationship with ICE. As with a number of the company's engagements, Palantir's work with ICE began in a moment of crisis. In February 2011, an ICE special agent named Jaime Zapata was assassinated by a Mexican drug cartel. Determined to apprehend the perpetrators as quickly as possible but hobbled by the fact that much of its intelligence was siloed in different places and could not be easily shared among investigators, ICE turned to Palantir for help. It took Palantir's engineers just eleven hours to merge all the data, and within two weeks, Zapata's murderer had been identified and arrested, part of sweep dubbed Operation Fallen Hero that resulted in over six hundred other arrests and the confiscation of 467 kilos of cocaine, 64 pounds of methamphetamine, and 282 weapons.

ICE subsequently awarded Palantir a contract to provide its technology to Homeland Security Investigations, or HSI, a subdivision of the agency that handled issues such as drug smuggling, human trafficking, financial crimes, and cybercrimes. In 2012, HSI began using a Palantir-designed system called FALCON for investigations. In 2014, ICE paid Palantir $41 million to design and maintain an electronic case management system for HSI. A privacy impact assessment conducted by the Department of Homeland Security in 2016 noted that although this new database, known as Investigative Case Management, or ICM, was built for HSI, agents from ICE's other major subdivision, Enforcement and Removal Operations, or ERO, which administered U.S. immigration laws, would have access to it.

Palantir's work with ICE attracted little notice prior to the first Trump presidency. But the relationship became controversial when Trump made good on his campaign pledge to go after illegal immigrants. Privately, Karp had been scornful of Trump's plans. During that same town hall meeting with Palantir employees in which he called Trump a phony billionaire, he also attacked his nativism. "Therefore we should throw out all immigrants—like, who is going to do all the work? It makes no sense," Karp said. He expressed dismay that Trump's scapegoating seemed to be resonating with voters: "You have to ask yourself—something that makes no sense, that is de facto bringing up the worst that a society can bring up, which is that, like, blame the people who work really hard and that we need and that are coming here at the risk of their life instead of, you know, the dysfunction that you may have helped create—why is that person so successful?"

But when those comments became public, in April 2017, Trump's clampdown was underway, and immigration advocates and human rights groups were voicing strong concerns about Palantir's work with ICE. Initially, Palantir tried to deflect criticism by emphasizing that its contracts were with HSI, not ERO. "We do not work for E.R.O.," the company said in a statement to *The New York Times* in 2018. The implication was that Palantir had no role in enforcing Trump's policies. But that was not true. A document obtained by *The Intercept*, a news site, and Mijente, an immigration advocacy group, showed that in 2017, HSI and ERO undertook a joint operation using the ICM database to arrest and possibly deport family members of undocumented children caught trying to cross the border. Palantir's effort to distance itself from Trump's immigration policies fell apart in August 2019, when HSI, deploying FALCON, led a raid on food-processing plants in Mississippi. Nearly seven hundred people were arrested. In an interview with CNBC a few months later, Karp acknowledged that Palantir's blanket denials had been misleading. However, he insisted that the company was not really involved with Trump's crackdown. "It is a de minimis part of our work, finding people in our country who are undocumented," he said.

By then, Palantir had become the object of protests nationwide. Demonstrations were held at its office in New York and Palo Alto, as well as outside Karp's Palo Alto home. During one nighttime gathering, activists projected the words "#Complicit with Genocide" and "#Never Again Is Now" on the façade of the company's Palo Alto headquarters. Palantir also found itself a pariah on college campuses. Students put up signs saying "No Tech for ICE" and encouraged their peers to shun Palantir recruiters. For years, Palantir had cosponsored an annual conference of privacy laws scholars hosted by the University of California, Berkeley. But in 2019, the organizers, under pressure from Berkeley faculty and students and outside groups, dropped Palantir as a sponsor. The company was also removed as a sponsor of the Grace Hopper Celebration, the largest conference for women in technology. Employees at Amazon sent two letters to company executives demanding that they no longer do business with Palantir, which ran its software on Amazon's cloud.

There was also internal dissent at Palantir. Some two hundred employees signed a letter objecting to the company's relationship with ICE. Another sixty sent a letter to Karp asking that the money that Palantir earned from its ICE contracts—around $16 million annually—be donated to a nonprofit charity (that didn't happen). On the company's Slack channels, as well as in staff meetings, Palantirians waged a vigorous internal debate about ICE. There were strong views on both sides. Some employees had no problem working with ICE and were frustrated by the controversy. "They talk about deportations, but they never talk about the stuff we've done to stop human trafficking and drugs," one executive said during an impromptu conversation with several colleagues that I happened to overhear. Complicating matters, for Karp and for Palantir, was Thiel's hardline immigration views. In 2019, for instance, he and the right-wing commentator Ann Coulter hosted a fundraiser for Kris Kobach, the Kansas secretary of state who was virulently anti-immigration.

Karp and I had a number of conversations about the ICE controversy as it was unfolding. Our most extensive one was when I visited him at his house in Vermont in the fall of 2019. It was the Saturday of Columbus Day weekend, and I figured he'd be staying there for a few days. But he had arrived the previous night and was heading to a meeting in Boston that evening before leaving for Europe. He had spent the morning roller skiing. I showed up in time for lunch, which was prepared by an Italian chef whom Karp had flown in from Washington. Afterward, Karp and I went for a hike on a nearby cross-country-skiing trail, two of his bodyguards trailing us as we walked.

Karp noted that other major tech companies, including Microsoft and Amazon, also had contracts with ICE but were not being vilified the way Palantir was. He suggested that it was a backhanded compliment—evidence of the superior quality of Palantir's products. "People understand we have these powerful platforms and that the platforms actually work," he said, adding that perhaps protesters were ignoring those other companies because their technology was "not as effectual." But the opprobrium directed at Palantir clearly irritated Karp. He was particularly angered by claims that Palantir was abetting a racist policy. It was during this period that he had disclosed—first to Palantir employees, then publicly—that his mother was black. But he said that he was reluctant to answer the racism charge by invoking his background because he didn't want to "instrumentalize" his mother, and also because he didn't think that the "emotional argument is as persuasive as people think."

Karp cited his own political views to defend Palantir. He said he was in favor of legal immigration and wanted the United States to remain welcoming of newcomers. "There are lots of reasons I don't support the president; this is actually one of them," he told me, adding that he was "personally very okay with changing the demographics of our country." But he believed that a secure border was important. "I've been a progressive my whole life, my family's progressive, and we were never in favor of open borders," he said. He claimed that progressives had historically opposed unfettered immigration because it tended to depress wages for working-class Americans. And even if liberals didn't care about border security, millions of Americans clearly did, and in Karp's judgment, Trump had won in part because he took their concerns seriously and the Democrats did not. "Having no border is the surest way to elect Trump," he said. It was the same way in Europe: the refusal of center-left parties to deal with legitimate worries about immigration had fueled the rise of the far right.

Trump's effort to curb illegal immigration, however, was notable mainly for its cruelty—in particular, the policy of forcibly separating migrant children, some of them infants and toddlers, from their parents. Many of the children were detained in steel enclosures—cages—and while thousands were later reunited with their parents, thousands of others were not. According to *The Atlantic*'s Caitlin Dickerson, this was because U.S. immigration officials had often failed to log basic information, such as where a child's parent was being detained. In 2024, six years after the child separation policy was discontinued in the face of public outrage, more than one thousand children had still not been reunited with their parents. Although the full disgrace did not become apparent until after Trump left office, it was clear enough at the time that human rights abuses were being perpetrated by immigration authorities.

Karp didn't deny that bad things were being done, although he pointed out that family separation was not illegal under U.S. law. He reiterated that Palantir was not involved in the crackdown at the border, but he also said that it had a duty to fulfill its contractual obligations to federal agencies, including ICE. Companies were free not to work with the government, but those that did couldn't renege on their contracts just because they didn't like a president or approve of certain policies. Trump had been elected in part on his promise to get tough on illegal immigration, and if Palantir decided to stop working with ICE, it would be defying the will of the voters and subverting the democratic process, which Karp was unwilling to do. This argument was Karp's justification for his decision in the summer of 2019 to renew Palantir's contract with ICE, a deal that would earn Palantir $50 million over three years.

During our conversation in Vermont, Karp also suggested that terminating Palantir's relationship with ICE would have jeopardized vital work that the company was doing with other parts of the government, notably the military. Karp said that if Palantir walked away from ICE, that might have marked it as an unreliable partner in the eyes of U.S. soldiers. "Why would a warfighter believe you aren't going to do the same thing to them when they're in the middle of a battle?" he asked rhetorically. (Others at Palantir did not share Karp's concern; several of his colleagues told me that if the company had opted to end its contract with ICE, it would have no repercussions for its military business.) But Karp admitted that if ICE had first sought Palantir's technology after Trump took office, he might have balked. "I'm not sure I would feel strongly about doing it," he told me. "We probably wouldn't do the contract. But that's different than pulling the plug."

But not pulling the plug had costs. Normally, Karp and his colleagues took pride in the idea that Palantir was the one company that didn't flinch in the face of controversy or run away from morally complicated engagements. "Our product is used on occasion to kill people," Karp told *Axios* in an interview in 2020, and his matter-of-fact tone suggested that he had no qualms with that. However, Karp couldn't show the same defiance over ICE; seizing children from their parents as a matter of policy was abhorrent, and even if Palantir wasn't directly complicit in those actions, being associated with the government agency perpetrating these abuses was a public relations fiasco. In September 2020, on the eve of Palantir's stock market listing, Amnesty International issued a fifteen-page report on the company's relationship with ICE. It said that there was "a high risk that Palantir is contributing to serious human rights violations of migrants and asylum-seekers by the U.S. government."

In December 2015, Britain's *Guardian* newspaper reported that a company called Cambridge Analytica, whose principal owner was Robert Mercer, a reclusive American hedge fund billionaire, had harvested the personal data of Facebook users in order to generate "psychographic" profiles of voters. The scheme involved a personality quiz designed by a Cambridge University lecturer named Aleksandr Kogan. Participants were told that the results would "only be used for research purposes" and would "remain anonymous and safe." Those were lies: the information was not anonymized, and it was shared by Cambridge Analytica with Ted Cruz's presidential campaign, presumably to help it microtarget voters. At the time, Mercer was backing Cruz. In addition, individuals who took the personality quiz unwittingly gave Cambridge Analytica access to personal information for their Facebook friends. Cambridge Analytica created profiles of over fifty million Americans.

Like Thiel, Mercer threw his support behind Trump after Cruz's White House bid sank. Steve Bannon, a senior Trump adviser, was close to the Mercer family and was a member of Cambridge Analytica's board. The data that Cambridge Analytica gave to Cruz was later shared with the Trump campaign. That story emerged in an investigative series published in March 2018 by *The New York Times* and two British newspapers, *The Guardian* and *The Observer*. Much of the information came from a Cambridge Analytica cofounder-turned-whistleblower named Christopher Wylie, who said that the information the company collected had been used to target individual voters with digital ads that tapped into their anxieties, anger, and bigotry. There was no way of determining the degree to which Cambridge Analytica helped Trump's 2016 campaign, but later studies found that online misinformation played a significant, perhaps decisive, role in his victory over Clinton.

The Cambridge Analytica controversy was a debacle for Facebook, which was harshly criticized for its failure to protect users' data. But Palantir was soon drawn into the scandal. The *Times* reported that a London-based Palantir employee named Alfredas Chmieliauskas, working with the Cambridge Analytica team, had come up with the idea of developing the mobile-phone app that was used to collect Facebook data. According to documents obtained by the *Times*, Chmieliauskas started corresponding with Wylie in 2013. Emails reviewed by the *Times* also showed that an unnamed Palantir executive had discussions with Cambridge Analytica about possibly collaborating on other election campaigns— even though Palantir had a policy against doing election work.

At first Palantir denied any connection to Cambridge Analytica. When reporters confronted Palantir with evidence of Chmieliauskas's activities, the company retracted its denial and issued a new statement: "We learned today that an employee, in 2013–

2014, engaged in an entirely personal capacity with people associated with Cambridge Analytica. We're looking into this and will take appropriate action." But testifying before British lawmakers on the same day that the *Times* published its story about Palantir, Wylie alleged that "senior Palantir employees" had also been involved with Cambridge Analytica. He said that "Palantir staff would come into the office and work on the data." In an interview with the *Times*, Wylie said that he and Cambridge Analytica's CEO, Alexander Nix, had visited Palantir's London office.

It was not the first time that Palantir blamed a misdoing on a rogue employee; it made the same claim during the HBGary Federal controversy. And fairly or not, the fact that Palantir's initial denial turned out to be untrue created the impression that the company was being evasive. Beyond that, Palantir worked in sensitive areas; having an employee moonlighting with a shady outfit such as Cambridge Analytica was a bad look. That his side hustle involved the harvesting and abuse of personal data, something that Palantir had emphasized over and over that it never did, made it all the worse. Being implicated alongside Facebook, of all companies, was especially embarrassing.

A few weeks after the *Times* story was published, Facebook CEO Mark Zuckerberg was called before the Senate Judiciary Committee to answer questions regarding the scandal. Senator Maria Cantwell, a Democrat from Washington, used her allotted time to question Zuckerberg about Palantir, which she claimed was now being referred to as "Stanford Analytica." Zuckerberg said that he knew of Palantir but was unaware of the accusations against the company concerning the improper use of Facebook's data. He told Cantwell he was "not really that familiar with what Palantir does," which seemed like a dubious claim. More likely, his comment was a put-down masquerading as a plea of ignorance, a way of saying that Palantir was too small and inconsequential to draw his attention. After years of being swiped at by Karp, the Senate hearing gave Zuckerberg an opportunity to hit back, and it appeared he took it.

For people who regarded Palantir as sketchy, the Cambridge Analytica imbroglio was just more evidence that the company was untrustworthy. Its connection to the scandal also fed into a broader narrative about Palantir being in the service of Thiel's political agenda. The immigration issue was seen in that light, and now Palantir had been linked to a plot to manipulate millions of people into voting for Thiel's chosen candidate. Meanwhile, in return for his support of Trump, Thiel had gained vast influence in Washington. Several of his acolytes got senior positions in the Trump administration. Michael Kratsios, Thiel's former chief of staff, was appointed chief technology adviser in the White House. Kevin Harrington, another former aide, was named to the National Security Council. Some people in Thiel's orbit referred to him as the "shadow president." And as Palantir began winning lucrative Pentagon contracts, many observers wondered if it, too, was benefiting from Thiel's donation to Trump.

Three weeks before the Cambridge Analytica scandal broke, the Army awarded Palantir and Raytheon a ten-year, $876 million contract to build the replacement for D-sigs. It was a surprising conclusion to Palantir's long and costly battle with the Pentagon, and it wasn't the only contract that the company got from the Army during Trump's first presidency: a year later, it won a $440 million contract to build Vantage, the database that tracked troop preparedness and supply availability. Palantir also landed an $80 million deal to aid the Navy with logistics.

Palantir executives bridled at suggestions that the White House was steering contracts their way. "Donald Trump wouldn't know how to spell Palantir," one said. According to Doug Philippone, the allegations of cronyism were unfounded. The Pentagon procurement process had its problems—no one knew that better than him—but between stringent rules governing how contracts were to be awarded and normal bureaucratic inertia (and with over three million employees, the Defense Department was the world's largest bureaucracy), it really couldn't be manipulated by blatant political interference. "That's just not how it works," said Philippone. For his part, Karp pushed back against the idea that Palantir was benefiting from Thiel's links to Trump. He said it was "completely ridiculous" and bemoaned the "unfairness it creates towards us." Whatever favor that Thiel enjoyed with Trump, said Karp, was more than offset by his own opposition to the president. "I think they already know my views at the White House," he said. "It's true that Peter is chairman, [but] I'm running the company, I don't have close ties with the Trump administration."

There were no specific allegations of impropriety regarding the military contracts awarded to Palantir. And certainly, it would have been hard to argue that the company didn't deserve the contract to replace D-sigs, given that its technology had proven to be superior on the battlefield. But Thiel's White House connections caused every Defense Department deal that Palantir won to be viewed with skepticism. Moreover, a lawsuit that Amazon brought against the Pentagon in 2019 alleged that Trump had indeed corrupted the procurement process.

Amazon claimed it had been passed over for a $10 billion cloud-computing contract with the military because of pressure from Trump. The president had repeatedly attacked Amazon's founder and chief executive, Jeff Bezos, and had publicly stated that he did not want the company to get the deal. He had supposedly conveyed the same message in private: Amazon's lawsuit cited a comment by Defense Secretary James Mattis's former speechwriter, who said that Trump had personally ordered the Pentagon chief to "screw Amazon." When Microsoft won the contract, Amazon decided to sue. In May 2020, the U.S. Court of Federal Claims, the same court that had found in Palantir's favor in its complaint against the Army, ordered the contract be put on hold until Amazon's case could be adjudicated. Just over a year later, the Pentagon announced that it was scrapping the deal and reopening the bidding process. It attributed the decision to "evolving requirements, increased cloud conservancy, and industry advances." However, in a press release, Microsoft indicated that the Defense Department had spiked the contract because it feared "a years-long litigation battle." For its part, Amazon issued a statement hailing the reversal but reiterating its charge that the contract had been awarded as a result of "outside influence that has no place in government procurement." Ultimately, the military split the new contract among four vendors: Amazon, Microsoft, Oracle, and Google.

As it happened, Google essentially handed Palantir what was arguably the most consequential military contract it won during Trump's first presidency. In 2017, the Pentagon started a program called Project Maven, which aimed to bring artificial intelligence and machine learning to the battlefield—specifically, for drone targeting. Google was awarded a $10 million contract to help the Defense Department build out this capability; it was a relatively meager amount as military contracts go, but Google executives thought it would lead to more lucrative opportunities. However, thousands of Google employees objected to the company's involvement. They believed that weaponizing AI was inherently wrong and ran counter to Google's ethos, expressed in its famous tagline, "Don't be evil." A handful of people quit in protest. For the better part of a year, internal protest racked Google. In June 2018, the company announced that it was pulling out of Maven.

For Karp, the controversy over Maven was an opportunity to try to shift some of the opprobrium that was being directed at Palantir to Google, and he lashed out at the search giant. He called it "borderline craven" and disparagingly referred to the employees who had protested as "super-woke engineers." Thiel joined in the criticism. Speaking at a conservative conference in Washington, he noted that while Google had backed away from its Pentagon contract, it had set up an AI lab in China, which was almost certainly going to be used to help China's military. He called Google's behavior "borderline treasonous," suggested that the company had been infiltrated by foreign agents, and called on the CIA and FBI to investigate that possibility in "a not excessively gentle manner."

In September 2019, Karp published an op-ed in *The Washington Post* excoriating Google and the rest of Silicon Valley over what he claimed was their betrayal of the U.S. military and, by extension, American democracy. He suggested that Google's decision to bail on Maven had undermined national security and had subverted the will of the voters. "The U.S. marine serves; the Silicon Valley executives walk," Karp wrote, adding, "This is wrong." He noted that Palantir, by contrast, had stood by its contract with ICE in the face of protests because it was not its place to try to thwart decisions that had been made by elected officials. He said tech companies could not be permitted to exercise veto power over actions taken by the government. "This is not the way consequential policy decisions should be made," Karp argued. "I don't believe I should have that authority." He said policy belonged to policymakers, not "unelected engineers running global businesses in a precious corner of a golden state."

When I visited Karp in Vermont a few weeks later, he was still bashing Google. In his view, Maven was nothing less than the Manhattan Project of the twenty-first century—as with the atomic bomb, the country that gained a military edge with AI would "determine the world order tomorrow," as he put it. Alluding to China, Karp said the choice was a stark one: "Do you want the world order to be materially shaped by people who do not have a significant commitment to human rights? It's an alternative worldview, but it doesn't include free speech, it doesn't include the rule of law, it doesn't include a protection of minorities, it doesn't include an independent judiciary, it doesn't include a sense of radical liberty." Karp's answer—Palantir's answer—was an emphatic no; the company was all-in when it came to defending the West. "We're making Western institutions strong and, in some cases, dominant," he said. "That's our narrative. Now, that's probably not a popular narrative in the Valley. It's a very popular narrative in the rest of America. What's Google's narrative? We destroy the media, we divide the country, we take away your job, we get rich, and by the way, when the country needs you, we're nowhere to be found." He added that if the "Google standard takes hold, the single biggest strategic asset America has, which is our ability to produce software platforms, will be taken out of the hands of our warfighters. And that de facto means our adversaries are in a much stronger position."

At that point, it was unclear if any other tech company had assumed Google's role in Maven. But as I listened to Karp, a thought occurred to me: Had Palantir replaced Google? Nothing Karp had said gave any hint that Palantir was working on Maven. Maybe it was just the added vehemence with which he spoke—he was always animated, but this topic had him especially riled—plus the fact that Maven was exactly the kind of project that would appeal to Palantir. As we walked along the cross-country-skiing trail, I asked him if Palantir had taken over for Google. "Well, I can't really comment on that," Karp replied. I took his answer to be a non-denial and later confirmed that Palantir was indeed now involved with Maven. In addition to the Maven news, I learned something else that afternoon in Vermont. I realized that Karp's diatribes against Google were not purely a strategic ploy; the guy also just liked to argue.

But if his aim, in repeatedly attacking Google, was to try to take some of the pressure off Palantir, it didn't work; the company remained an object of scorn and mistrust. This feeling was due in no small part to Thiel, as even many Palantirians acknowledged. "Peter is our biggest problem," one Palantir executive told me. And it wasn't just Thiel's support for Trump that was causing difficulties. A month after I saw Karp in Vermont, I attended a conference in Washington where he was one of the keynote speakers. During his talk, Karp was asked about facial-recognition technology and gave an unequivocal answer: he thought it should be used by the police only for exculpatory purposes, to exonerate people who were suspected or falsely accused of crimes. A few months later, *The New York Times* reported that Thiel had secretly backed a start-up called Clearview AI, whose facial-recognition app was being used by police departments nationwide to charge individuals. Thiel's investment in Clearview AI contradicted Karp's position and also raised doubts, not for the first time, about the sincerity of the views that Thiel had expressed regarding civil liberties and privacy.

For a long time, the perception that Karp and Thiel were ideological opposites had redounded to Palantir's benefit: it suggested that the company was a broad church internally and was doing work of such critical importance that it transcended partisanship. That Karp, a self-declared progressive, was the CEO helped assuage concerns about Thiel's involvement with Palantir. But that was before Trump. Now some Palantirians wondered how Karp, having claimed that fascism was his biggest fear, could abide his cofounder's embrace of right-wing populism. It puzzled Karp's family, too. They understood that Karp and Thiel were friends, but a lot of friendships had splintered over Trump—and Thiel, of course, was no ordinary Trump supporter. (Every time he heard his brother railing against "wokeism," Ben Karp couldn't help but wonder if that was the way one needed to talk to be part of the so-called Thielverse.)

Moreover, if you took Karp at his word, he and Thiel were now working at cross-purposes. Karp insisted that keeping the far right out of power was part of Palantir's mission. Yet its chairman of the board was now using his wealth and influence to promote the far right, and this wasn't a Hegelian contradiction that could just be ironed out. Palantir was devoted to the defense of the West, but Thiel appeared to have a different view than Karp about what that meant—about what was worth defending. Based on what he had written and said, as well as the candidates he had supported, it could be surmised that Thiel thought of the West principally in terms of cultural identity—as a group of nations bound by their Judeo-Christian heritage and, in varying degrees, by a commitment to free enterprise. For him, defending the West was about protecting these bedrocks of Western life; it clearly did not mean safeguarding multiracial, pluralistic democracy. Karp might have been fine with America's changing complexion, but judging by his support for highly restrictive immigration policies, Thiel plainly was not.

Thiel recognized that he had become a public relations liability for Palantir, and not long after Trump took office, in 2017, he told Karp that if he ever wanted him to step down from the company's board, he would. But Karp had no interest in asking for his resignation. As he later explained to me, he benefited enormously from Thiel's counsel and believed it was essential that he remain formally involved with Palantir. "I think Peter is invaluable as an intellectual asset," Karp said. "He's an irreplaceable intellectual asset." He said Thiel was also a cherished friend and that he was not going to let a spate of bad press come between them. In addition, he felt indebted to Thiel and thought it would have been an act of betrayal to part ways with him just because it might have been expedient. "Peter brought me into the game; no one else would have brought me in as a cofounder, no one else would have supported me as CEO," Karp said.

When I suggested to Karp that the conversation about Palantir might have been a little different had Thiel not been associated with the company, he rejected the premise. In his view, the better question was: Where would Palantir have been *without* Thiel? Karp believed that Palantir had profited not just from Thiel's business savvy but also from his fame, including the controversy that he generated. Palantir, particularly when it was still a fledgling start-up, needed to establish a strong brand identity; Karp, by virtue of his leadership role in the company, had obviously contributed more than anyone else to building Palantir's brand. But Thiel's name recognition and notoriety had helped.

Beyond that, Karp thought that people were reading too much into Thiel's support for Trump. During our conversation in Vermont, he suggested that Thiel had embraced Trump in 2016 because it was an opportunity to *épater les bourgeois*—to shock the establishment. "Peter is a provocateur," Karp told me. Backing

Trump reflected the same impulses that had guided Thiel when he edited *The Stanford Review*. Karp refused to believe that Thiel was attracted to the darker aspects of Trumpism, specifically the bigotry that had animated his candidacy. A year after I visited Karp in Vermont, on the eve of the 2020 presidential election, it was reported that Thiel had met with several well-known white nationalists during the 2016 campaign. When I asked Karp about those claims, he dismissed it as a nonissue and suggested that the fact that he, a biracial Jew, was Palantir's CEO was proof that Thiel was not himself a white nationalist. "I wouldn't be in this position if it were true, would I?" he said.

Trump's presidency brought even greater scrutiny to Palantir's work with police departments. Fears about civil liberties were now joined to concerns that the police would be enlisted to help with the immigration crackdown. Those worries were not unwarranted: in 2019, the ACLU of Northern California released the results of an investigation it had conducted that found that around eighty police departments in that region alone had shared with ICE data gathered from automatic license plate readers. According to *Bloomberg Businessweek*, ICE detained at least two immigrants in Chicago because their names were in a police database of gang members, even though neither man belonged to a gang. Chicago was a sanctuary city, and it was unclear how ICE obtained the erroneous information. *Bloomberg Businessweek* suggested one possibility: Palantir had a contract to help the Cook County Sheriff's Office pull in additional data, including gang lists compiled by police departments throughout Illinois.

But it was Palantir's work with the New Orleans Police Department that became a particular flashpoint during Trump's first presidency. As with ICE, the relationship predated Trump. It started in 2012 and was brokered by James Carville, the Democratic consultant and a native of Louisiana. Palantir, as part of its effort to win more government business, had hired Carville as an adviser. It was an unlikely match: Carville was a campaign operative, the mastermind behind Bill Clinton's 1992 presidential run, with no background in technology. But he was a popular figure in political circles and was seen as another person who could possibly help Palantir navigate Washington.

However, he ended up leading Palantir to an opportunity in his hometown. Carville was appalled by the violence plaguing New Orleans at the time. While the city had largely recovered from the devastation of Hurricane Katrina, it had the highest per capita murder rate in the United States. It had been that way for years, defying all manner of effort to reduce the number of homicides. But Carville thought that Palantir's technology could possibly succeed where human intervention had failed; it seemed worth a shot, anyway, and he arranged for the city's mayor, Mitch Landrieu, scion of a Louisiana political dynasty, to meet with Karp. They spoke for about an hour; at the end, Karp said he thought that Palantir could help and offered the city free use of the company's software, which Landrieu accepted.

New Orleans looked to be a particularly challenging engagement. On the one hand, there was wide agreement among scholars that data-driven policing, dependent on algorithms developed by human beings, tended to reflect and reinforce existing biases—which is to say, it inevitably involved racial profiling and often led to even more of it. On other hand, 90 percent of the homicide victims in New Orleans were black, and 90 percent of the perpetrators were black. If the goal was to reduce the city's murder rate, there was no getting around the fact that it was overwhelmingly a problem of black-on-black violence. And at least according to some people in Karp's orbit, his decision to assist New Orleans was rooted to a degree in his own identity: he wanted to help a black community in need.

Palantir made its technology available to New Orleans with the stipulation that it could not be used for predictive policing, but rather, only for preventive policing. It might have seemed like a hairsplitting distinction (and in the view of many civil libertarians, it was), but there was a difference. Predictive policing is primarily about identifying places where crimes are likely to be committed—so-called hot spots—and upping the police presence there in the hope of thwarting robberies and murders. Preventive policing, by contrast, uses data to intervene at an earlier stage—to identify individuals who, because of where they live, whom they associate with, or their previous behavior, seem at greater risk of committing or falling victim to violent crimes. The police attempt to guide these individuals away from potential trouble—by, for instance, offering those with known gang connections inducements to steer clear of trouble. Courtney Bowman, Palantir's head of privacy and civil liberties, says that preventive policing is "more ameliorative than punitive."

Between 2012 and 2015, the murder rate in New Orleans fell by 25 percent. But according to Jeff Asher, who worked as a crime analyst for the City of New Orleans from 2013 to 2015, it had little to do with Palantir. Much of the violence in New Orleans was gang-related, and Asher, a former CIA analyst, was attached to what was known as the Multi-Agency Gang Unit. In that capacity, Asher made frequent use of Gotham, the software platform that Palantir was supplying the city. At the CIA, he had used Analyst's Notebook and had no difficultly figuring out how to operate Gotham. But he said he was the only person he knew in the gang unit who used Palantir. While the software performed well, it did require some technical skill and training to operate. "It was intuitive," said Asher, "but not for cops." The detectives he worked with would attend tutorials with Palantir engineers, but they didn't really need the software for their work and also struggled to understand how to use it. "It was like trying to teach your grandfather," he quipped. In his view, the drop in the city's murder rate was mostly the result of the successful prosecution of gang members on racketeering charges, which had a deterrent effect, at least for a time. He said the fundamental problem for Palantir in New Orleans was that the police department didn't have a dedicated team of analysts; it was just him. A bigger department that had more analysts and that took data-driven policing more seriously would have been a better fit for Palantir.

In 2018, three years after Asher left his job, the online tech magazine *The Verge* published an article that alleged that the New Orleans Police Department was operating a secret anti-crime program with the help of Palantir and that the company was using New Orleans as a testing ground for developing predictive policing technology. The article was marred by some erroneous claims. Although a number of New Orleans officials insisted that they were unaware of the city's relationship with Palantir, it wasn't a secret: Palantir's 2015 annual report discussed its work in New Orleans, and the mayor's office likewise noted Palantir's involvement on a website it had set up that detailed its effort to combat violent crime. *The Verge*'s allegation about predictive policing technology was also wrong. It was based on a patent that Palantir filed in 2014 for what it called a crime risk forecasting system. However, Bowman says that the patent was for a program that Palantir had developed with a European law enforcement agency and made no use of the company's work in New Orleans.

Palantir also disputed *The Verge*'s claim that it had facilitated predictive policing in New Orleans. In a seven-page response to the article that he posted on Palantir's in-house blog, Bowman said the company "did not develop or deploy *any* predictive policing algorithms or capabilities" during its collaboration with the city of New Orleans and had, in fact, rejected a request from the police department for help in that regard. He pointed to an email exchange, cited in *The Verge* article, that he had with a department crime analyst (not Asher), who had compiled a "gang member scorecard" in which individuals were ranked according to the number of gun-related incidents they had previously been involved with. In one email, Bowman explained to the analyst that he had "serious concerns about instituting a ranking or numeric scoring approach" and that "an opaque scoring algorithm substitutes the veneer of quantitative certainty for more holistic, qualitative judgment and human culpability." Bowman told me that the analyst wanted help integrating the scorecard into the data pool that Palantir had created for the police department but that he turned down the request precisely because Palantir was unwilling to abet anything that smacked of predictive policing.

But *The Verge* article caused an uproar among civic organizations in New Orleans, and within days of its publication, the city announced that it was terminating its relationship with Palantir. The controversy infuriated Karp. When I brought it up several years later, he remained bitter. "I will go to my grave never accepting the critique of our work in New Orleans as being anything but an abysmal embarrassment for the people who made it," he said. He insisted, pace Asher, that Palantir's software had helped cut the murder rate and said that the company's critics were "very misaligned with the people they claim to protect."

Contrary to what some of his colleagues had told me, Karp

denied that his own identity had factored into his decision to help New Orleans. He said that while he was "very happy to stop black-on-black genocide," it was simply a humanitarian gesture, something he would have done for any other community. Karp said he was still dumbstruck that something that had been so well-intentioned and—at least in his telling—effective had been portrayed in such a nefarious light. "How do you make saving lives into anything other than what it was?" he asked. "It is mind-boggling to me that the advocates of human rights are so theologically attached to their view that they would rather that the genocide continues than to have a mild intervention that largely was around meeting with the friends and of people who are likely to engage in violence and calming them down. Shutting down that program, I'm certain, between now and then, cost hundreds of lives."

To Karp, the New Orleans fracas was emblematic of what he saw as the left's descent into mindless dogmatism. He said that many liberals now seemed "to reject quantification of any kind. And I don't understand how being anti-quantitative is in any way progressive." They also appeared more interested in posturing than in improving the lives of the people they were ostensibly seeking to assist. Karp said that he was actually the true progressive. "If you are championing an ideology whose logical consequence is that thousands and thousands and thousands of people over time that you claim to defend are killed, maimed, go to prison—how is what I'm saying not progressive when what you are saying is going to lead to a cycle of poverty?"

He conceded, though, that partnering with local law enforcement, at least in the United States, was just too complicated. "Police departments are hard because you have an overlay of legitimate ethical concerns," Karp said. "I would also say there is a politicization of legitimate ethical issues to the detriment of the poorest members of our urban environments." He acknowledged, too, that the payoff from police work wasn't enough to justify the agita that came with it. And in truth, there hadn't been much of a payoff; indeed, Palantir's technology was no longer being used by any U.S. police departments. The New York City Police Department had terminated its contract with Palantir in 2017 and replaced the company's software with its own data analysis tool. In 2021, the Los Angeles Police Department had ended its relationship with Palantir, partly in response to growing public pressure. (Palantir still had contracts with police departments in several European countries.)

But as fraught as Trump's first presidency was for Palantir, it yielded what became arguably the company's most consequential deployment. During the Covid-19 pandemic, Palantir's software was used by the U.S. government to track the spread of the disease and to manage the distribution of personal protective equipment, or PPE, such as gloves and masks. It was also an integral part of the vaccine roll-out. The pandemic became Palantir's ultimate proof-of-concept moment and a transformative event in the life of the company, a point accentuated by Karp's decision to take Palantir public at the height of the global health emergency.

EIGHT

PROOF OF CONCEPT

On a weekend morning in late February 2020, Karp was cross-country skiing near his New Hampshire home. He was joined by one of the Norwegians, but there was little conversation; in general, Karp liked to be alone with his own thoughts when he was skiing, and there was a lot on his mind that day. A novel coronavirus that had started in China a few months earlier was spreading around the world. In Europe and North America, the first deaths had been reported, and the data indicated that the doubling rate—the number of days that it took for the case count to double—appeared to be getting smaller, which meant the virus was propagating at an increasingly rapid pace. As Karp contemplated these developments, it became clear to him that it was no longer possible to prevent Covid-19 from becoming a global pandemic.

As soon as he returned to the house, he called other Palantir executives and told them that he was closing the company's offices indefinitely and that employees were to begin working from home. Karp had been accompanied to New Hampshire by two of his Austrian assistants, Gabriel and Günter, as well as several bodyguards. Karp was a germophobe, and he was already requiring everyone to wear surgical masks and to keep their distance from one another (and, most importantly, from him). Now he told them that they were all going to have to hunker down in New Hampshire, possibly for some time. On Karp's instructions, members of the security team drove to a nearby supermarket and bought several months' worth of canned foods, which after being wiped off with disinfectant were stored in the basement of the house. Karp, worried about possible civil unrest, also had them stock up on ammo. "We bought a lot of bullets," he says.

Over that same weekend, Dr. Deborah Birx was in Johannesburg, South Africa, for a conference on AIDS. Birx was the U.S. global AIDS coordinator and oversaw PEPFAR, which stood for President's Emergency Plan for AIDS Relief. This $100 billion program, started under President George W. Bush, funded AIDS treatment, prevention, and research in Africa and other parts of the developing world. But although AIDS was ostensibly the focus of the meeting in Johannesburg, Birx and other attendees were keeping close watch on Covid-19. While in South Africa, she received a call from White House aide Matt Pottinger, who worked on the National Security Council (he had previously been a Marine and had coauthored with Lieutenant General Michael Flynn the "Fixing Intel" report that had caught Doug Philippone's eye). Birx and Pottinger were friends, but this was not a social call: he asked if she would be willing to serve as the White House coronavirus response coordinator, a position created to help the Trump administration handle what was rapidly metastasizing into a crisis.

Birx agreed to take the job and flew to Washington to assume her new duties. She knew that the only hope of containing the virus was to marshal as much data as possible as quickly as possible. "You control pandemics through the use of data," she said. "That's how you do it." But it would not be easy. Despite being the world's most prosperous and technologically advanced nation, the United States had a Rube Goldberg system when it came to health care data—every state did things a little differently, and between antiquated and disconnected reporting systems, inconsistent or incomplete data gathering, and enormous disparities in how data was collected, formatted, and stored, trying to accurately track the spread of the virus was going to be difficult. A *New York Times* article about the case of an Alaska woman who caught Covid described the challenge:

> After the woman was tested, her workplace transferred her nasal swab to the Fairbanks state laboratory. There, workers manually entered basic information into an electronic lab report, searching a state database for the woman's address and telephone number. The state lab then forwarded her case report to the state health department's epidemiology section, where the same information had to be retyped into a database that feeds the C.D.C.'s national disease surveillance database. A worker logged in and clicked through multiple screens in yet another state database to learn that the woman had not been vaccinated, then manually updated her file. The epidemiology section then added the woman's case to a spreadsheet with more than 1,500 others recorded that day. That was forwarded to a different team of contact tracers, who gathered other important details about the woman by telephone, then plugged those details into yet another database. The result was a rich stew of information, but because the contact tracers' database is incompatible with the epidemiologists' database, their information could not be easily shared at either the state or the federal level. For example, when the contact tracers learned a few days later that the woman had been hospitalized with Covid, they had to inform the epidemiology section by email, and the epidemiologists got the hospital's confirmation by fax.

This was one case in one sparsely populated state, involving a virus that would sicken millions of people across all fifty states.

After Birx's appointment was announced, Julie Bush, who ran Palantir's health care business, emailed her offering the company's assistance. Bush and Birx were acquainted because Palantir had supplied its technology free of charge to PEPFAR, which used it to analyze the efficacy of its work down to the level of individual clinics. Birx had found Palantir to be a valuable resource, and she arranged to see Bush. They met on March 7 in the Old Executive Office Building, next to the White House, where Matt Pottinger joined them. Birx was blunt: she needed help, urgently. The Centers for Disease Control and Prevention, or CDC, was trying to track the virus, but the decrepit and slapdash state of America's health data infrastructure—including the CDC's own systems—made it almost impossible to generate accurate numbers. (A joke in public health circles was that CDC stood for "Can't Do Computers.") It was so bad that Birx and others had decided that open-source information was more reliable. "I'm getting my data off CNN," Birx told Bush.

A few days later, Bush returned to the Old Executive Office Building, this time accompanied by two colleagues: Aki Jain, who now oversaw Palantir's U.S. government operations, and Hirsh Jain (no relation), a forward-deployed engineer. The three Palantirians met with Birx and the team she had hastily assembled. One of the people she had recruited was Amy Gleason, a former nurse who worked for the United States Digital Service. USDS was an office of the executive branch established by the Obama administration in the wake of the bungled rollout of Healthcare.gov, the online portal for Obamacare. USDS provided information technology consulting for federal agencies and was staffed in part by outside experts who would join the government for a few years before returning to the private sector.

Gleason specialized in healthcare technology, with a focus on interoperability—making it easier for health care professionals to obtain and share data. For her, it was a personal issue: her daughter had a rare disease that required her to see a dozen physicians spread over six different health systems in three states, and the difficulty those doctors encountered when trying to share information with one another electronically had led Gleason to change careers. She, as much as anyone else, was acutely aware of the data challenge that Covid posed. Gleason had never heard of Palantir and was, by her own admission, "extremely skeptical" going into the meeting with Bush and her colleagues. Palantir had limited experience in the health care sector, and this was a once-in-a-century pandemic in a country that struggled to collect and disseminate population-wide medical data. Gleason had come to see that even basic information—how many total beds a hospital had, for instance—was not readily accessible. "We had no way to know anything about our health care system," she says. The self-assurance of the Palantirians only deepened her skepticism. She says, "Everything I asked, they were like, 'Yeah, we can do that,' and 'Sure, we can do that.' And I was like, 'No, that's impossible.'"

But the Palantir team hadn't overpromised. Using Foundry, the software platform that had replaced Metropolis, around sixty Palantir employees began integrating the data that Birx's team needed to find emerging hot spots and get resources to them. The data they pulled in included case counts, testing numbers, hospitalizations, and hospital bed availability, as well as supplies of ventilators, personal protective gear, and therapeutic treatments. The Palantirians broke up into teams—one group for cases, another for supply chain issues—and worked around the clock (employees in Australia and Europe contributed to the effort). Most worked remotely, but Julie Bush and Hirsh Jain were on-site with Birx's team—first at FEMA headquarters, later at the Department of Health and Human Services, or HHS. Bush, who was pregnant at the time, says it was a harrowing experience. "There was a lot we didn't know about the virus, there was no vaccine yet—it was scary," she says. For social distancing, they used microphones to talk to one another.

The raw data, gathered from all three thousand counties in the United States, was often a mess, and there was no consistency in how it was reported. It came via Excel spreadsheets, PowerPoints, and PDFs. Palantir's engineers harmonized the data into a standardized structure. "It was one of the hardest technical challenges I've seen," says Jain. Even so, within a matter of days, Palantir had built a dashboard, later christened HHS Protect, that was yielding daily, comprehensive updates for Birx and her team. By the third week, the system had incorporated around three hundred different data sources, merging roughly two billion data elements, and had become the most up-to-date and reliable gauge, public or private, tracking the spread of the virus and efforts to contain it. Gleason was struck not just by Palantir's efficiency, but also by the "intelligence" of the company's software. There was a lot of bad data coming in, which was often just the result of typing mistakes or clerical errors. "Someone would fat-finger a daily case count," says Gleason. Foundry would flag numbers that seemed off, which was critical to ensuring that the totals were correct.

This work took place in the background. What the public saw was a daily shit show in the White House briefing room, in which President Trump, surrounded by members of the Covid response task force, including Birx, downplayed the severity of the outbreak and peddled quack remedies, such as UV lighting ("it will kill it in one minute," Trump said) and a drug used to deworm horses and other livestock. Sadly for Birx, one of the defining moments of the Covid crisis was at a briefing on April 24, 2020, when Trump turned to her and asked her to investigate whether injecting disinfectant into the body would eliminate the virus. Birx was seated in a chair to the side of the podium, and the pained expression that fell across her face went viral. By that point, Birx had the data she needed to mount an effective response to the pandemic; what was missing was competent leadership at the top.

It was public knowledge that the government was using Palantir's software to manage the pandemic. However, some of the reporting was erroneous or incomplete. Claims that Palantir had been brought in at Trump's behest, as another gift to Thiel, were untrue—it was Birx who enlisted Palantir's help, and it was her decision alone (and Gleason says that among civil servants, there was some resistance to Palantir—she says that she received messages from a handful of colleagues urging Birx's team not to use Palantir because they thought that the company was shady and also because of the ICE controversy). Some critics noted that the two contracts that Palantir was awarded to assist with the Covid response, worth a combined $25 million, were not subject to competitive bidding. That was partly correct—the country was facing an unprecedented public health emergency, and there was no time to follow the normal procurement process. But Palantir was initially hired on a thirty-day trial basis, and Birx's team considered several other software vendors before going with Palantir. Meanwhile, immigration activists raised concerns that patient information that was being funneled through Palantir's software could be used to apprehend undocumented workers. That did not happen, nor was it possible: the Covid data was anonymized.

Amid all the craziness with Trump (and the scrutiny that it brought to Palantir), the effort to track and contain the virus became ever more refined. Hirsh Jain says that despite the sometimes unhelpful messaging from the White House, behind the scenes, among the civil servants at HHS and other government agencies who were drawing on insights derived from Palantir's technology, there was a level of "operational excellence" that remained undiminished. This proved especially true during the vaccine rollout, which also involved Palantir and was a resounding success. In June 2020, the company was contracted to build a dashboard for Operation Warp Speed, the public-private joint venture to expedite the creation of a Covid vaccine. As with HHS Protect, Foundry was the software for the dashboard, which was called Tiberius and that was provided to all fifty states to help them manage vaccine supplies and distribution, as well as to monitor vaccine uptake.

The United States was not the only country that used Palantir's software during the pandemic. The company provided Foundry to around twelve other nations. Initially, Palantir gave it to most of them at no cost, which in addition to being an altruistic gesture was also a shrewd one—a way of potentially drumming up business amid crisis. Palantir charged Great Britain's National Health Service, or NHS, £1 for the software, which it used for the same functions that the U.S. government did—to trace the spread of the virus, to collect testing and hospitalization data, and to help with the disbursement of critical supplies. The British likewise turned to Palantir's technology for their own vaccine program. The British government later rewarded Palantir with a nearly $600 million contract to revamp the NHS's data infrastructure.

Palantir also played a central role in the most important humanitarian effort undertaken during Covid. In early 2019, the World Food Programme, or WFP, signed a five-year, $45 million contract with Palantir. The collaboration grew out of a pilot project that Palantir did with the WFP involving a supply chain optimization tool. According to the WFP, the program yielded nearly

$30 million in savings, and on the back of that success, it entered into a long-term agreement to use Palantir's technology in its operations. Several aid groups denounced the deal, citing Palantir's ties to the CIA, as well as the Thiel connection. They also expressed mistrust of Palantir and questioned whether it would keep the data anonymized. Some suggested that the company, stung by the controversy over ICE, was trying to launder its reputation through the tie-up with the WFP.

But officials at the WFP were undeterred. Pierre Guillaume Wielezynski, the WFP's chief of digital transformation services, says that it was clear to him and his colleagues that Palantir was genuinely interested in helping with its relief efforts. Through experience, he had developed a good sense for when potential partners were looking to reap a PR benefit. "We've had folks who have wanted to partner with us because they want the press release, the tweet, the photo," Wielezynski says. "But with Palantir, that never came across as one of their objectives. They never asked us for a communications campaign, they never asked us for visibility."

Palantir's software proved to be a critical asset when Covid hit. As the global economy came to a halt, supply chains froze, disrupting shipments of wheat, corn, and other staples. There was grave concern that the pandemic would cause mass starvation across large swaths of Africa. But through its use of Foundry, the WFP had a comprehensive view of where food supplies were located, where they were needed most urgently, and the most expeditious way to get them there, and it was ultimately able to prevent widespread famine. Not only that: the WFP's ability to deliver emergency assistance was so robust that the World Health Organization (WHO) used it to send personal protective gear to health professionals throughout Africa. While there is no way to calculate how many lives the WFP saved during Covid, the number was enormous, and Palantir proved essential to this effort. "Without Palantir, we wouldn't have pulled it off," says Wielezynski. In October 2020, the WFP was awarded the Nobel Peace Prize for its work on combating hunger. The Nobel committee cited the Covid response as one of the reasons it had selected the WFP as that year's recipient.

While all this was happening, Karp was in isolation in the woods. He had personal assistants with him as well as his security detail, but in his mind, he was effectively alone. He didn't like running the company remotely—it was antithetical to his management style, which was built around making himself accessible (that was why he insisted that he needed to be on the road some three hundred days a year). But Palantir continued to function well even though all 3,500 employees were working from home.

While the pandemic was wretched for most people, Karp found it blissful. He recognized that millions were suffering, and he was sympathetic (and took pride in the help that Palantir was providing). But he savored the downtime that Covid gave him, as well as the quiet. "In the beginning, it wasn't clear whether everyone was going to die," he says. "But once I knew that I wasn't going to die, I was in heaven. It was the best thing ever in my adult life. I was so happy, and it underscored my certitude that I am a deeply introverted person." Had he not felt a strong attachment to his colleagues and the company, he would have happily remained in seclusion.

As he was enjoying this solitude, Karp decided that the time had come to take Palantir public. While it was a move that was likely to make him extraordinarily rich, it had the potential to undermine the company's culture. Palantir was nothing if not idiosyncratic; it had been built in Karp's image, and unconventionality was arguably its greatest strength. Now, though, Karp was prepared to put that at risk.

In early April 2020, as Covid was ravaging much of the planet, Palantir held a virtual board meeting. As soon as the executive session was over, Karp called Dave Glazer, Palantir's de facto CFO. In typical fashion, Karp skipped the pleasantries and got right to the point. "Oh, hey," he said, "we're going to need to go public in two months." Glazer, a lawyer who had specialized in IPOs before joining Palantir, suppressed the urge to laugh and told Karp it couldn't happen that quickly. "Well, what about three months?" Karp asked. That would also be impossible, Glazer explained, adding that the Securities and Exchange Commission, or SEC, would ultimately determine the timing. But by that point, it was clear to Glazer that Karp, after resisting the idea for so long, was suddenly ready to take Palantir public.

It had occurred to Karp that the pandemic might actually be an ideal time for such an offering. He recognized that the company was an oddity: it derived around 50 percent of its revenue from government contracts, and much of its work involved matters that couldn't be disclosed publicly. Moreover, Wall Street still struggled to make sense of Palantir and whether it was truly a technology company or a consulting firm masquerading as one. On top of that, Palantir had been in business for seventeen years and had yet to turn a profit. Under normal circumstances, it might have been a hard sell. But Karp figured that other companies that had been contemplating IPOs were likely to put off going public until the pandemic was over and that amid a dearth of new listings, perhaps investors would be more inclined to overlook or downplay what they didn't like about Palantir. "In this environment, maybe our warts mattered a little less now," as Glazer put it. (As it happened, though, other companies also saw opportunity in the Covid crisis, and the second half of 2020 brought a wave of IPOs.)

Another factor was that year's presidential election. Between Thiel's support for Trump and the controversy over ICE, Palantir had incurred the wrath of many people on the left, including prominent figures like U.S. Senator Elizabeth Warren and U.S. Representative Alexandria Ocasio-Cortez, and there was concern that the company's business might suffer under a Democratic administration. (On the eve of Palantir's public listing, Ocasio-Cortez wrote a letter to the SEC asking it to delay the stock's debut and to investigate a broad range of problems that she identified with the company. The SEC did not comply with her request.) In June 2020, *The Intercept* noted that an online biography of Avril Haines, one of Joe Biden's chief foreign policy advisers, no longer noted that she had served as a consultant to Palantir; the implication was that Palantir was now so toxic that Democrats were afraid to be associated with the company. Going public before the election seemed like a wise move given the blowback that Palantir might face if the Democrats reclaimed the White House.

But Palantir also had some points in its favor. Its government business was booming—between all the defense contracts that it had won and its frontline role in the battle against Covid, the company was reaping a bonanza in Washington. On the commercial front, its relationships with Airbus and BP continued to deepen. By 2020, Palantir was approaching $1 billion in annual revenue and was still privately valued at around $20 billion; it was a flourishing business, if not yet a profitable one. It had also had a significant technological breakthrough, via the introduction of a software platform called Apollo, which enabled Palantir to deploy and update its technology remotely, thereby reducing—or, in some cases, eliminating—the need to dispatch engineers to work in situ with clients. Apollo had been in development before Covid, but it was rolled out during the pandemic, when most workplaces were shuttered and it was difficult to send forward-deployed engineers out into the field. But more than just solving the problem posed by the Covid lockdowns, Apollo seemed to hold the key to answering a long-standing critique of Palantir—that its products were not scalable.

Still, the decision to go public marked an abrupt reversal for Karp. Even just a few months earlier, he had still been resistant to the idea. In September 2019, when I was working on the Palantir article that I wrote for *The New York Times Magazine*, I met with Karp in Paris, where the company was hosting a conference for its European corporate clients. He and I took a walk one afternoon from Le Bristol Paris, the hotel where he was staying, to the Luxembourg Gardens, where he planned to do tai chi. As we cut through the Tuileries, Karp explained that he remained hesitant to take Palantir public because he worried that it would undermine the company's egalitarian spirit, which in his view had been essential to its success. "My main skepticism is whether it could be done while maintaining Palantir's culture," he said.

From the earliest days of Palantir, he had effectively asked employees to accept a trade-off—in exchange for the opportunity to work on consequential issues, they'd earn less than they might have at other tech companies. But it stood to reason that going public would be lucrative for Karp and other executives, and he worried that this would diminish the sense of shared purpose that had always prevailed. Karp also thought that going public would be a distraction: employees would inevitably follow the daily gyrations of the company's stock price, which itself might have a corrosive effect on Palantir's work.

Privately, Thiel had been pushing for an IPO for several years. Publicly, though, he expressed solidarity with Karp. A few months after I saw Karp in Paris, I met with Thiel at his office in Los Angeles. He said it was still too soon for Palantir to seek a stock market listing. "There's always a question of who benefits from an IPO," he told me. "The investment bankers benefit massively, as do all the people who help you with the process. Then certainly early investors and early employees benefit, but then if you think of the company itself as an entity or as a person—maybe that's too anthropocentric—but if you think of what's actually in the interest of the company, it's not at all clear that IPOs are the best thing for companies."

Thiel acknowledged that there were upsides to going public, and not just the potential financial reward: it imposed a greater degree of transparency on companies and also obliged them to adopt better managerial and corporate governance practices. He said that IPOs made sense "once you're at a certain scale, when you have all these customers locked in, and it's sort of a steadily growing business." But Palantir was still innovating and was "nowhere near" achieving its potential market share. He noted, as well, that Palantir was not the only tech company that had put off going public: in the two decades since the dot-com bust, companies had been much slower to seek public listings. They could raise the money they needed privately and could let their businesses mature without having to submit to the exigencies of the quarterly earnings cycle.

Indeed, since the 1990s, the number of publicly traded companies in the United States had fallen by more than half—from a peak of around 7,500 in 1997 to around 3,500 in 2020. This decline happened even as the U.S. economy had doubled in size over the same time period. Some companies had gone out of business, and others had been swallowed up through mergers and acquisitions. But the decline had also been driven by the growing allure and financial muscle of private capital. Private equity had become a $4 trillion business, an eightfold increase since the early 2000s, and the U.S. venture capital industry had around $1 trillion in assets under management. Start-ups—even mature ones like Palantir—could now easily obtain the funding they needed without having to meet the strict regulatory requirements of the public equity markets or answer to Wall Street analysts. Many young companies were now opting to stay private for longer, a shift in sentiment reflected in the dwindling number of IPOs. In the mid- to late 1990s, there were five to six hundred IPOs a year. In retrospect, that was arguably excessive, a byproduct of the dot-com boom and the irrational exuberance of that era. But by the late 2010s, there were fewer than two hundred IPOs annually, and what was once a cherished rite of passage for companies—and a symbol of the enduring vitality of American capitalism—had become almost an option of last resort.

In this regard, at least, Palantir was not an outlier. But Karp knew that he couldn't continue to put off an IPO. Investors who had backed the company were clamoring for one, and while his cofounders had generally been supportive of his decision to keep Palantir private, they were not going to wait forever. Nor were Palantir employees, especially those who had been with the firm a long time. "When you are twenty years into a company, people start to get antsy about equity and the equity value of the company," Karp said that afternoon in Paris. "And the thing I'm most sensitive to is, how do you ensure that the people who are building Palantir now are fairly compensated, and that really does presuppose a liquidity event." He understood why his colleagues were eager to see the company go public. "How do you explain to your kid that he can't go to the college of his choice because Karp won't IPO?"

Karp, of course, didn't have kids and was seemingly content with being an undercompensated CEO—on a relative basis—and a paper billionaire. For him, the whole notion of an "exit strategy"—the idea that the ultimate aim for a start-up was to go public or be acquired—was anathema. Palantir was his life's work; it was the only place he could imagine working, and he had no desire to cash out and move on. It seemed, too, that becoming a plutocrat just didn't fit his self-image as a scrappy outsider (or his desire to be seen as such) and also didn't quite square with his political leanings. As we were exiting the Tuileries, there was a commotion in front of us: a bunch of street vendors were scrambling to pack up their knockoff Gucci and Dior handbags because the police were apparently coming. Watching the merchants racing to avoid the gendarmes, Karp quietly remarked, "I'm on their side."

But just seven months later, in April 2020, Karp decided that it was time to take Palantir public. The company's investors were delighted, and Thiel was, too. When he and I spoke again in 2023, he said that Karp's previous resistance to the idea had been "actually somewhat charismatic," in that it showcased Palantir's determination to walk its own path. But he now acknowledged that he thought it had taken too long to go public. He had come to feel that Palantir would benefit from the discipline imposed by having to answer to shareholders. He also believed it would help the company's bottom line. Thiel suspected that some clients had been hesitant to enter into bigger, longer-term contracts with Palantir because they worried about its staying power—the company's reluctance to go public inevitably raised questions about the quality of its business and its financial viability. A stock market listing would give Palantir added legitimacy.

Major investment banks had long hoped to underwrite a Palantir IPO. But even though two of them, JPMorganChase and Credit Suisse, had been Palantir clients, Karp hated Wall Street, animus rooted in the frosty reception that Palantir had received from Silicon Valley's venture capital community. Karp still nursed a grudge over the way Palantir had been treated, and it colored his view of investment bankers and institutional investors more generally. Several investment banks wrote pitchbooks for a Palantir IPO, but the prospectuses all fell flat with Karp. He claimed that he even burned one of them because it seemed indistinguishable from the dealbook for WeWork, the scandal-plagued office-sharing company that had to cancel its IPO in the face of investor skepticism. "I'm against burning books because I'm from a progressive Jewish family," he said. "I've actually only burned a book a couple times in my life. I took the draft that the bankers wrote, and I went to my massive fireplace and I dumped it in."

Karp ultimately opted to take Palantir public not through an IPO but, rather, via a direct public listing, or DPO. In a DPO, the company doesn't issue new shares; it just makes it possible for the public to buy existing ones. Spotify had gone public through a DPO in 2018, and Slack did the same the following year. Investment banks play an advisory role in DPOs but earn much less in fees—millions less—than they do from IPOs. Karp also made another important call: after years of excoriating Silicon Valley, he decided that Palantir would use the occasion of its public listing to move its headquarters from Palo Alto to Denver.

The company's footprint in Palo Alto had already been declining. In the mid-2010s, Palantir was the single-largest tenant in the city, renting space in seven different buildings. ("There's more Palantir paraphernalia in downtown Palo Alto than there is Patagonia," a local venture capitalist told CNBC in 2016.) But by the time the pandemic struck, New York, Washington, and London had become the company's hubs, and Palantir was using just a single office building in Palo Alto. However, moving the headquarters to Denver, as opposed to, say, Washington or New York, was also a statement, a way of signifying that Palantir was in sync with Middle America in a way that the rest of Silicon Valley was not (even if Denver was a fairly progressive enclave in a state that had been trending Democratic). In 2018, Thiel moved from the Bay Area to Los Angeles because he was frustrated by what he regarded as Silicon Valley's "monoculture" (never mind that Los Angeles was a liberal stronghold, too). Now Palantir was also bailing on Northern California.

Internally, the push to take Palantir public was referred to as "GN," which supposedly stood for "Go Now." But Karp told several associates that it actually meant *goyim naches*, a Yiddish phrase that loosely translates as "goyish games"—a gentile pursuit. It was his way of expressing the mixed feelings he had. The actual prep work was done over the summer, at Karp's house in New Hampshire. A number of employees relocated there to strategize and draft the necessary paperwork. Dave Glazer, who brought his family with him, said that it was "kibbutz-style living." During breaks, he used Karp's front yard as a driving range.

One priority was devising a share structure that would allow Karp, along with Thiel and Stephen Cohen, to retain a controlling interest in Palantir. This practice was now common among tech companies. In Silicon Valley, founders were kings, and most felt that they should be able to continue running their businesses as they saw fit even after taking their companies public. Prior to its 2004 IPO, Google created dual-class shares for its cofounders, Larry Page and Sergey Brin, to ensure that they could never be outvoted by other shareholders. Facebook did the same for Mark Zuckerberg before it went public in 2012. But Palantir already had a special category, so-called B shares, whose holders enjoyed ten times the voting power of people who owned regular shares. While Karp, Thiel, and Cohen held most of the B shares, some had been granted to other Palantir executives as well as several outside investors, and the three cofounders now controlled only around 30 percent of the company's outstanding stock.

In the lead-up to the DPO, Palantir created a third category of shares, which were awarded only to Karp, Thiel, and Cohen. These so-called F shares had a variable number of votes—in essence, they gave the three of them as much voting power as they needed in any given moment to ensure that they controlled 49.999999 percent of the total vote on any issue put before shareholders (and yes, it was exactly six 9s in the decimal place). While it wasn't quite 50 percent, it was enough to guarantee that the three would almost certainly never lose a shareholder vote (and Thiel, in addition to his personal stake in Palantir, also owned shares through Clarium Capital, his hedge fund, and Founders Fund, one of his venture capital funds). This structure would remain in place until the last of the three died, and their voting power would remain determinative even if their total share of Palantir stock declined to the low single digits. Insiders jokingly referred to the F shares as "fuck-you shares."

The F shares were controversial. Michael Weisbach, a professor at Ohio State University's Fisher College of Business, suggested that Palantir was seeking all the benefits of being a publicly traded company without the responsibilities—but like other commentors, he evidently believed that Thiel, not Karp, headed Palantir. "They set it up so Peter Thiel can still sort of run it like a private company and still have the advantage of being public," Weisbach told *Bloomberg*. Beyond that, the creation of the F shares seemed like another swipe at Wall Street—a statement that Palantir made its own rules. (After Palantir went public, a disgruntled shareholder filed a lawsuit in Delaware, where the company was incorporated, challenging the legality of the F shares and alleging that the share structure had turned Karp, Thiel, and Cohen into "emperors for life." The case was settled in 2022, when Palantir agreed to change its bylaws to ensure that any future sale of the company as well as certain transactions involving the cofounders would have to be approved by other members of Palantir's board of directors and a two-thirds vote of all the company's shareholders.)

The process of taking Palantir public became just one extended middle finger. In keeping with its very male culture, the company had always had an all-male board. But under California law, publicly traded companies based in the state needed to have at least one female director, and since Palantir would still be headquartered in Palo Alto at the time its stock began trading, it had to add a female director. In June 2020, it announced that Alexandra Wolfe Schiff would be joining its board. The daughter of the novelist Tom Wolfe, she was a *Wall Street Journal* reporter; more significantly, she was a close friend of Thiel's and had written a book about Silicon Valley that portrayed him in glowing terms. According to Thiel's biographer, Max Chafkin, someone in Thiel's orbit reached out to him to ask about Schiff's nomination to the board, and he replied with a wink emoji.

As a precursor to going public, Palantir was required to file a document called an S-1, which formally registered the company's shares with the SEC. For Karp, the S-1 was an opportunity to enunciate Palantir's worldview, and the document that he and his team drafted would become, in their minds, a canonical text. "Our work and the use of our software present difficult questions," it said. "The construction of software platforms that enable more effective surveillance by the state of its adversaries or that assist soldiers in executing attacks raises countless issues, involving the points of tension and tradeoffs between our collective security and individual privacy, the power of machines, and the types of lives we both want to and should lead. The ethical challenges that arise are constant and unrelenting. We embraced the complexity that comes from working in areas where the stakes are often very high and the choices may be imperfect. The more fundamental question is where authority to resolve such questions—to decide how technology may be used and by whom—should reside."

In the S-1, Palantir disclosed that it was relocating its headquarters to Denver, and it took aim at Silicon Valley: "Our society has effectively outsourced the building of software that makes our world possible to a small group of engineers in an isolated corner of the country. The question is whether we also want to outsource the adjudication of some of the most consequential moral and philosophical questions of our time. The engineering elite of Silicon Valley may know more than most about building software. But they do not know more about how society should be organized or what justice requires." The S-1 included broadsides against Facebook and Google: "From the start, we have repeatedly turned down opportunities to sell, collect, or mine data. Other technology companies, including some of the largest in the world, have built their entire businesses on doing just that.... For many consumer internet companies, our thoughts and inclinations, behaviors and browsing habits, are the product for sale. The slogans and marketing of many of the Valley's largest technology firms attempt to obscure this simple fact."

The S-1 went on to suggest that Palantir was aligned with American interests and values in a way that other tech companies (read: Facebook and Google) were not: "The bargain between the public and the technology sector has for the most part been consensual, in that the value of the products and services available seemed to outweigh the invasions of privacy that enabled their rise. Americans will remain tolerant of the idiosyncrasies and excesses of the Valley only to the extent that technology companies are building something substantial that serves the public interest.... Our software is used to target terrorists and to keep soldiers safe. If we are going to ask someone to put themselves in harm's way, we believe that we have a duty to give them what they need to do their jobs. We have chosen sides, and we know that our partners value commitment. We stand by them when it is convenient, and when it is not."

Palantir's DPO brought additional scrutiny to the company and also highlighted a stark divide among its detractors. Many observers—immigration activists, civil libertarians, politicians such as Ocasio-Cortez—believed that Palantir's technology was every bit as effective as Karp claimed and saw the company as uniquely menacing for that reason. They regarded its public listing as an ominous bellwether—capitalism concretizing the emergence of a surveillance state. Other critics, however, suggested that Palantir's software wasn't as good as advertised and that the company was essentially peddling pixie dust. A few weeks before the DPO, *New York* magazine ran a story that all but called Palantir a sham. In a blog post, Scott Galloway, the influential podcaster and a New York University professor, slammed Palantir as a "shitty" business and said it had "all the calories of Facebook (scaled sociopathy) with none of the great taste (profits)." He later told CNN that Palantir was "crap being flung at tourists to the unicorn zoo."

Palantir went public on September 30, 2020, opening at $10 per share. The DPO got off to an inauspicious (and ironic) start: trading in Palantir shares was delayed for several hours because of a software glitch. However, it wasn't Palantir's technology that malfunctioned; rather, the snafu involved an online trading platform operated by Morgan Stanley. Despite the interruption and the fact that the stock finished slightly down on the day, at $9.50, it was a triumphant debut in the minds of Karp and his senior colleagues. They had all gathered in Germany, where Karp was attending a conference. The Palantirians celebrated with champagne. Shyam Sankar said later that it was the first time in his almost twenty years with Palantir that he felt completely confident that it would survive as a business.

For Karp, the DPO was both validation and vindication. It conferred legitimacy on Palantir—it could no longer be called a start-up, a label that always implied a risk of failure, but was truly an established company now. The public listing was proof, as well, that Karp had succeeded on his own, highly differentiated terms. When he and I first started talking, in 2019, he projected confidence, but there was also an undercurrent of anxiety. Although he was convinced he was the right person to lead Palantir internally, he worried that in his public-facing role he was more of a liability than an asset. He was clearly not a standard-issue CEO, and he believed this was detrimental to Palantir. "We're an enterprise company with enterprise clients," Karp said. "You think it is helpful having a fluorescent praying mantis coming into their office, telling them about German philosophy? Do you think that's helpful? I can tell you, it's not helpful." He freely admitted that from an image and messaging standpoint, Palantir might have been better-off with a more conventional CEO—someone who actually looked and sounded like a captain of industry.

His lifestyle fed into the anxiety that he felt. He recognized that it was unorthodox, and he seemed almost apologetic about it. During one of our first conversations, he confessed that he wished he could be more "norm-conforming." When asked what exactly that meant, Karp replied, "The way I see your life." It was true that I had a fairly bourgeois existence—I resided in a suburb and had a wife, two kids, and a dog. Did he think he could ever have a life like mine? He shook his head. "I fantasized about being norm-conforming, but I don't know how to do that," he said. "I just don't know how to do that, I don't know how it works, I wouldn't know how to be not transgressive. I try. I try really hard, really I do, but it's not working out." It was a surprisingly candid and raw comment.

But after Palantir's public listing, Karp no longer felt the need to express regret for his unconventionality. It was a lifestyle that suited him, and he had come to believe that it suited Palantir, too—that, far from being a burden, it had actually benefited the company. He was now convinced that Palantir would not have been as successful with a more typical CEO—the job was too demanding to be done by someone with a full life outside the office, or at least could not be done as well.

Likewise, he now recognized that his distinctive personality was good for Palantir's brand. That became clear to him in the months following the DPO. While Wall Street continued to express doubts about Palantir, retail investors piled into the stock, mostly on account of a sudden infatuation with Karp. Participants in the subreddit known as wallstreetbets found Karp very entertaining and began referring to him as "Daddy Karp" and "Papa Karp." Palantir became a so-called meme stock—a stock that soars in value thanks to social media. In its first three months of trading, it nearly quadrupled in price, peaking at $35 per share in late January 2021. Karp liked the nicknames and delighted in the adulation (and the effect it was having on Palantir's share price). That the wallstreetbets crowd shared his contempt for the professional investment community made it all the sweeter. Karp regarded Palantir as a kind of pirate ship, and the fact that its stock had surged thanks to small-fry investors who prided themselves on their own iconoclasm played into that image. It was also confirmation, in Karp's mind, that in contrast to investment bank analysts, the man on the street had no trouble understanding Palantir: it was the company defending America and the West.

With the DPO, Karp officially became a billionaire, and even as he reveled in—and played up—his sudden populist appeal, Karp also took pleasure in the enhanced stature that he now enjoyed in elite circles. Since the mid-2010s, he had faithfully attended the annual Allen & Company conference in Sun Valley, Idaho, a gathering of media and tech moguls referred to as "summer camp for billionaires." But Karp sensed a change in how his fellow tycoons perceived him when he took part in the 2022 edition (the conference had been canceled the previous year because of Covid). While he hadn't necessarily felt like a gate-crasher before, he could tell that he was now seen as one of their own. He was also a figure of curiosity in a way that had not been the case previously; other Sun Valley stalwarts seemed more eager to talk to him and to make his acquaintance.

Karp's biggest indulgence after Palantir went public was buying his own airplane, a Bombardier Global 7500 for which he paid over $50 million. He had leased a business jet for years before deciding that he wanted to own one. He also used his windfall from the DPO to add to his collection of homes. He purchased a place in Boulder, to be close to Palantir's new headquarters in Denver, and also the house near Washington, D.C. In addition, he acquired a home near Anchorage and one in Sun Valley (he had grown to love the area), and he added 1,500 acres to the New Hampshire property. But none of the homes were palatial—most were modest—and despite his enormous wealth, Karp continued to lead a fairly streamlined existence. Apart from the plane, he evinced little interest in billionaire trophies, which didn't surprise those who knew him best. His cousin Mat Johnson said Karp had always had a "total lack of material obsession" and jokingly suggested that his vast riches were wasted on him.

But if Karp wasn't necessarily as avaricious or acquisitive as other billionaires, he also didn't seem to have any moral qualms about his extreme wealth. That billionaires were generally scorned by the intelligentsia and other liberal elites only enhanced the satisfaction that Karp derived from his economic status; it brought out his innate contrarianism. When Palantir's board of directors awarded him $1.1 billion in total compensation in 2020, making him the highest-paid CEO of a publicly traded company that year, he took some pleasure in the controversy that it kicked up. (A billion-dollar pay package was outrageous under any circumstances, but it was especially provocative amid a global pandemic.) It played into his self-image as a renegade. And while he never boasted of his net worth, in the wake of the DPO he discovered a favorite new word: *tendies*. It was a term popularized by wallstreetbets that essentially meant profits, gains, *getting paid*. Karp loved the phrase and began making promiscuous use of it.

In contrast to other freshly minted billionaires, Karp did not establish a charitable foundation; he told associates that the philanthropic phase of his life would come later. Privately, though, he was generous with his personal fortune. Over the years, he had given a lot of Palantir stock to his parents and his brother and had created trusts for all three. He took particular care of his mother, who never remarried. He bought her an apartment in suburban Philadelphia. Beyond the financial benefits, Palantir's public listing had yielded another dividend for Leah. She liked to check Palantir's stock price each morning—not so much because she wanted to see how the company was doing, but rather because she thought Alex would be checking it, too, and the idea that they were sharing this daily ritual gave her a sense of connection to her son. "It makes me feel closer to him," she said.

For Karp, the wealth he reaped from Palantir's public listing also afforded him the opportunity to repay some debts from the past. To express his gratitude to the family friends who took in Leah and Ben after Bob refused to pay for an apartment for them, Karp made an anonymous donation in the family's name to a Philadelphia-area university. Leah and Ben were eventually able to get their own place because a landlord was willing to give her a lease even though she couldn't show sufficient income. The landlord owned a jewelry shop in the town of Bryn Mawr, and the store was still in his family; as a thank-you for the kindness shown his mother, Karp began periodically dispatching an assistant to the shop with instructions to make large purchases. His affluence also came in handy when he made an unusual request of the people who now resided in the house that he grew up in on Lincoln Drive in Mount Airy. Karp's childhood dog, Rosita, had been buried in the yard, and he wanted to rebury her on his New Hampshire property. The homeowners, both college professors, initially balked but then agreed to have the dog exhumed, and Karp subsequently made a donation to the university where they taught.

One thing that Karp's financial success couldn't get him, however, was an invitation to speak at our alma mater. In his years at the helm of Palantir, he had never been asked to talk at Haverford, and now that he had taken the company public, the college's apparent unwillingness to recognize his accomplishments formally became a source of extreme irritation for him. He was also baffled by Haverford's failure to cultivate him as a donor. He joked about it, but there was an undercurrent of bitterness. "Maybe next year they can get the librarian at Northwestern to speak at graduation," he remarked sarcastically during one of our conversations.

He assumed that Haverford was shunning him because Palantir was anathema to many students and faculty. (Karp did visit Haverford during the summer of 2022; he was seeing his mother, who lived just up the road, and dropped by to look around. He ran into his old professor Mark Gould while there, but otherwise seemed to go unnoticed.)

Haverford's reluctance to embrace Karp fed into his growing disenchantment with the left—over what he saw as its censoriousness, its refusal to take seriously issues like immigration and border security, and its fixation with identity politics. At the same time, his relationship with his own identity seemed to grow more complicated in the wake of the DPO. Media outlets now routinely listed him among the world's black billionaires, but he had no interest in putting himself forward as someone representative of the black experience in America. He told me that he was proud of his mother's heritage and would be "happily claimed by the black community" if it wanted to claim him. However, he didn't believe that blacks saw him as one of their own. Partly, it was a function of appearance: he looked "mostly Jewish with a tan," as he put it, and also had a Jewish surname, so his authenticity would inevitably be called into question. He also thought that people would suspect that he was embracing his black identity "to get some benefits I didn't deserve. I do think descendants of slaves from the underclass of our country deserve special benefits, but do I?" He added, "If I went out there and said, 'Yeah, I'm a black man,' it would be uncomfortable for the black man, justifiably. It would be like proxy saying that I'm going through the same thing the black community's going through, but I'm not."

His unwillingness to identify himself more fully and enthusiastically as black puzzled his brother. In early 2023, Karp was in Davos for the World Economic Forum, where he was interviewed by David Rubenstein, the billionaire founder of the Carlyle Group. Rubenstein made a joking comment about Karp's hair. "So do you comb that or it just goes that way?" he asked. "It just goes that way," Karp replied. "I have this hair naturally." Rubenstein, not quite ready to move on, asked if Karp's mother ever called him to tell him to comb his hair. Karp didn't answer the question but replied instead that his parents wished he had become an academic. Ben Karp watched the interview and thought his brother should have responded by saying that his hair was that way because *his mother was black*. Karp did, however, mention his German Jewish heritage, and Rubenstein, engaging in some billionaire-on-billionaire fluffing, noted that "a very, very smart German, Albert Einstein, had a hairdo not unlike yours."

Ben had also hoped to persuade his brother to be a guest on Harvard professor Henry Louis Gates's PBS show *Finding Your Roots*. Given Karp's prominence, there seemed little doubt that he could have snagged a guest slot, and with their family's rich history on both sides, Ben thought that Alex would be a particularly intriguing subject. The history on their mother's side was especially compelling, and profoundly American. Karp was, in fact, the descendent of a slave: his great-great-grandfather William Alonzo Janes, a native of Tennessee, was a slave who resettled in central Illinois after being freed. He was also a highly accomplished fiddler and banjo player whose songs were later popularized by Mel Dunham, an acclaimed bluegrass musician who befriended Janes. But Alex had no desire to be on Gates's show, and even though he was closer to his mother than his father, the curiosity he had about his German Jewish roots did not extend to his African American heritage. "For him, it sort of ends with our mother," Ben said.

Ben kept in touch with some of his brother's black friends from Haverford, but Alex showed no inclination to reconnect with them. The issue wasn't a source of tension between the two; Ben just didn't understand why Alex was downplaying half his lineage. This rejection stood in contrast not just to Ben, but to their cousin Mat Johnson—also the son of a black mother and white father—who had won acclaim for his incisive explorations of race and identity in novels such as *Loving Day* (a title drawn from the 1967 U.S. Supreme Court decision striking down prohibitions against interracial marriage) and *Drop*. Over the years, Alex and Ben had had candid exchanges about race. Alex thought that Ben had a stronger claim to being black in part because he was more knowledgeable about African American history and black culture. But at one point, he suggested that identity was as much a choice as it was a matter of bloodlines. "You've overdialed the blackness," he told Ben. "I've dialed it back."

NINE

THE BATSHIT-CRAZY CEO

It was a chilly March morning in Washington, D.C., in 2022, war had broken out on the other side of the world, and Karp couldn't suppress his triumphant mood. While Russia's attack on Ukraine horrified him, it was also, in his mind, a moment of vindication. For one, it affirmed the wisdom of the decision that he had made years ago to not do business in Russia or with any Russian companies—to treat Russia as an enemy of the West. But he was also feeling ebullient because Palantir's technology was being used to help the Ukrainians stymie the Russian offensive. "Bad times are good for Palantir," he had said during an earnings call a few weeks earlier. As if on cue, bad times had arrived, and Karp had a bounce in his step that morning.

Dressed in his standard attire—ski pants, a ski jacket bearing the insignia of Team Veidekke Vest, the Norwegian professional cross-country team whose clothing he liked to wear—Karp had arrived at the office just after daybreak. The office was coming back to life after two years of remote work, and Karp was eager to catch up with his colleagues. However, the first item on his agenda was finalizing a salvo that he was aiming at, well, anyone who had doubted Palantir. Karp planned to release a letter saying that Ukraine was proof that history had not ended in 1989, that it was time to wake up from the delusion that sweet reason and soft power would inevitably prevail, and that he and Palantir had been right about basically everything.

As he walked into his office, Karp summoned his usual ghostwriter, Nick Zamiska, from down the hall. Zamiska, a lawyer who headed up corporate affairs for Palantir, grabbed his laptop and hustled across the room, accompanied by a lanky Swiss-British employee. Karp had met him a few months earlier in the Zurich office, and struck by his ability to craft elegant sentences, had drafted him into some writing duties. But he couldn't remember the young man's name; instead, he referred to him as "our Swiss friend" and "our Yeats." As Zamiska read aloud the latest version of the letter, Karp slumped slightly in his chair, listening intently. Early-morning sunshine filled the room, and the Washington Monument was visible through one of the windows.

The letter was a curious document—it was the sort of thing that a veteran diplomat might publish under a pseudonym in some starchy foreign policy journal, but it also had a slight Unabomber vibe. It was full of sweeping declarations ("the war in eastern Europe stems from a collective suspension of disbelief by those whose overconfidence in recent decades in the raw power of their ideals enabled the balance of power in Europe to shift") and self-congratulatory asides ("Our business has grown over the years precisely because we refused to build what the market thought it wanted and make real the misguided fantasy of an omniscient state"). It included a nod to Karp's academic background, citing—in German—Max Weber's dictum about the state's monopoly on the use of force (*das Monopol legitimer physischer Gewaltsamkeit*). The most noteworthy part of the letter was the third-to-last sentence, which read, "Our software is in the fight in Ukraine."

After Zamiska finished reading, Lisa Gordon, Palantir's head of communications, suggested that the letter was too long. Karp disagreed—he said its length and somber tone were virtues and indicated that he saw it as another way in which Palantir would be distinguishing itself. "We're going for a new frame," he explained. "The last frame is Elon [Musk] and Trump. It's short. It's tweets. We're doing something unique. It's long, dense, unique and can't be copied—that's valuable in business." He instructed Zamiska to get the letter posted on Palantir's website that morning, and also to email it to journalists in the United States and Europe.

A short while later, Karp needed to retrieve something from his hotel room, which was near the office. (He hadn't yet purchased a home in Washington.) As he and I walked along the C&O Canal, his bodyguards following us, I was hoping to ask him about Ukraine and the exact role that Palantir was playing there. But Karp had a more pressing matter that he wanted to discuss: Haverford. He told me that someone from donor relations had finally written to him, but the outreach was "so lame" it would have been better had they not even tried. At this point, he had pretty much given up on our alma mater. "I don't even want to speak at graduation there," he said. "But what kind of idiotic institution does not invite me to speak?" Trying to humor him, I said that it seemed a little crazy. He cut me off. "It's not crazy—it's suicidal."

Back at the office, I saw that Karp's letter had been published on Palantir's website but that the reference to Ukraine had been changed. Instead of "Our software is in the fight in Ukraine," it now read, "Our software is in the fight around the world." The revision was done out of caution: at that point, it didn't serve the interests of either Ukraine or the United States to tell the world what assets were being utilized against the Russians. But Karp's desire to trumpet Palantir's role was understandable. It was the first time in a while that Palantir's work in the realm of national security and defense was not bound up in controversy or ambiguity. The failed war efforts in Iraq and Afghanistan, coupled with human rights violations and concerns about privacy and civil liberties, had tainted the fight against terrorism. The Trump years had been fruitful but challenging for Palantir. With Ukraine, however, there were no complicating factors (so far)—it was good versus evil, and Palantir was unequivocally on the side of good.

Karp was also eager to talk about Palantir and Ukraine because it was a way of deflecting attention from the company's sagging stock price and Wall Street's deepening skepticism. After trading as high as $45 per share in early 2021, Palantir's stock had steadily declined, and by the time Russia invaded Ukraine, it was barely above $10. True, it had been swept up in a general sell-off of tech stocks, but it was also the case that the market just didn't see Palantir as a winning investment. A headline in the *Financial Times* took Karp's words and used them against the company: "Palantir: Built for Bad Times (But Maybe Not These Bad Times)." The disconnect between the importance of the work that Palantir was doing and the value that the market placed on that work was large—and, for Palantirians, not a little maddening.

For Karp, the war in Ukraine was an opportunity, as well, to rally his own troops. The company was still full of industrious, ambitious people, but two years of Covid lockdowns, as well as the controversies that had dogged Palantir, had sapped morale—that was how Karp felt, anyway. The challenge on this front was evident in a town hall meeting he held that afternoon in Washington. With the pandemic still causing widespread illness, the meeting took place under a tent in the courtyard of Palantir's office. As his colleagues ate lunch, Karp, using a handheld microphone, riffed on a variety of topics, including himself. "Everyone thinks

I'm insane," he said. This perception, he went on to explain, had contributed to Palantir's success. "The thing about being viewed as bonkers is that people don't want to compete with you." He continued in this vein for around forty minutes. His quips drew polite laughter, but he seemed to struggle to connect with his audience. True, it was early March and a little chilly for an al fresco lunch (there were heaters in the tent, but they weren't offering much warmth), which might have muted the response. Still, it felt as if there was distance now between Karp and the rank and file, a point he acknowledged in his talk. "We've been separated for two years," he said. "It's very hard to build a culture, to keep a culture, when you don't interact with people in person." He added, "We just have to try to get back together in the office." Much had changed during Covid: the company had gone public, work habits had been altered, and Karp had officially become a billionaire. He was also now a lot older than most of his employees. Could he still relate to them? Could they still relate to him?

Three years before Russia invaded Ukraine, Palantir started working on Project Maven, the Pentagon's artificial intelligence program, taking over for Google. According to Doug Philippone, Defense Department officials approached other tech companies first and reached out to Palantir only as a last resort because they were put off by the turmoil surrounding the firm at that time. For his part, Philippone was wary of getting involved with Maven. While the future of warfare undoubtedly revolved around AI, Maven had become a costly flop—the AI technology just wasn't good. Philippone says that the algorithms that were supposed to be able to identity, say, objects being surveilled by a drone were not up to the task: a sheep standing in a field would be mistakenly flagged as a man—that sort of thing. "The dirty secret of Maven was that this shit didn't even work," says Philippone.

Palantir didn't solve the AI problem—that task fell to other companies that were contributing to Maven. Instead, Palantir filled other gaps. Initially, it provided the project with a sophisticated mapping tool called Gaia. Not long thereafter, it occurred to Philippone and some of the engineers he worked with that Foundry could possibly deliver the data integration and analytic capabilities that Maven still lacked. That proved to be the case, and Foundry soon became Maven's operating system. Philippone says that Palantir "built the infrastructure that would allow the AI to be useful" and gave the officers who were running Maven "breathing room" until the AI technology was workable.

By the time Russia invaded Ukraine, Maven had become a formidable asset, dramatically improving the military's situational awareness in combat zones and accelerating the so-called kill chain, the time between the identification of a target and its destruction or liquidation. The Biden administration sought to aid Ukraine without putting the United States in direct conflict with Russia, and Maven was integral to this strategy. Operating out of a secret site in Germany known as "The Pit," the Army's 18th Airborne Corps, under the direction of Lieutenant General Christopher Donahue (who would later oversee the evacuation of Kabul Airport), used Maven to track Russian troop movements. The system ingested and analyzed vast quantities of satellite and drone imagery to show where Russian forces were attacking or massing in preparation for an assault; where Russian munition depots were located; and other vital intelligence. The U.S. shared this information with the Ukrainians, which helped them mount unexpectedly effective resistance during the first months of the war.

But via Foundry, Maven was able to deliver much more than just an exquisitely detailed view of the battlefield. Palantir's technology also enabled Donahue's team to pull in cellular data. As it happened, many Russian soldiers—including, it turned out, commanding officers—were using their personal cell phones to communicate because their military-issued phones didn't work. This allowed the Americans to identify their precise locations, information then shared with the Ukrainians. "It was the war on terror all over again," Philippone says. "I mean, the one thing we know how to do, we know how to pinpoint you anywhere in the world and kill you. The terrorists who learned to live without their phones survived. Those who couldn't, didn't." A number of Russian generals were dispatched to the front to try to salvage the sputtering war effort, and Ukrainian forces killed several of them in the first months of the conflict. They were located with the help of Maven, too, but the American military was cagier about how it passed along that information. The Ukrainians were given coordinates and told, in so many words, that they would be pleased with the result.

Karp was not quite as circumspect. "Palantir is responsible for most of the targeting in Ukraine," he said at a conference that the company hosted in Palo Alto. Karp had grown tired of having to always be so discreet about what he considered Palantir's most important work. In the past, he had talked only in vague terms about the terrorist attacks that Palantir had supposedly helped foil. His inability to offer specifics meant that the company never got the credit that he believed it deserved. It was, he said, a "twenty-year frustration." But after deleting that passage in his letter referencing Palantir's involvement in Ukraine, he had now decided that it was time for Palantir to get the recognition that it deserved: the world would know that it was helping Ukraine. (The Pentagon was not thrilled about his outspokenness and eventually asked him to dial it back, which he did.)

In May, I joined Karp at the World Economic Forum in Davos. The WEF was normally held in January, but the organizers had decided to delay the 2022 edition until spring in the hope that Covid would be subsiding by then. It was a hectic few days for Karp—he had a couple of speaking engagements, a number of private meetings with current and prospective clients, and also put in an appearance on CNBC's *Squawk Box*. During previous visits to Davos, he decompressed by escaping to nearby cross-country skiing trails. But the only snow in May was on the mountaintops.

Ukraine dominated the discussion at Davos. Although he was now in his early nineties, Davos stalwart George Soros was back in the Swiss Alps to give his annual state-of-the-world address, and his message was basically: hide under your bed. Russian government officials and businessmen had been barred from attending the WEF, and Russia House, the building on the main thoroughfare that had served as the Kremlin's de facto consulate in Davos, a place where members of the Russian contingent threw back vodka and cut deals, had been rented out by a Ukrainian tycoon named Victor Pinchuk and renamed Russian War Crimes House. It now contained a gruesome photo exhibit documenting atrocities that had allegedly been committed by Russian troops during their initial assault.

In Davos, Karp met with several Ukrainian officials. He told me later that he was considering traveling to Ukraine. He said it offhandedly, and while he was clearly serious, I figured he meant that he might go when things had settled down. But it turned out that he was intent on going sooner than that: a few days after the WEF ended, Karp was in Kyiv, meeting with Ukrainian President Volodymyr Zelensky. The trip to Ukraine was an odyssey. To get there, Karp flew to Poland and was then was driven in a three-car convoy to Kyiv. It took around ten hours to reach the Ukrainian capital. Although Karp had left his electronic devices behind and was accompanied by a group of Ukrainian soldiers and his own security detail, he assumed that the Russians were aware of his presence and admitted that the drive to Kyiv was nerve-racking. "I was pretty worried," he said.

Louis Mosley, the head of Palantir's London office, organized the trip and accompanied Karp. He said the Ukrainians that Karp met with in Davos had issued the invitation. While they seemed trustworthy, Mosley was worried about whether they could deliver on a promised visit with Zelensky. His concern grew when they arrived in Kyiv and were told that the president was unable to see Karp that day. Karp had not planned to spend the night; he wanted to return to Poland as soon as the meeting was over. But he agreed to stick around until the following day. He and Mosley stayed in a hotel in central Kyiv. With the city under curfew, they couldn't go anywhere. Karp passed some of the time doing tai chi and didn't seem all that troubled about the delay. Mosley, however, was stressed: he had put Karp at some physical risk, and if a visit with Zelensky didn't happen, it was going to look bad. But the next morning, his Ukrainian interlocutors told him that the meeting was on, and a group of security officials arrived at the hotel and brought Karp and Mosley to the fortified presidential compound.

Karp and Zelensky spent about an hour together. While Karp could be an excellent conversationalist, he didn't normally bond with people—even in his most engaging moments, you never had the sense that he wanted to form a connection. But he immediately felt a sense of kinship with Zelensky, rooted in their shared Jewishness. He saw in the Ukrainian leader a recognizable figure—the "gruff but genial Jewish businessman you'd meet in synagogue," as he described him. Karp was also drawn to Zelensky because he viewed him as the embodiment of the Tough Jew—someone with no illusions about how the world worked and who did not shrink from a fight (which was how Karp saw himself). Karp was struck, too, by Zelensky's intelligence: he later said the Ukrainian leader had the kind of agile mind that would have made him a successful entrepreneur.

At one point during the drive back to Poland, Karp's security team thought that their convoy was being tailed, which made for some harrowing moments. But it was a false alarm, and six hours after leaving Kyiv (they made better time on the return trip), Karp was safely in Poland. By then, news of his trip—and photos of his meeting with Zelensky—had broken, generating headlines worldwide. The visit to Kyiv was Karp's way of highlighting Palantir's support for Ukraine and also its commitment to defending liberal democracy. The West was on the side of Ukraine, and Palantir was on the side of the West. The unstated reason for the trip was because Karp wanted it known that Palantir was indeed *in the fight* in Ukraine. (Later that year, Karp would find a novel way to demonstrate that Palantir stood with Ukraine: the company began sponsoring the Ukrainian tennis star Elina Svitolina.)

A few weeks after Karp saw Zelensky, Palantir began supplying its software to the Ukrainians free of charge. (As the war dragged on, it became harder for Palantir to continue providing the technology at no cost; ultimately, four European governments paid the company $55 million per year on Ukraine's behalf.) The Ukrainians used the software for a range of activities. They deployed it on the battlefield, to do their own targeting, independent of the U.S. military. They also used it to try to clear the country of land mines, to collect evidence of Russian human rights violations, to help resettle civilians displaced by the war, and to try to keep the country's schools open and students safe amid the ongoing conflict. "It's like a superpower," is how one Ukrainian official described Palantir's software to *Time*.

Louis Mosley started traveling to Ukraine on a monthly basis. Other Palantirians were also sent in to help train the Ukrainians on the company's software. In addition, Palantir hired a number of locals. There was a lot of technical talent in Ukraine, and it was not hard to find software engineers eager to contribute to the war effort without being put in harm's way, although some of them ended up there anyway: on several occasions, Palantir employees were present at Ukrainian military facilities when those sites were struck by Russian missiles (none were injured). Palantir was also directly targeted by the Russians: it was the object of a spear phishing attack that the company traced back to Russia. A handful of accounts were compromised.

Karp's visit to Kyiv thrust him into a new and somewhat unique role: the statesman CEO. When he traveled to the Baltics, heads of state met with him and he was given police escorts. Amid fears that Russian President Vladimir Putin had designs on their countries, the Baltic republics were eager to obtain Palantir's software, thus the VIP treatment. And Karp recognized that he was now seen in a different light—as a person of gravitas. For years, he had played up his image as an oddball. He took pleasure in the idea that people considered him "batshit crazy," a phrase that he regularly invoked to describe how he thought he was regarded. To Karp, it was a backhanded compliment, an acknowledgment that he was a mad genius.

But after the trip to Kyiv, he decided to ease up on the "batshit-crazy" schtick. Perceptions of him had changed, he realized, and the faux-self-deprecatory stuff was now off-key. Putin's invasion of Ukraine had destabilized the world, and the moment demanded a different kind of public engagement on his part. His reputation was also enhanced because he projected seriousness at a time when other figures in the tech world were seen as increasingly absurd. While Karp was talking about war and peace, Mark Zuckerberg was trying to transport humanity to the metaverse, and Elon Musk was embroiled in a soap opera over his proposed acquisition of Twitter. The contrast with Musk and Zuckerberg flattered Karp.

But the one place where Karp could not bring himself to show a different face was during quarterly earnings calls. He made no effort to hide his disdain for Wall Street analysts, and with Palantir still not turning a profit and investors growing more dubious, the stock price continued to plummet even as the company was playing a central role in the biggest land war in Europe in nearly a century.

In early May 2022, Palantir released its first quarter earnings. Karp was in London for the earnings call. It did not go well. Dressed in off-white jeans and a skin-hugging white undershirt, he seemed distracted, even a little rattled. In the not-so-distant past, Karp's casual garb and stream-of-consciousness riffing, which often included an expletive or two, was entertaining. Now, not so much. Investors wanted a reason to believe in Palantir's prospects. What they got instead was an orgy of free association and strange digressions. "We at Palantir are not flying to a different world," Karp said, "whether the metaworld [a dig at Facebook] or a theological world or a financial version of a theological world or a grad school version of a theological world, which isn't even actually academic because academic presupposes interacting with the object from a theoretical perspective, differentiate from the object, not importing a theological preconceived version of the object onto the theory and reimporting that onto the object." Within minutes, Palantir's stock had dropped another $2 and was trading below $10, the price at which it had debuted in 2020.

The pace of Palantir's deal flow—the amount of time it took to develop and close deals—concerned investors. They worried, too, about scalability, and whether Foundry, the software platform that was now central to Palantir's long-term prospects, could really become a dominant product in the corporate sector. This anxiety was tied to the perennial question of whether Palantir was a software company or a consultancy—if clients still required lots of hand-holding from Palantir's forward-deployed engineers, it was going to be difficult for Foundry to achieve the kind of market penetration that Karp insisted it would. But it also seemed that professional investors were souring on Karp, and while he was expounding on the fate of the West, he was doing nothing to assuage the concerns they had about his leadership.

A few months after the London earnings call, a viewer asked CNBC's Jim Cramer for his thoughts about Palantir. Cramer recommended selling the stock if it got back above $10 and said, "They are just not a company that I think can be relied upon. When they appear on TV, they make me feel like it's just a big joke and I'm not in on it." Following Palantir's third-quarter earnings call, in November 2022, another viewer asked Cramer about Palantir. Cramer cut him off before he finished his question. "Sell!" Cramer bellowed. He then chastised Karp for using obscenities during earnings calls. "By the way, you don't curse, especially when you're doing lousy. Hey, maybe you can curse when you're doing well. But when you're doing lousy, SHUT UP!"

Cramer was speaking, loudly, for a lot of Wall Street. Even among investors and analysts who thought well of Palantir, Karp's routine was becoming tiresome. One analyst with a major investment bank, who insisted on anonymity when we spoke, said that he was a Palantir true believer: he was convinced that the software was transformative and that Palantir was, on balance, a force for good. "I tell people this is Tesla all over again," he told me. "What they are doing is so different and unique. No one has ever seen this." But he was increasingly put off by what he regarded as the arrogance and juvenile attitude of Karp and those around him. "You look at this company—they have this mission to protect the world, to do these things that no one else does, and yet they act like they are in college," the analyst said. This disconnect was killing Palantir with investors. He had pitched Palantir to his hedge fund clients as an attractive long-term play, but they wanted no part of it. "They tell me, 'This management team is absolutely crazy, I can't be near this,'" he said. He couldn't understand why Karp had no interest in changing this perception and said it called into question whether it made sense for Palantir to be a publicly traded company. "It is like they spray repellent all over their bodies," he said. Maybe the company's executives had made so much money from the stock market listing that they didn't care. Whatever the case, the analyst was exasperated. He compared Karp to the super-antihero Deadpool and suggested that a change at the top would benefit Palantir—that investors might be more willing to get behind the company if it had a "professional CEO," as he put it.

But Karp had no interest in placating institutional investors: in his opinion, they didn't understand Palantir, and he was not going to waste any more time trying to help them make sense of the company. He said he cared only about retail investors—"my fans," as he called them—and Palantir's clients. He acknowledged that some clients were not charmed by his persona, either, but had remained customers because Palantir's software was too good to give up. During one earnings call in 2022, Karp said that the company had clients who "quite frankly, didn't like us" but who had signed new contracts anyway. "The product brought them back," he said.

It did appear that Palantir was difficult to replace. In 2021, ICE had announced that it was not renewing its contract with Palantir because it was developing its own, similar technology. For Palantir, it was a bitter coda to the immigration imbroglio. But a year later, ICE reversed course and signed a new deal with the company. And despite the controversy over Palantir's work with ICE, the Biden administration had continued to use the company's software to track Covid-19 and to expedite the distribution of vaccines. One online commentator observed that when Karp touted Palantir's indispensability, he sounded a lot like Colonel Nathan Jessep, Jack Nicholson's character in *A Few Good Men*. ("My existence, while grotesque and incomprehensible to you, saves lives. . . . You want me on that wall, you need me on that wall.")

In addition to frustration with Karp's attitude, Wall Street had legitimate concerns about how Palantir was being managed. In 2021, the company purchased around $51 million worth of one-hundred-ounce gold bars. Shyam Sankar told *Bloomberg* that this was to hedge against "black swan events." At the time, some companies were dabbling in bitcoin—in 2021, Tesla bought $1.5 billion worth of the cryptocurrency and also made it possible for customers to pay in bitcoin. While gold was a more traditional store of value than bitcoin, Palantir's bullion investment struck many observers as bizarre, even suspect. "Give me your best conspiracy theory," one CNBC host asked some panelists. "It feels kind of CIA-ish," one replied. During an earnings call in November 2022, Karp proudly described Palantir as "a prepper company." It was a comment that played well with his retail investor fanboys, but not with Wall Streeters. The CEO of a major investment management company shuddered when I mentioned Palantir. "It's just so dark," he said.

In late 2022, Palantir found itself in the spotlight over another unorthodox move. Starting the year before, the company had invested $450 million in around two dozen start-ups that had gone public via special purchase acquisition companies, or SPACs, which are essentially shell companies created for the purpose of buying other companies or merging with them. Palantir gave all the companies it invested in free access to its software, on the understanding that they would eventually purchase the technology. The start-ups included a German flying taxi company and a grocery delivery service. It was a growth hack, a way of superficially boosting Palantir's commercial business at a time when it was trying to reduce its dependence on government contracts.

Unfortunately for Palantir, it backfired: by late 2023, one of the companies had gone under, and nearly a dozen others were running short of cash. *Bloomberg* calculated that Palantir had lost some $330 million on the investments. While no one claimed that Palantir had acted illegally, some corporate law experts thought the company had behaved in an ethically dubious way, and several activist investors threatened to bring class-action suits against it. When Lisa Gordon learned that *The Wall Street Journal* was planning to run a feature about the SPAC investments, she and others at Palantir went into crisis mode. Peter Thiel even dispatched his own spokesperson, Jeremiah Hall, to New York to help Gordon and her colleagues fashion a response. Privately, Thiel had grown tired of Palantir's inability to book a profit and had made his frustration known to Karp and other members of the board. The *Journal* story noted in passing that short sellers had pocketed more than $1 billion betting against Palantir's stock over the previous year.

The night before the *Journal* piece ran, Karp and I talked about the SPAC debacle in his New York office. It was just after 5 p.m., and he was eating dinner. He was more annoyed than distressed about the situation. He said that he had farmed out too much authority in this instance and hadn't done enough due diligence himself to see the potential pitfalls to these investments. He said that "the negative side of my unusual cognitive structure" was a tendency to assume that problems obvious to him would be equally apparent to others. He readily took the blame for the SPAC mess. "It's an indictment of me," he said.

Karp was still struggling to reanimate Palantir's culture in the aftermath of the pandemic, a task made harder by the DPO. Karp had feared that taking Palantir public might undermine its cohesiveness, and when the company filed the S-1, some employees were irritated to learn just how much senior management had been paid. While no one expected rank-and-file engineers to be making as much as Karp and other executives, the gap between their compensation and everyone else's was jarring, and all the more so because it was at odds with the egalitarian vibe that Karp had cultivated. One longtime Palantirian, who by any measure had made out well from the DPO, spoke bitterly of the leadership's haul. While he knew their paydays would exceed his, he was surprised by how much more equity they had received and admitted that he felt suckered.

Now, in a company that had prided itself on its nonhierarchical structure, there was a hierarchy, and it revolved around wealth. The money was a source of resentment and also became a cudgel. In the fall of 2022, Palantir's London office was in turmoil after the company said that it was considering slashing the amount that it contributed to the pensions of some UK employees. During a conference call that Shyam Sankar held with the London staff to discuss the proposed change, several participants cited the windfall that he and other executives had reaped from the DPO. The angry response—and a spate of unfavorable press—ultimately prompted Palantir management to drop the idea.

For Karp, the wealth effect was also playing out in more subtle ways. His status as a confirmed billionaire seemed to be coloring his interactions with junior colleagues. When, in the past, he had tried to persuade Palantirians who were thinking of leaving the company to stay, he didn't always succeed, but his efforts were taken in good faith—the employees knew that he really did believe that it would be better for them to remain at Palantir. Now, however, he sensed that some people were more skeptical of his advice. "'Oh, here's Moneybags, telling me what to do with my life,'" Karp said, describing the way he thought they were responding to him now.

Karp admitted that something had changed in the company's culture. He spoke wistfully of the "cult spirit" that he and others had nurtured during Palantir's early years, and he wanted to rekindle it. The company had planned to resume HobbitCon, an annual retreat in which employees from all over the world gathered for a weekend of parties and team-building exercises; the last one had taken place before the pandemic. But Karp scrapped the idea: with the stock price still below $10 and the company under mounting pressure to show a profit, he couldn't justify the expense, and it might have raised more concern about how Palantir was being run.

His frustration over company morale became apparent on a weekend in November 2022, when he was in New York to prepare for the release of Palantir's quarterly earnings that Monday. Karp spent all of Saturday and Sunday in the office, as did other senior executives. But it was hard not to notice that they and their staffs were the only ones around; otherwise, the office was empty. On Sunday, Karp dipped into a conference room to join a pre-earnings call with a journalist. It had just been reported that Meta, the parent company of Facebook, was laying off eleven thousand employees, or around 13 percent of its workforce, which gave Karp an opportunity to take a shot at Mark Zuckerberg. "It's cold in the metaverse," he exclaimed in a singsong voice as he walked down the hall. A bit later, Karp told several colleagues that Zuckerberg had "picked a fight with us; he had a special operation going to make Palantir more hated so that people would focus on us and not him. He denied it to Peter [Thiel], but I have this on very good authority." Karp didn't identify his source, nor did he provide any details about the alleged scheme. He suggested, in a joking/not-joking way, that Zuckerberg had made a big mistake. "Don't pick a fight with us," he said. "It's like prison, we're going to be shanking you every day." (Through a spokesperson, Zuckerberg said that he was "not aware of any such operation and if such a thing did exist at Facebook, he definitely didn't support it.")

Karp spent twenty minutes on the call with the reporter. Afterward, he lingered in the doorway. He had also noticed the dearth of people around the office and was ticked off. He thought the rows of empty desks showed a lack of commitment. "When people complain," he said, "I'm going to tell them that you can complain as much as you want, but how many weekends did you work? Every other weekend? Three weekends of every four? What's so exciting about going out with your friends? You can be here, which is much more entertaining." Karp was puzzled by the apparent lack of careerism—from a purely opportunistic standpoint, why would Palantirians not want to be in the office that weekend? Lisa

Gordon interjected to say that Covid had changed people's ideas about work-life balance and that employees had also gotten out of the habit of turning up when he was in town. Karp wasn't buying it. "You have this company that has succeeded for over twenty years, and every single person who built it is here," he said. "What could be more interesting than that?"

The next day, Palantir reported that it had failed to turn a profit yet again. It would be the last time that the company fell short. Three months later, Palantir announced that in the fourth quarter of 2022, after almost two decades in business, it had finally turned profitable. Nor was that a one-off: Palantir went on to notch profits in all four quarters of 2023, which helped lift its stock price and, more importantly, erased what had become almost a stigma for the company. No one was happier than Karp, but the pleasure that he took in the achievement, and the peace of mind that it conferred, proved fleeting. The world was about to become a vastly more dangerous place in his eyes.

TEN

A SURVIVAL SITUATION

It was several days after Hamas murdered 1,200 Israelis, and Karp planned to issue a statement reaffirming Palantir's support for Israel. He was intent on striking a hawkish tone, and the original draft included a line that read, "Certain kinds of evil can only be fought with violence." But his aides suggested replacing "violence" with "force"—it would convey the same thought but without sounding quite as bloodthirsty. Karp agreed to the edit, and shortly thereafter, the message was posted on X, the social media platform formerly known as Twitter that Elon Musk had purchased for $44 billion the year before. Although it was a public declaration of solidarity with Israel, the audience that Karp was really addressing was an internal one: he was signaling to any Palantirians who disagreed with his position on Israel to keep it to themselves. The X post was "a way of putting up a guardrail," he told me later. He had tolerated the spirited in-house debate over Palantir's work with ICE because employees, unnerved by Trump, needed the chance to vent, and also because he agreed there were legitimate ethical and moral concerns. But in his mind, there was no ambiguity when it came to the terrorist attack in Israel, and he wanted it understood that open disagreement would not be permitted. "If you don't like it," Karp said, "then I would say that Palantir is probably not the right place for you."

As important as the war in Ukraine was to Palantir, the October 7, 2023, pogrom in Israel was far more consequential in Karp's view. It was certainly more personal. He had been haunted from the time he was a kid by the precariousness of Jewish existence. He had always staunchly supported Israel precisely because it seemed to represent a safe harbor for Jews. He didn't approve of every policy or prime minister, but because of his anxiety about his own place in the world, Israel's security and well-being mattered greatly to him. "If you're me, you recognize the danger of fascism and the importance of having a place to go," he said. But now, Israel had been the scene of the deadliest massacre of Jews since the Holocaust. For Karp, it was a shattering event, but also a galvanizing one. A few days after Karp's message on X, Palantir took out a full-page ad in the Sunday *New York Times* that said, "Palantir Stands with Israel."

The company also had a business relationship with the Israeli government. For nearly a decade, the Mossad had been using Palantir's technology. The spy agency had sought out Palantir, a request that surprised Karp. After all, Israel had a robust tech sector, and the Mossad was famously resourceful (and lethal). Karp was so sure the Israelis didn't need Palantir that he suggested they try Gotham before purchasing it. When they came back and said they wanted it, he sold them the software at a discount. Some employees objected to the contract, citing Israel's treatment of the Palestinians. Karp tolerated the pushback because the Israeli-Palestinian conflict was at a low boil then and Israel didn't seem to be in mortal danger. But after October 7, its continued existence was very much in doubt, at least in Karp's mind.

The Mossad is Israel's equivalent of the CIA—it focuses on external threats. Israel's domestic intelligence service, Shin Bet, did not have Palantir at the time of the Hamas attack, nor did the Israel Defense Forces, or IDF, the country's military, and this quickly became a source of recriminations. A few weeks after the massacre, at a memorial service in Jerusalem for the wife of Dan Meridor, an influential political figure (her death was unrelated to October 7), one attendee sharply commented to several senior Israeli officials that the massacre "wouldn't have happened" if Shin Bet and the IDF had been using Palantir. That was debatable, but both services sought to obtain Palantir's software in the wake of October 7. The demand for Palantir's assistance was so great that the company dispatched a team of engineers from London to help get Israeli users online. Palantir ended up having to rent a second floor in the building that housed its Tel Aviv office to accommodate the intelligence analysts who needed tutorials.

Palantir's software was also used by a large group of retired Israeli intelligence analysts who offered their services following the massacre. The ad hoc effort was organized by Joab Rosenberg, who had been the IDF's deputy head of intelligence before leaving the military and launching an AI-focused start-up that was backed in part by Mithril Capital, one of Peter Thiel's investment funds. In 2014, while still with the IDF, Rosenberg had been part of a pilot program using Gotham. He thought that the technology was good but was missing certain higher-level analytical functions that he believed it needed, and in the end the IDF decided to stick with a software system developed internally.

Now Rosenberg and his fellow volunteers were equipped (free of charge) with Foundry, and he was struck by how easy it was to learn and operate and also by its advanced capabilities. "It was a much better machine," he says. He and his colleagues had an urgent task. In recent years, the Israelis had scaled back their open-source intelligence gathering. But the Hamas militants, using their phones as well as GoPros that they had attached to their bodies, had filmed their murderous rampage, and many of the videos were being posted to social media. These were important pieces of evidence as the Israelis tried to identify the 250 or so people kidnapped by Hamas and taken to Gaza. There were also a lot of messages and still pictures posted on sites like X and Telegram, some of which yielded clues.

Rosenberg's team supplemented the data that they scraped from social media with commercially available satellite imagery. The volunteers were a source of critical intelligence early in the crisis. They reconstructed the attack on Kibbutz Nir Oz, where around one hundred residents were killed or kidnapped. Rosenberg was the group's liaison to the IDF, and the results that he and his team produced convinced active-duty intelligence analysts that they needed Palantir, too. "They really wanted it for themselves," he says. In this, there were echoes of Palantir's experience with the U.S. military, when it was American troops on the ground in Iraq and Afghanistan who led the push to get the company's technology. But in the case of the IDF, the top brass was more than happy to oblige in the aftermath of October 7. Josh Harris spearheaded Palantir's work in Israel, and as he listened to Israeli military officials marveling at the speed with which the company's technology merged and analyzed data, he couldn't believe that the software was such a revelation for them. He recalled thinking, "Are you guys being paid to say this?"

While Palantir scrambled to help Israel, Karp was perturbed that he seemed to be the only American business leader speaking out forcefully. A week after the *Times* ad ran, he and I talked by video. He was at his place in New Hampshire; he was seated at his desk, wearing a knit cap and drinking tea. There were two Rubik's Cubes on the desk. For the first time that I could recall, he appeared deflated, and he admitted that he was "a little depressed." Like many people, he was appalled by the brutality of the Hamas attack, and while he said that he was never under any illusions about how Jews were perceived, the outpouring of antisemitism following the massacre had surprised him. "It's worse than I thought, and I thought it was worse than anyone I know," he said. He expressed disappointment over what he saw as the failure of other tech executives to defend Israel. He didn't name names, but clearly referring to Musk, a prolific poster on X, he said he found it "weird" that "certain people in tech who comment online about everything that moves" had nothing to say about what had happened in Israel. Karp was certain that most tech moguls supported Israel, but their reticence annoyed him. "Why am I the only one defending the Jews?" he asked.

He was irked, too, by the silence of other Jewish business executives. He said that we had all grown up hearing the phrase "never again," but now, in the face of a slaughter that had, on a per capita basis, claimed the equivalent of fifty thousand American lives, he was the only Jewish head of a publicly traded company who was standing up for Israel and denouncing antisemitism. Apart from him, it was "like crickets out there." He put the silence down to cowardice. "My personal view is that they don't want to be yelled at and unpopular," Karp said. He speculated that some of them also didn't want to risk falling out "with their progressive friends. And their progressive friends do not like Israel. And a higher proportion than anyone wants to admit don't actually like Jews."

The reticence of Jewish business leaders was a recurring theme for him in the weeks following the Hamas attack. In private, he acknowledged the contempt that many American Jews felt for Israeli Prime Minister Benjamin Netanyahu and his far-right government and said that he had no inclination to defend Netanyahu. "If Netanyahu got pushed out of a helicopter, I wouldn't ask any questions," he commented to a friend. "If I had the chance to push Netanyahu out of a helicopter, I might." But however repugnant the Israeli leader was, that didn't account for the spasm of antisemitism, nor was it an excuse to keep quiet. Karp was planning to go to Israel as soon as possible. He wanted to demonstrate his support for the embattled nation, but he admitted that he also wanted to embarrass others in the American Jewish community who were in positions of power and authority but were being cravenly silent.

With the outbreak of war in Gaza, Karp put off traveling to Israel. In early November, he attended a summit on AI security hosted by the British government. He did Palantir's third-quarter earnings call while in London. He used his opening remarks to claim, again, total vindication for the dystopian outlook that had always guided Palantir's work and to reiterate the company's pro-Israel stance. "Obviously, current events and the performance of our business are absolute validation of our strategy of building the world's most aligned and powerful enterprise products," he told analysts and investors before launching into a peroration about October 7. "We have been building products for a world that is violent, disjointed, and irrational, a world in which you have to show strength, a world in which if you do not show strength, people who are biased, xenophobic, dare I say it antisemitic, will rear their head [*sic*], a world in which you really have to pick sides," Karp said.

He went on to say that it was no longer tenable, or defensible, to sell products to friends and enemies alike. "Palantir is the first major company, in my view, to have said from the beginning a thing that is obviously true—there is no such thing anymore of being on all sides. Palantir only supplies its products to Western allies. We've never supplied our products to enemies. We proudly support the U.S. government. I am proud that we are supporting Israel in every way we can. And we also support plain English speaking. So when people are massacred to the equivalent of almost fifty thousand people, in Israel, we view it as a terror act. We call it terrorism. We supply our product to people who are fighting terrorism and we have no problem with describing it as it is or sticking up for our allies, and we don't provide false context. All of a sudden, you need a lot of context for describing what it means to kill Jews or persecute Jews across the world. I believe in context, in places where you actually need to provide it. But at Palantir, we have seen that our view of the world, which is that there really are people that are violent and not conformant with morality need to be fought."

In a sense, October 7 brought Palantir back to its roots. The company had been founded for the purpose of combating terrorism, and specifically jihadism. But Islamic terrorism hadn't proven to be as cripplingly pervasive as many had feared in the wake of 9/11, and with the damage that the United States and its allies had inflicted on Al Qaeda and, later, ISIS, it was possible to imagine that the danger had been mostly neutralized. In the meantime, Palantir had expanded into realms far removed from the war on terrorism. The Hamas attack was horrifying proof that the terrorism threat had not been extinguished. For Karp, it also showed that the world was still okay with the slaughtering of Jews and that it remained a perilous place for Alex Karp. Even with his phalanx of bodyguards, he felt personally threatened. "This is a survival situation," he said.

In early December, two months after the atrocities in Israel, Karp attended the annual Reagan National Defense Forum, held at the Ronald Reagan Library, near Los Angeles. He had become a regular at the event, which brought together cabinet secretaries, members of Congress, senior Pentagon officers, and representatives of the defense industry. Karp took part in a panel discussion and used the opportunity to talk about antisemitism. "There were unfortunately way too many people on October 7th who were happy, and we have to acknowledge we have a huge problem in the Western world with antisemitism," Karp said. "Not all criticism of Israel is antisemitism, but a larger portion of it is than we realized. We have to call it out. And I'm one of the largest donors to the Democratic Party, and quite frankly I am calling it out and I'm giving to Republicans and if you keep up this behavior I'm going to change and a lot of people like me are going to change."

That comment went viral; Republicans were trying to appeal to disaffected Jewish Democrats, and here was a major Jewish donor telling the Democratic Party that he was about to stop. In truth, even though Karp continued to call himself a progressive, he had been drifting away from the Democrats for a while. He rarely had anything positive to say about them and his criticisms often echoed right-wing talking points; if Karp wasn't watching Fox himself, it seemed as if he was getting some of his information from people who were. For instance, he blamed President Biden for the inflation spike that started in 2021, even though it was a global phenomenon caused mainly by supply chain disruptions during the pandemic. Sometimes, Karp strained to find reasons to dump on the Democrats. Noting that anti-vaxxers had appropriated the "my body, my choice" slogan used to defend reproductive rights, he suggested that the backlash against Covid vaccine mandates was a case of liberals having their own argument turned against them. It was a surprisingly poor analogy coming from Karp, whose logic was usually unimpeachable even if you disagreed with the point that he was making. Covid was a public health emergency that threatened the lives of millions. Abortion was a private decision that posed no such danger.

His estrangement from the Democrats had nothing to do with his personal wealth, at least not directly. He wasn't resentful of the taxes that he had to pay, nor was he one of those whiny plutocrats who thought that the Democrats were trying to punish him for his success. To the extent that being a billionaire was a factor, it was mostly because he spent much of his time now surrounded by other extremely rich people, and in those circles, expressing contempt for the Democrats was almost a rite of initiation. But Karp's main grievance with the Democrats wasn't economic, it was ideological. He thought they were generally weak on foreign policy and that the party had been captured by the identarian left and "wokeism" (and his animus toward both had increased as a result of the ICE controversy and the furor over Palantir's work in New Orleans). The anti-Israel protests that erupted after October 7 caused Karp to feel even more alienated from progressives. By contrast, he praised the Republican Party for its strong support of the Jewish state. "I'm now very willing to overlook my disagreements with Republicans on other issues because of the position they have taken on this one," he said. Karp had soured on the Democrats in part because of identity politics. Yet it was his own identity politics that was now driving him even further away.

At the same time, though, some powerful voices on the right had embraced nakedly antisemitic views after October 7. In mid-November, Elon Musk had finally weighed in on events in the Middle East, via a discussion on X. Someone posted a comment saying that Jews had been "pushing the exact kind of dialectical hatred against whites that they claim to want people to stop using against them. I'm deeply disinterested in giving the tiniest shit now about western Jewish populations coming to the disturbing realization that those hordes of minorities that [they] support flooding the country don't exactly like them too much." The implication was that Jews were behind the so-called Great Replacement—the alleged plot to make whites a minority in the West, a conspiracy theory that had become an article of faith in far-right circles. Musk responded with a pithy "You have said the actual truth."

His comment sparked outrage. After months of speculation about whether Musk was an antisemite—conjecture prompted by his attacks on George Soros and the Anti-Defamation League, as well as his re-platforming of neo-Nazis on X—many observers concluded that they now had an answer. As Musk sought to defuse the controversy by traveling to Israel to meet with Netanyahu and to visit a kibbutz that had been attacked by Hamas, two leading right-wing commentators, Tucker Carlson and Charlie Kirk, chimed in with sentiments similar to those expressed by the poster on X. Carlson claimed that wealthy Jewish Americans had been bankrolling people who advocated for "white genocide." Kirk, in his daily radio show, seconded Carlson's comments. "The philosophical foundation of anti-whiteness has been largely financed by Jewish donors in the country," Kirk told his audience.

When I brought up these comments to Karp, he didn't deny that they were troubling—or, indeed, antisemitic. But he didn't think that they sprang from genuine hostility to Jews. Carlson's main grievances were immigration from the developing world and a belief that the left was sanctioning discrimination against white people. As Karp saw it, Carlson had a problem with Jews only to the extent that some of them provided money to groups that promoted immigration, and also to universities and other institutions that had become platforms to inveigh against white privilege. And *Karp* had a problem with those Jews, too: the people they had thought of as allies had turned on them viciously after October 7, and at the same time, their actions risked inviting the wrath of those who actually were their friends. "The least antisemitic people in the history of civilization are white Americans," Karp said.

While he wasn't suggesting that Carlson spoke for all white Americans, millions of them clearly shared his views, and to Karp, it was self-evidently not in the interest of Jews to make enemies of these people. Before October 7, he had considered the border crisis bad for the Democrats; now he saw it as bad for the Jews. He said that 80 percent of Americans thought well of Jews (he didn't cite a source for this claim). "They might not want to hang out with Jews, but they respect and admire them," he said. In his opinion, the health of a society was commensurate with its tolerance of "Jewish overachievement," as he put it, and Karp believed that most white, Christian Americans were disposed favorably to Jews. By almost any measure, Jews had themselves become an in-group. But Karp surmised that the people trying to enter the United States now were probably more hostile toward Jews, or at least not as friendly, which in his mind was all the more reason to secure the border and keep them out.

Karp had been convinced for some time that Donald Trump would win the 2024 election. He thought that immigration had become an almost insurmountable liability for Biden. Karp saw Vice President Kamala Harris as a further drag on the Democrats: she was not popular, and because there was a good chance that the eighty-year-old Biden would be unable to serve out a second term, the election was likely to be as much a referendum on Harris as it was on him. Karp also believed that the effort to prosecute Trump for crimes that he had allegedly committed was a mistake and had backfired, only strengthening his hold over the GOP. He assumed that the October 7 massacre would likewise redound to Trump's benefit: it had put terrorism back on the front page, and when voters felt scared, they usually turned to the right.

Despite his frustration with the Democrats, Karp was still giving money to Biden's campaign, in part because of the support that his administration had shown for Israel. He said he couldn't vote for Trump because of the turmoil that he would inevitably unleash—it would be four more lost years for the country. In his judgment, the biggest problem with Trump wasn't his malevolence but, rather, his shambolic personality. To me, at least, Karp had always insisted that Trump wasn't as dangerous as he was made out to be and that people were too easily triggered by "the orange man," as he called him. He also went to lengths to credit Trump for what he believed the former president got right, such as his claim that the pandemic had been caused by a lab leak in China, a view that Karp shared. Privately, though, Karp didn't always project the same equanimity toward Trump. Over the years, he had encouraged several colleagues to seek second passports, as a form of insurance.

But following the massacre in Israel, Karp was even more intent on downplaying the threat posed by Trump. When I saw him in Washington a week after the Hamas attack, Trump's name came up. "I don't think Trump is a fascist," Karp said, explaining that he was too obsessed with money to be one. In an increasingly defiant tone, he added, "I don't think Trump is an antisemite. In fact, I don't think he's a racist." Karp usually spoke with total conviction—it was part of what made him such an effective salesman—and maybe he really did believe that Trump wasn't any of those things. However, his unprovoked combativeness suggested that it wasn't me he was trying to persuade but, rather, himself—that he *needed* to believe that Trump, despite abundant evidence to the contrary, wasn't a bigoted authoritarian. Perhaps it was his way of bracing for Trump's possible return to power and of preemptively justifying whatever that might require of Palantir.

On December 5, 2023, the presidents of Harvard, MIT, and the University of Pennsylvania appeared before a congressional committee to discuss antisemitism in academia. When asked if statements calling for Jews to be killed violated the codes of conduct at their universities, all three gave legalistic, carefully hedged answers. Their evasiveness sparked outrage, and Penn's president, Liz Magill, was soon out of a job. A few days later, Karp announced via X that Palantir was creating 180 positions for students who "because of antisemitism fear for their safety on campus and need to seek refuge outside traditional establishments of higher education." The statement added, "our software embodies our values and commitments. These include high performance, efficiency, transparency, fairness, and a rejection of narrow thinking, including fear and skepticism of the other and outright bigotry." It went on to condemn "the egregious levels of antisemitism in our society, especially at our most elite educational institutions. Some of these organizations seem structurally incapable of taking any steps to reform themselves."

I was with Karp that morning. He had told me a few minutes ahead of time that he was about to make some headlines ("keep an eye on X"), and when the statement went live, he was ecstatic. He clearly found pleasure in piling on the Harvards and Penns and putting Palantir at the center of this particular news cycle (later that day, Fox Business would have him on to talk about the unusual jobs program, as well as other topics). He acknowledged that the recruitment effort, which would soon be christened Operation Safe Haven, was possibly illegal—presumably, one had to be Jewish to apply, but it was against the law, of course, for companies to discriminate on the basis of race, religion, or ethnicity. As far as Karp was concerned, Palantir's legal team could sort that out. "My lawyers are having heart attacks," he said with a satisfied grin.

Karp believed that DEI was at the root of the problems on campuses. DEI—diversity, equity, and inclusion—was a framework, adopted by universities, corporations, and other organizations, to redress the insufficient representation of minorities in their ranks. At the heart of DEI, Karp said, was a belief that America's claim to being a meritocratic society was a lie—that for all the social progress that we had made as a country, systemic discrimination against women, blacks, gays, and other out-groups was a persistent factor in American life and could be remedied only by imposing DEI standards on institutions. But Karp said that Jews stood as inconvenient evidence to the contrary—they had "started below anyone else" and were now "arguably the most successful group in America," a distinction they had achieved without assistance and often in the face of great hostility. "Jews unravel the whole ideology of DEI," he said, and this, in his judgment, accounted for the hatred now being directed at them on campuses. Karp claimed that DEI was "the precursor to antisemitism" and needed to be dismantled.

He went on to say that the self-made success of American Jews was the reason for the rift between Jews and blacks; blacks, in his view, resented and envied Jews. This wasn't just true of blacks, he added—there were competing narratives between Jews and people of color more generally, which was why hostility to Jews was so much more intense than that directed at "normal white males," as he put it. I told him that this was an odd thing to hear from someone who was biracial. Karp admitted that his views were complicated and perhaps controversial. But he insisted that he was as aligned with blacks as he was with the Jews; the difference, he said, was that "the Jews know it." He suggested that fighting antisemitism was beneficial for blacks, too. "The health of a society is most easily measured in inverse proportion to the level of antisemitism," he said. "If you want a strong black community, you fight antisemitism."

The conversation about colleges led to more dunking on Haverford. Karp said that our alma mater was probably doomed now. Jewish students nationwide were going to be suing colleges and universities for discrimination. Harvard, with its $50 billion endowment, could withstand a wave of lawsuits, but a place like Haverford was vulnerable. "This could end Haverford permanently," Karp said. "It could take their endowment down to two hundred million dollars. They would drop out of the top fifty. It would basically become an annex of Bryn Mawr." (Bryn Mawr is an all-women college closely affiliated with Haverford.) He asked if I had seen the latest alumni email from Haverford; it was about upcoming events at the school, with no reference to the situation in the Middle East or the turmoil engulfing academia. "Are they fucking nuts?" he asked, growing agitated. "For universities, this is a moment like Martin Luther King walking through Memphis and being attacked by dogs—you can't send out something like this." (Haverford did end up getting sued by a group of students, parents, and alumni for allegedly creating an environment that was hostile to Jews.)

According to Karp, the college was foolish not to seek his counsel. "If you are Haverford, you need someone like me to explain how the world actually works," he said. But Haverford's president, Wendy Raymond, had never reached out to him personally, and he assumed she wouldn't be doing so now. He figured it was because she feared having him become to Haverford what his fellow billionaire, the hedge fund manager Bill Ackman, had been to Harvard. Following that disastrous congressional hearing, Ackman helped lead the (ultimately successful) effort to oust Harvard's president, Claudine Gay.

In Karp's view, Haverford wasn't just guilty of moral obtuseness; it was also being daft. The college's endowment was $600 million; Karp said that he and Howard Lutnick, a Haverford grad who was the CEO of the financial services firm Cantor Fitzgerald and who would serve as commerce secretary during the second Trump administration, had a combined net worth significantly larger than that. Any rational institution would try not to piss off people who could write hefty checks (Lutnick, though, was already a major donor to Haverford). Karp had long ago concluded that Haverford's administrators were inept, but what he saw as their failure to adequately denounce terrorism and to confront antisemitism on campus had destroyed any chance that he would make a gift to the school. "They will never get a dime out of me," he said.

Nor, it seems, were Haverford students going to be landing jobs at Palantir. During his appearance at the Reagan National Defense Forum, Karp took aim not only at the Democrats, but also at student protesters who were demonstrating against Israel. "I am not a legislator," Karp said, "but I am running one of the coolest companies in the world, and I'm telling young people, you are breathing the vapors of a dangerous new fake and self-destructive religion when you are sitting at your elite school pretending because you watched TikTok twice and got an A-plus on some crazy paper because your professor couldn't get a job anywhere else that you actually understand the world. And you are not welcome at my company." The last line elicited laughter and loud applause.

In early January 2024, Karp finally made it to Israel. He had decided to call attention to Palantir's support for the country in a dramatic way: by holding a board meeting in Tel Aviv. Not every board member could attend in person, but the most prominent one did: Thiel joined Karp in Israel. Before the board convened, it met in Jerusalem with Israel's president, Isaac Herzog, who expressed his gratitude for Palantir's assistance. Karp and Thiel also met privately with Netanyahu, a meeting that neither Palantir nor the prime minister's office publicly disclosed. During the trip, Karp, along with other Palantir executives, visited Kfar Aza, a kibbutz near Gaza where over sixty Israelis were murdered and nineteen were taken hostage. The group also toured an Israeli military installation. While in Israel Karp signed a contract with Israel's Ministry of Defense, formalizing a relationship that had started in the weeks after the terrorist attack. Karp's trip received a lot of local coverage, but didn't get much press back home, although *Bloomberg* published a story under the headline "Thiel's Palantir, Israel Agree Strategic Partnership for Battle Tech." A film crew had been hired to follow Karp in Israel, and several of his aides wanted to post the video on Palantir's website. But Lisa Gordon talked him out of it; she said it would seem crass.

The World Economic Forum took place the following week. Davos had become such a punch line that Karp would have preferred to skip it. But he recognized that it was another opportunity to highlight Israel's suffering. To that end, he hosted an event in which several former hostages of Hamas, along with the families of a couple of Israelis still being detained in Gaza, discussed the horrors they had experienced. (Karp covered the group's travel costs.) Karp got several fellow CEOs to take part: Amazon's Andy

Jassy, Salesforce's Marc Benioff, and Dell Technologies' Michael Dell were among those in attendance. The front display of Palantir's pavilion in Davos showed pictures of all 150 Israelis who were still being held hostage, along with the message "Bring Them Home Now."

Almost from the start of the war in Gaza, there was speculation about the role that Palantir was playing in the conflict. In April 2024, the Israeli online magazine *+972* published a lengthy investigation into a trio of AI-driven targeting programs that Israel was allegedly using in Gaza: one was called Lavender, the other two were called The Gospel and Where's Daddy? Citing military sources, the magazine said that the IDF had essentially outsourced decision-making to the algorithms and that thousands of innocent Palestinians had been killed as a result.

Although the *+972* article made no mention of Palantir, suspicion immediately fell on the company, with some analysts and critics suggesting that it had furnished technology for Lavender, The Gospel, and Where's Daddy? But according to people at Palantir who were intimately involved with its work in Israel, that was untrue; the company did not contribute to any of the targeting systems. In the spring of 2025, the UN special rapporteur on the Palestinian territories, Francesca Albanese, prepared a report that accused major tech companies of being complicit in what she characterized as Israel's genocidal war in Gaza, and an early draft repeated these claims about Palantir. In response, the company enlisted the British attorney Anthony Julius (best known for representing Princess Diana in her divorce from Prince Charles), who wrote a strongly worded letter accusing Albanese of recycling falsehoods.

But Palantir was assisting Israel in other ways. Its software was used by the Israeli military in several raids in Gaza in which hostages were freed, and it also helped facilitate the handover of detainees who were released by Hamas. In addition to hostage extraction, the company's technology was deployed by the Israelis during military operations in Lebanon in 2024 that decimated Hezbollah's top leadership. It was also used in Operation Grim Beeper, in which hundreds of Hezbollah fighters were injured and maimed when their pagers and walkie-talkies exploded (the Israelis had booby-trapped the devices). Via the U.S. military's Project Maven, Palantir also helped repel large-scale Iranian missile attacks on Israel in October 2024 and June 2025.

Back in the United States, meanwhile, Palantir hired dozens of students under Operation Safe Haven. To ensure that the program was legal, the company had opened it to Jews and non-Jews alike, and a number of non-Jews received offers. Safe Haven was not dissimilar to a program that Thiel had started some years earlier, in which he paid students to drop out of college to pursue innovative projects. The idea was born in part of Thiel's disdain for academia, a contempt that Karp shared even before October 7. With Karp, however, it seemed deeper and more personal. He had chosen not to become a professor, yet when he talked about the universities, he often sounded like someone who had been denied tenure—there was an undercurrent of rancor.

But while Palantir was welcoming the refugees from Columbia, Dartmouth, and other schools, it was facing some in-house dissent over its support for Israel. The debate on Palantir's Slack channels grew so heated at one point that the company shut down the discussion. Palantir executives made some effort to turn the controversy into a teachable moment. They announced that the company would initiate a speaker's series to help educate Palantirians on the history and nuances of the Israel-Palestine conflict. But the first guest was John Spencer, a scholar at the Modern War Institute, a think tank affiliated with West Point and one of the staunchest defenders of Israel's military campaign in Gaza. In opinion columns and media appearances, Spencer argued that Israel was not committing war crimes and was, in fact, showing excessive restraint. He believed that pressure from the United States and other Western countries was hindering Israel's ability to defeat Hamas and, as such, was putting Gaza residents at even greater risk. By no means was Spencer a crank, but choosing him to be the inaugural speaker served only to reinforce the impression among some employees that Palantir wasn't interested in having a robust discussion about Israel and the role the company was playing there—and, of course, Karp *wasn't* interested in having a debate. While very outspoken publicly, he was conspicuously silent internally: he didn't hold any town hall meetings or otherwise address the misgivings that Palantirians might have had about the company's work with Israel. Some colleagues thought he was remiss in not speaking directly to employees, but others believed that it was probably just as well that he didn't—that he was apt to say things that would aggravate tensions.

In Karp's inner circle, there was unabashed support for Israel, and the non-Jews seemed especially strident. Several executives wanted to fire the more vocal dissenters. But even though Karp had previously signaled his unwillingness to countenance any protests, he vetoed the idea; he thought the optics would be bad and that people who couldn't abide the company's position would quit. A handful did. One circulated a letter explaining his decision. "After 5 memorable years as a Hobbit, today is my last day at Palantir," he wrote. He spoke of his affection for his colleagues and of the pleasure that he took in the work before getting to the heart of the matter: "This is who our Palantir leadership has officially chosen to ostentatiously support: a government that is and has been in clear violation of international law, and an army that has been actively carrying out war crimes with complete impunity. While rightfully condemning the atrocious October 7th terrorist attacks, mourning Israeli civilian lives, and calling for the release of Israeli hostages, they had absolutely no word of sympathy for Palestinians, no condemnation of the attacks on the civilian population of Gaza, and no denunciation of the tens of thousands of Palestinians held illegally in Israeli detention and subject to systematic abuse. It is as if Palestinian lives are worth less than Israeli lives: the selective indignation is so obvious, and these double standards are unacceptable." He suggested that Palantir was acting in a way that contravened its own mission: "This is not what supporting the West should be about. Our stance and involvement are only aiding administrations and special interests who are betraying western and universal values of human rights, human dignity, and the right to freedom, justice and a lasting peace."

But Karp was unmoved by that argument or any other opinions that diverged from his own. In his view, Israel's fight *was* the West's fight—the battle against Hamas was a battle for the civilized world and in defense of the values that the West enshrined and represented. And Karp was convinced that those values weren't just under assault in the Middle East, but also on American college campuses. In May 2024, he spoke at an AI conference in Washington. He was joined onstage by Eric Schmidt; General Mark Milley, the former chairman of the Joint Chiefs of Staff; and David Cohen, the deputy director of the CIA. CNBC's Andrew Ross Sorkin moderated the conversation, and Karp used much of his time to once again rail against the students protesting the war in Gaza. He said they were in thrall to a "cancerous, corrosive ideology" that rejected Western thought and that if their ideas were not challenged and defeated, the West would be disarming itself.

"If we lose the intellectual debate, we will not be able to deploy any army in the West, ever," Karp said.

The next morning, CNBC's *Squawk Box* aired a clip of his remarks. Afterward, an amused Joe Kernen, one of the cohosts along with Sorkin, commented that Karp was "an enigma wrapped in a riddle. He always emphasizes 'I'm a progressive' and then he goes on to sound like just a huge right-winger."

ELEVEN

THE REBELS WIN

Before Palantir went public, Thiel was careful never to openly air any concerns that he had about how it was being run. He expressed faith in Karp's leadership and gave every indication that the two of them spoke with one voice when it came to Palantir. But after the stock market launch, he was more willing to acknowledge that there had been points of disagreement between him and Karp and that certain things about how the company operated had troubled him. He admitted, for instance, that he had wanted to take Palantir public sooner than Karp. He conceded, too, that he had been frustrated by the company's struggle to land deals—"It shouldn't have taken ten years to get the D-sigs contract," Thiel said, referring to the Army's battlefield intelligence system—and its inability to turn a profit. "If you had told me in 2004 that our first profitable quarter of business would be in the fourth quarter of 2022, that would've been very surprising," he said.

Thiel thought that the company had been hindered at times by its own underdog mentality. He said there was a "self-narrative" that Palantir was on this "very heroic" quest in which everything had to be an epic struggle, even if that wasn't necessarily true. Although he didn't use this exact metaphor, he was saying that given a choice between walking through the front door and trying to squeeze down the chimney, Palantir had always opted for the chimney. Thiel suggested that this pattern of behavior was rooted to some degree in Karp's personality. "My riff on Alex is that's he working out some psychological issues where he has to do things in this really, really hard way versus the straightforward, easy way," Thiel said. He didn't downplay the challenges that Palantir had faced but believed it shouldn't have been so difficult to achieve sustained success. "In theory, there were ways to build this that would have been far better, far faster, far less chaotic," said Thiel. The chaos, he added, had extended to the pursuit of new revenue streams: "There were ways that we pivoted too much from sector to sector."

He made that comment just weeks after Karp had announced that Palantir was plunging into another area that suddenly seemed full of promise. In early April 2023, Karp published a letter touting the imminent debut of Palantir's Artificial Intelligence Platform, or AIP. Six months earlier, OpenAI had released ChatGPT, a chatbot that brought generative artificial intelligence—algorithms that can create new content, be it text, images, video, music—to the masses. ChatGPT was at the vanguard of a group of bots—Google's Bard, later renamed Gemini; Microsoft's Copilot—that were trained on large language models, or LLMs. They had hoovered up enormous quantities of data (books, newspaper and magazine articles, photos) to learn human speech and thought patterns and were capable of giving increasingly sophisticated answers to complex questions. LLMs were widely regarded as a massive leap forward in the quest to achieve artificial general intelligence, or AGI, the long-anticipated moment when machine cognition might surpass human brainpower.

In his letter, Karp hailed LLMs as revolutionary. "At the most foundational level," he observed, "software provides an interface, a means of interacting, between the human mind and a computational machine. There has always been some degree of friction in translating the desires and creative instincts of a human operator into direction that a computational system can understand and apprehend. The development and refinement of large language models alongside our existing machine learning capabilities has now opened up a whole new means of interacting with machines that has never existed." He said that for business and industry, "the deployment of these new technologies will be transformative." But he also acknowledged that AI carried enormous risks for humanity. "It is clear that the sophistication and complexity of these latest systems will only continue to increase," Karp wrote. "The challenge will be to ensure that such technologies remain subservient to our collective will. We must impose our values on the software that we create."

The introduction of AIP was another instance of Palantir chasing the new new thing, but in this case, it paid off to a degree that even Karp hadn't anticipated. AIP led to an unprecedented surge in business, consistent profitability, and a run-up in the company's stock price that ultimately led to Palantir's ascension to the S&P 500. Karp had once told me that he believed Palantir was poised to become the new IBM—to achieve the kind of market dominance that IBM had enjoyed in the 1960s and '70s, when its mainframe computers were the backbone of corporate America and the U.S. government. At the time, Palantir's stock was under $10, and his confidence seemed, if not delusional, then at least fanciful. However, AIP proved to be a moon shot for Palantir, and the idea that the company's software might indeed become the de facto operating system of the West's most important institutions no longer sounded quite so far-fetched.

Along with Karp and Thiel, Stephen Cohen was one of the three cofounders who was still actively involved with Palantir when it went public. Joe Lonsdale left Palantir in 2009, eventually launching a venture capital firm. Nathan Gettings stayed at Palantir until 2012, when he quit to start a consumer lending company with Max Levchin, his old PayPal colleague. Cohen, by contrast, opted to remain, becoming Palantir's president. Even though the DPO had also made him a billionaire, Cohen personally had never gotten out of start-up mode. He wore the same outfit pretty much every day—a black polo shirt and jeans (shorts in warmer weather). He normally ate the same lunch, too: peanut butter and jelly on Wonder Bread. Like Karp, he was quirky. He preferred his room temperature ice-cold, and his office in Palo Alto felt like a meat locker. His discipline was legendary: he would sequester himself in a conference room and not emerge for hours—not even for bathroom breaks. He still pulled all-nighters.

Cohen had a long-standing interest in artificial intelligence, which he called "the final frontier in computing." He said that his biggest regret, upon graduating from Stanford, was that he had not taken a popular course on natural language processing. (He later audited the class.) While intimately involved in Palantir's product development, which included a number of machine-learning functions, he kept close watch on the AI research being done by companies like Google, Meta, Microsoft, OpenAI, and Anthropic. When ChatGPT came out, Cohen was struck by how much it seized the public's imagination. "The thing about ChatGPT wasn't just the technological progress, which was sublime," Cohen says. "Seeing the way the whole world got excited about it, seeing the human element awaken at such a collective scale—it was electric."

Bob McGrew, one of Palantir's original engineers, was now OpenAI's chief of research. Not long after ChatGPT was released, he stopped by Palantir's Palo Alto office and met with Karp and Cohen. They had a simple question: Was there true intelligence to ChatGPT, or was it just persuasive mimicry? McGrew couldn't tell them that OpenAI would soon be releasing an updated version of ChatGPT that had shown the ability to reason, but he said the intelligence was coming. "I just kept repeating that the models are going to get better, this stuff is real, and Palantir should prepare," says McGrew. Karp and Cohen, joined by Shyam Sankar and other Palantir executives, began brainstorming. It seemed clear to them that, as Cohen puts it, "a giant technological revolution" was at hand, and that this presented Palantir with an opportunity. Corporations and other institutions were going to want to integrate LLMs into their workflows and their broader digital infrastructure, and Palantir seemed ideally positioned to play an intermediary role.

But building an entirely new set of tools that would enable organizations to take advantage of LLMs was going to require a significant investment of time and money, and would also pull people away from other work. "You have to stand up teams—it's turning the ship," says Akshay Krishnaswamy, Palantir's chief architect. Karp made the decision to proceed. It was a risky move, a two-pronged wager: it was a bet that generative AI would fundamentally alter how companies manage their businesses, and it was a bet that Palantir could become the dominant enterprise software provider in the age of AI. In an earnings call, Karp announced that ambition with characteristic bravado, saying that Palantir's "strategy on AI is just to take the whole market."

AIP was developed in a matter of weeks and was incorporated into Foundry. Through AIP, companies could utilize LLMs for a host of functions—from financial modeling to communications and marketing to data analysis. In June 2023, Palantir hosted the first of what would become a quarterly event known as AIPCon, which drew dozens of attendees to the company's Palo Alto office for a day of demos and testimonials. It also began holding "boot camps" for existing and potential clients; Palantirians would visit companies to provide AIP tutorials for employees and allow them to experiment with it. Ultimately, Palantir did more than one thousand boot camps, which underlined its commitment to the new product and also the intense demand for AI capabilities—demand that yielded a trove of business.

During that first year, Palantir signed up around 150 new U.S. commercial users, roughly doubling the number it had before AIP. The new customers spanned a range of industries: they included Lowe's, the home improvement chain; General Mills; United Airlines; CBS; Aramark, the food services giant; the American Association of Retired Persons, or AARP; and Selkirk Sport, which manufactures pickleball equipment. Two companies that had dropped Palantir years earlier, JPMorganChase and Coca-Cola, became clients again. Several major hospital groups, among them Cleveland Clinic, also signed on; by the end of 2023, almost 20 percent of the nation's hospitals were using Palantir's software, an outgrowth not just of AIP, but also of the company's central role during the pandemic.

Palantir's year-on-year revenue increased by nearly 30 percent after AIP was introduced, and the company continued to report quarterly profits, a winning streak dating back to the fourth quarter of 2022. Some perennial Palantir skeptics on Wall Street were still unpersuaded: they saw AIP as little more than a sugar high and remained doubtful about the company's longer-term growth prospects. One analyst, Rishi Jaluria of RBC Capital Markets, suggested that Palantir was trying to hoodwink people. "Palantir messages that they are this cutting-edge generative AI company and very deliberately targets retail investors," Jaluria told Yahoo Finance. "It's a good data pipeline, it's a good data ontology company, I'm not saying it's not a useful company, but it is not what they claim it is." Jaluria found himself frozen out by Palantir—the company wouldn't take his calls or let him attend AIPCon. Other dubious Wall Street analysts were likewise shunned.

However, Wall Street's most prominent Palantir bear seemed to be changing his mind. In October 2023, Jim Cramer was asked by a *Mad Money* viewer for his thoughts about the company. "Palantir actually has real business," he said. "I was a little skeptical about those fellas... but they had a really good quarter and actually lived up to their hype. So I'm reluctant to say anything bad about them, and they are going to make money. So two cheers for Palantir." Several weeks later, he went further. "I disliked these guys for a long time, but not anymore," he told his audience. "I am on the Palantir team. I am Mr. Palantir." A few months after that, Cramer reiterated his bullishness and said he wanted to attend an AIP boot camp. He added that he hoped Karp or another Palantir executive would appear on his show. "I'm not begging them to come on," he said. "I'm simply imploring them to come on." (Neither Karp nor anyone else from the company took him up on the invitation.)

But Palantir's army of Karp fanboys didn't need Cramer to tell them that the stock was a buy, and partly on the backs of retail investors, the company's share price rallied sharply in the months following AIP's launch. When Palantir released AIP, its stock was under $8. A year later, it was $22 and rising; by late summer 2024, it was trading at over $35 per share. Palantir had seen an even bigger jump in its share price back in 2021, when it topped out at $39 before plunging back below $10. But Palantir was just a meme stock in that instance, driven higher by wallstreetsbets participants, their infatuation with "Daddy Karp," and their desire to stick it to professional investors. The Karp cultists were responsible in no small part for the stock's AIP boom, but in this case the fundamentals seemed to justify the price action—Palantir was now delivering solid numbers.

For his part, Karp was putting Palantir at the forefront of the debate over AI. In July 2023, three months after AIP debuted, Karp wrote an op-ed for *The New York Times* about AI. The film *Oppenheimer* had just been released, and Karp's article was titled "Our Oppenheimer Moment." But the headline really should have been "My Oppenheimer Moment," because the clear subtext was Karp's desire to be a thought leader on AI. At the time, more than a thousand tech executives, researchers, and scholars, including Elon Musk, had called for a six-month moratorium on AI development, citing the potential danger posed by these new technologies, not least the risk of human extinction.

Karp, in his *Times* piece, dismissed calls for a pause. He claimed that the United States and its allies were in a new global arms race, the outcome of which hinged on whoever could achieve dominance in the realm of AI. He said that America should not "shy away from building sharp tools for fear they may be turned against us" and that "a reluctance to grapple with the often grim reality of an ongoing geopolitical struggle for power poses its own danger. Our adversaries will not pause to indulge in theatrical debates about the merits of developing technologies with critical military and national security applications. They will proceed." He urged against complacency, writing, "The ability of free and democratic societies to prevail requires something more than moral appeal. It requires hard power, and hard power in this century will be built on software."

While the essay was thought-provoking, Karp's snarkiness undermined his case. He took aim yet again at what he called the "wunderkinder of Silicon Valley" who he said had "drifted meaningfully from the center of gravity of American public life" because of their reluctance to work with the U.S. military. He added, "The preoccupations and political instincts of coastal elites may be essential to maintaining their sense of self and cultural superiority but do little to advance the interests of our republic." That line caused consternation in Palantir's Washington office; it was seen as a needless swipe that undoubtedly alienated a lot of readers and might well have also ticked off some people on Capitol Hill.

But any irritation that may have been felt on the Hill was quickly forgotten. Two months later, Karp was among the tech executives invited to take part in a daylong summit on AI regulation convened by Senate Majority Leader Chuck Schumer. When Karp joined other tech moguls at the Trump Tower meeting in December 2016, he seemed out of place—Palantir was a relatively small company, and while it arguably punched above its weight in reach and importance, it didn't merit inclusion alongside the likes of Apple, Amazon, Alphabet, and Microsoft (and Karp admitted as much). Just seven years later, though, no one questioned why Karp had been asked to join Musk, Bill Gates, Mark Zuckerberg, and other luminaries to discuss AI. Indeed, he was given a place of particular prominence, next to Musk.

Karp had a dyspeptic take on the seating arrangement. As he and the Tesla and SpaceX CEO made small talk during the press gaggle that preceded the conference, he asked Musk if he knew why they were next to one another. Musk said he had no idea. "It's because the shotgun blast radius will only take out the two of us," Karp said with a laugh. Whether Musk got the joke and found it funny was unclear. But it was an attempt at humor that reflected Karp's desire to be seen as an inconvenient, resented interloper, as someone the "establishment" would gladly off if only it weren't so dependent on his software. Even at an event that affirmed his insider bona fides, Karp still wanted to tell himself (and Musk) that he was an outsider.

In fact, though, he was now a major figure in Washington, a point vividly demonstrated when I caught up with him one day at Palantir's office there. It had been an exceptionally hectic morning for Karp, and he said the only opportunity for us to talk would be if I joined him for his midday workout. So just after noon, we piled into two cars and were driven to the start of the Capital Crescent Trail, by the Georgetown waterfront. From there, Karp roller skied five miles to the house he had recently purchased in the Maryland suburbs. I accompanied him on bike, as did a bodyguard; one of the Norwegians roller skied alongside Karp. It was not the easiest way to conduct an interview—I held my phone in one hand to record his comments and used my other hand to steer the bike, trying to avoid cyclists and joggers coming in the other direction and to keep my front tire from running into Karp's ski poles. But we made it to his house without any spills. As we walked inside, he mentioned that former CIA director George Tenet would be dropping by shortly. That Tenet, without whom Palantir might not have existed—Tenet, after all, created In-Q-Tel—was paying a visit to Karp rather than vice versa seemed emblematic of the stature that Karp now enjoyed.

When Tenet arrived, Karp was showering. I chatted with the ex-spymaster as one of Karp's assistants set a single place at the dining room table—Karp was going to multitask and eat lunch while meeting with Tenet. A short time later, Karp came downstairs, his hair still dripping. I joined them as Karp gave Tenet a quick tour of his library, but I wasn't allowed to sit in on their conversation. As I showed myself to the door, I heard Karp offering Tenet some of his hummus.

Karp's profile wasn't just rising inside the Beltway. In 2024, the German filmmaker Klaus Stern released a documentary called *Watching You: Die Welt von Palantir und Alex Karp* (translation: *The World of Palantir and Alex Karp*). It premiered at the Munich International Documentary Film Festival and drew a lot of press coverage in Germany. Karp did not cooperate with the film, but Karola Brede, his doctoral adviser, was among those who spoke to Stern. Karp, it seemed, was transcending the business world and becoming, like Musk if not quite to the same degree, a figure in the culture. In the summer of 2024, he was the subject of a flattering Maureen Dowd profile in *The New York Times*. A few weeks later, Karp was a guest on *Real Time with Bill Maher*. While in Los Angeles, Karp met with entertainment lawyers to discuss a possible feature film about him and Palantir. At around the same time, Karp's importance was acknowledged in another, different way: the Russian Foreign Ministry banned him from entering Russia.

For Karp and for Palantir, signs of validation—and of vindication—were everywhere. Following Palantir's lead, other tech companies, including OpenAI, were now hiring forward-deployed engineers of their own. Even more significant—and from Karp's view, gratifying—was the emergence of a Palantir Mafia, the growing number of start-ups founded by people who had previously worked at Palantir. While the list wasn't yet as illustrious as the PayPal offspring (LinkedIn, YouTube, and more), it was impressive and increasingly extensive. It included companies such as Affirm, OpenSea, Handshake, and Ironclad, all of which had attracted significant venture capital money. But the biggest success of the Palantir Pack, as it was called, was a company called Anduril (another Tolkien name; in the *Lord of the Rings* trilogy, Anduril is a sword with magical powers). Anduril specialized in defense technology; it produced autonomous and semiautonomous weapons. It was founded in 2017 by Palmer Luckey, a colorful entrepreneur who made his original fortune with the virtual reality headset company Oculus, and a trio of ex-Palantirians: Brian Schimpf, Trae Stephens, and Matt Grimm. Peter Thiel's Founders Fund was a major investor in Anduril, which by 2025 was valued at over $30 billion.

It was no exaggeration to say that Palantir spawned Anduril, and not just because it supplied three of its cofounders; the slew of military contracts that Palantir was awarded in the years following its lawsuit against the Army encouraged other tech players to launch defense-oriented start-ups. The disruption wrought by Palantir gave rise to a subindustry of new tech companies seeking to win business from the Pentagon, a renewed gold rush accelerated by the war in Ukraine. Between 2021 and 2024, venture capital firms poured around $130 billion into firms developing hardware and software for the battlefield, part of Silicon Valley's pivot to "patriotic capital."

The news, in the summer of 2024, that Eric Schmidt had started a company producing military drones seemed symbolically important. While Schmidt had long been an advocate for closer ties between the Valley and the Pentagon, his move into weapons manufacturing highlighted the degree to which warfare was now in vogue in tech circles—and it was largely due to Karp and Palantir. The scramble for Pentagon dollars was fueled in part by hawkishness regarding China, and on this score, too, Karp could claim vindication. For years, Palantir had been an outlier in the Valley because of its unwillingness to do business in China. The VC community, by contrast, had no hesitation about backing Chinese start-ups, and tech giants such as Apple and Google had major investments in China.

But by 2024, the mood had shifted. It was partly in response to political pressure: first under Trump and then under Biden, there was a growing recognition that the U.S. relationship with China was fundamentally antagonistic and that giving China access to strategically important advanced technologies was not in America's national interest. The Biden administration also placed restrictions on U.S. investments in certain Chinese tech sectors, such as AI and quantum computing. In Washington, there was now bipartisan consensus that the United States and China were at the dawn of a new Cold War. The defense tech sector was eager to play up the China threat because it was good for business, and no one played it up more than Karp. But in his case, it wasn't just opportunism at work; he had been dubious of China for two decades and had long believed that conflict was inevitable.

And Karp was now at the center of the debate over AI, China, and U.S. national security. In May 2024, he attended a dinner in Washington that capped a daylong conference devoted to that topic. The dinner, held in an ornate room in the Library of Congress, drew a sizable number of U.S. senators and members of the House of Representatives, including JD Vance, Kyrsten Sinema, Joe Manchin, and Lindsey Graham. But Karp was the star attraction. Chuck Schumer delivered remarks during the cocktail reception and lauded Karp for his leadership on AI (while also needling him about his hair). Later, Karp was the interviewee in a fireside chat with U.S. Representative Richie Torres, a Democrat from New York. The acoustics were terrible, which made it impossible for many guests to hear what Karp was saying, but the fact that Torres was interviewing him, rather than vice versa, spoke to the kind of power and influence that he now wielded. Not long thereafter, one of Torres's colleagues, Mike Gallagher, a Wisconsin Republican known for his hard-line stance on China, resigned from Congress and joined Palantir as the head of its defense business, replacing Doug Philippone, who had left to focus on his own defense-focused venture capital fund. Gallagher had been frustrated by legislative gridlock and by extremism in his own party. Even so, that a sitting member of Congress would quit to take a job with Palantir said something about the cachet that the company now enjoyed.

Yet Palantir still had the spirit of a start-up. It employed fewer than four thousand people, a head count that had essentially remained unchanged for almost a decade. And in contrast to Apple, Amazon, Google, and Facebook, which had fueled their continued growth mainly by buying other companies—as of 2021, according to *The Washington Post*, the four tech giants combined had swallowed up at least six hundred other firms—Palantir's growth remained almost entirely organic. In its two decades of existence, it had quietly acquired a few companies, but every new product that it kicked out was developed in-house, by people who had been hired by Palantir (and many of whom had only ever worked for Palantir).

And, of course, Palantir was still headed by one of its cofounders. Karp was now fifty-seven. Some of the biggest names in tech—Jeff Bezos, Larry Ellison—had remained at the helm of the companies they started long after they had earned their fortunes. But they were exceptions, and Karp was, too. Although he was busier than he had ever been as CEO—he was back to traveling as much as he had before the pandemic, and taking Palantir public had greatly increased his workload—he was giving no thought to stepping away. When I asked him if there was a succession plan, Karp broke into a broad grin. "Are you trying to tell me something?" he asked in mock horror. "Am I, like, going to get hit by a bus tomorrow?" Turning serious, he said he didn't have a designated successor because he had no intention of dying or retiring anytime soon. In truth, it was hard to imagine Palantir under a different CEO, given the degree to which the company's identity was bound up in Karp's, and also because it was difficult to believe that anyone else would have the singular focus that Karp brought to the job.

Near the end of the summer of 2024, Paul Graham, a prominent Silicon Valley investor, published a blog post in which he said that the most effective corporate leaders were those who remain in what he called "founder mode"—who stay intimately involved with nearly all aspects of their businesses no matter how large their companies grow to be. Graham contrasted this with "manager mode," in which CEOs, as their enterprises increase in size and complexity, provide instruction and guidance to their lieutenants but leave the implementation up to them. He claimed that founder mode had proven to be the more effective approach—there was no substitute for the vision, knowledge, and experience that a founder could bring to the factory floor, as it were. Graham's observation immediately became received wisdom in Silicon Valley, as entrepreneurs and investors alike affirmed the advantage conferred by founder mode. And while Graham didn't name-check Karp, few people in the tech industry embodied the idea more than Palantir's CEO.

A few weeks after Graham's post went viral, Palantir was added to the S&P 500. For Karp, this was incontrovertible proof that he had led Palantir wisely and well. He released a video to mark the occasion. It was filmed on a cross-country-skiing trail, but there was no snow; he and the Norwegian accompanying him were running, using ski poles to push off between strides. When Karp addressed the camera, he talked about the long journey that saw Palantir go from a start-up shunned by venture capitalists to membership in what he called the "most elite institution in economic life," the S&P 500. He threw the usual jab at Wall Street, saying that it had wrongly dismissed Palantir as a "Frankenstein monster powered by a freakshow leader, me." Karp said that he was "really, really fucking happy" and was proud that the company had forged such an unconventional path. "We did it our way," he exulted, adding that Palantir employees and the retail investors who supported the company had reason to feel triumphant. "The rebels won," Karp said. "The rebels won."

In April 2023, I met with Peter Thiel twice—first, at his home in Los Angeles, then just over a week later at a hotel on Maryland's Eastern Shore. I had assumed he was there for a political event, but it turned out he was hosting a symposium on René Girard, his old Stanford professor. When he and I spoke that afternoon, Thiel told me that he was stepping away from politics. He said he had been shaken by the hostility that he had drawn because of his previous support for Donald Trump and that it had been even more stressful for his husband, Matt Danzeisen, who was now insisting that he sit out the 2024 presidential election. "Matt is of the strong view that I'm not allowed to do anything at all," Thiel said. "He wants no more. I am really, really determined to stay out of all of it in 2024. We'll see if I can. I'm really, really determined to do it. I'm married, he's really put his foot down, and I have to listen to what he's saying."

But Thiel went on to tell me that he was done with Trump regardless. While he didn't regret his decision to back the real estate developer in 2016, it had proven to be a mistake. Even though he had recognized that Trump was a flawed figure who said things that "had a very bad relationship with the truth," as he put it, Thiel had thought that his campaign slogan, "Make America Great Again," could serve as a call to national renewal. However, winning an election was one thing, governing was another, and Thiel said that Trump had failed as president. He brought disruption but did little to cure the country of the lethargy that Thiel believed was plaguing it. "We needed to stop being distracted from the important problems, and Trump ended up being a terrific way to distract us from the important problems," Thiel said. He did not donate to Trump's 2020 reelection campaign and turned down an invitation to speak at that year's Republican National Convention. "The criteria was that I had to say something that was basically truthful, basically positive, and moderately impactful, and I couldn't figure out anything," he said. "I think even one of those things was hard, all three was impossible."

Thiel said that he was not supporting Trump's 2024 White House bid and wanted to see the GOP move on from the twice-impeached former president. He had contributed to a handful of Republican candidates during the 2022 midterm elections, but said that only two races had mattered to him: the U.S. Senate campaigns of JD Vance and Blake Masters, friends and former protégés of his, who were running in Ohio and Arizona, respectively. He suggested that the backing he gave to other candidates, notably Harriet Hageman, who defeated Representative Liz Cheney, a Trump nemesis, in the Republican primary for Wyoming's lone congressional seat, was purely strategic: he wanted to placate Trump in the hope that he would endorse both Vance and

Masters (which he did). Masters lost in the general election, but Vance won, helped in no small part by the $15 million that Thiel donated to his campaign. But Thiel indicated that his checkbook was now closed, especially to Trump.

For Karp, Thiel's break with Trump was as unhelpful as his support for Trump had been in 2016. Karp was convinced that Trump was going to be returned to the White House, and the former president was nothing if not vindictive. Soon after I met with Thiel in Maryland, Trump reached out to him asking for a contribution. Thiel said no, and Trump replied that he was "very, very sad to hear that." Thiel told *The Atlantic* that Trump, in a subsequent conversation with Blake Masters, called him "a fucking scumbag." The rift between Thiel and the once-and-possibly-future president seemed like bad news for Palantir.

When 2024 arrived and Trump swept the early Republican primaries and caucuses, Karp decided that he had to move proactively in anticipation of a Trump restoration. "I've got to get the company ready for Trump," he told me. Palantir had become a more MAGA-friendly place in the years since Trump had left office. It employed even more ex-servicemen now and had also hired a handful of former Republican congressional staffers and political appointees. The changes to the rank and file were reflected in Karp's decision not to impose a vaccine mandate at Palantir (this even though he still wore a mask whenever he stepped into an elevator). He knew there were anti-vaxxers on staff now, and he didn't want to cause internal friction.

With Thiel inactive, Karp sought to establish links to Trump World in other ways. At his direction, employees in the Washington office fanned out across the capital seeking to build ties to people who were likely to score jobs in a second Trump administration or wield influence over it. They attended conferences at right-wing think tanks, cocktail receptions with conservative luminaries, and other events where they could chat up former and possibly future Trump officials. And it wasn't just Washington employees: in March, Louis Mosley traveled to Palm Springs to spend a weekend at the BNP Paribas Open tennis tournament with Robert C. O'Brien, who had served as one of Trump's national security advisers and who owned a home in the area. O'Brien was one of the few "conventional" appointees who had left the White House on good terms with Trump, and he was thought to be in line for another senior position if he won back the presidency.

As Trump moved closer to claiming the Republican nomination, there was other bridge-building. Joe Lonsdale, who was now based in Austin, had hosted a fundraiser for Florida Governor Ron DeSantis's presidential bid, in part because he was skeptical that Trump could win the general election. But after DeSantis stumbled, Lonsdale set aside his doubts and became an enthusiastic Trump supporter. Even bigger help came in May when Jacob Helberg donated $1 million to Trump's campaign. Helberg was a foreign policy analyst who served as a paid consultant to Karp. He was linked to the PayPal Mafia and the Thielverse; his husband was the venture capitalist Keith Rabois, a *Stanford Review* alum who had gone on to work at PayPal and, later, at Thiel's Founders Fund. Helberg and Rabois had married in 2018; OpenAI CEO Sam Altman had officiated.

Helberg had recently been the focus of a *New York Times* story about the AI arms race. Some people at Palantir were troubled by the article: they thought that he was trading off the company's name and had overstepped his bounds. But it seemed that he was useful for Karp: he was well-connected in Washington, especially on the Republican side, and he also now had Trump's ear. Helberg organized the conference on China and AI where Karp was the keynote speaker, and he got Trump to deliver a videotaped message. The former president recalled meeting Helberg and urged attendees to "keep your chin up." A few weeks later, Helberg announced his $1 million contribution to Trump. On X, he posted a link to a *Washington Post* article about his donation and wrote, "This one's for Israel." From Palantir's perspective, his seven-figure check made up for the one that Thiel was not writing this time around. In contrast to Thiel, Helberg was not given a speaking slot at the Republican National Convention, but he did address a Trump rally in Georgia in October.

At the cocktail reception following the China and AI conference, Karp huddled with JD Vance. Two months later, after an intense lobbying effort by some of Silicon Valley's biggest names, including Elon Musk, Trump selected Vance as his running mate. Thiel, who had introduced Trump to Vance in 2021, reportedly also pushed hard to have the Ohio senator added to the Republican ticket. In August, Thiel told *The New York Times* that he was thrilled that Trump had chosen Vance, who prior to entering politics had worked for Thiel's Mithril Capital, and that he was warming to the idea of a second Trump administration. He was also so certain now that Trump was going to triumph that he didn't think a donation was needed. "Trump is locked on a massively winning race," he said. "And the Democrats are locked on a massively losing race. And that's why the money doesn't matter."

By that point, Biden had dropped out, and Vice President Kamala Harris had replaced him as the Democratic nominee. When I visited Karp at his suburban Maryland home in August, he was less caustic than usual about Harris. He acknowledged that she had performed well at the Democratic National Convention earlier that month and that she seemed to be generating real enthusiasm. He still thought that Trump was likely to prevail, but it was now going to be a much closer race, and despite the misgivings that he had previously expressed about Harris, he intended to contribute to her campaign. When I asked him about Vance, he demurred. "I'm not going to comment on that," he said.

The Sunday before the election, Karp was back in Washington; Palantir was releasing its third-quarter earnings the following afternoon, and he needed to prepare (it was another stellar quarter, and Palantir's stock would jump $10 on the news, to $51.13, a record-high close). Karp was now certain that Trump was going to reclaim the presidency; immigration was a toxic issue for the Democrats, and he said that Harris had also failed to adequately distance herself from the unpopular Biden. I was confident enough in a Harris victory that I suggested a bet: if Trump won, Karp would get half of my net worth; if Harris won, I would get half of his. Fortunately, he didn't take me up on the offer.

A few days after the election, Karp called me to gloat about his correct prediction and to discuss the result. I said that if Trump made good on his threat to launch an even bigger immigration crackdown, Palantir would inevitably face another backlash. Karp professed not to care—he was not backing away from ICE this time, either. I was curious, too, to know what he made of Trump now. Trump's campaign had been marked by incendiary rhetoric. He called his political opponents "vermin" and spoke darkly of "the enemy within," language that in the judgment of many scholars was not just fascistic, but evocative of Nazi Germany. Karp had written his dissertation on the rhetoric of fascism and could claim legitimate expertise in this area—and as someone who said that his greatest fear was fascism, he surely had a keen ear for what it sounded like. So I asked Karp if he still believed that Trump was not a fascist. He ignored my question and said only that he was uncertain about what the next four years would bring.

EPILOGUE

In early December 2024, a few weeks after the presidential election, Palantir hosted an AIP event in its New York office. When I arrived that morning, Karp was deep in conversation with Amit Kukreja, an amateur stock commentator who was possibly Palantir's (and Karp's) biggest fan in the retail investment community. He was now regularly invited to the company's events and had become its de facto human mascot. As Karp chatted with Kukreja, he noticed a woman approaching from across the room and exclaimed, "Oh, to what do we owe this honor? I hear congratulations are in order." Reaching Karp, the woman gave him a peck on the cheek. Feigning disappointment, Karp insisted that she give him a kiss on the other cheek, as well, which she did. The woman was Monica Crowley, the Fox News commentator who had just been nominated by President-elect Trump to be the Chief of Protocol of the United States. She had also served in the first Trump administration. As a pundit, she had amplified conspiracy theories about President Obama—suggesting, for instance, that he was a Muslim seeking to impose sharia law on the United States. Karp considered her a friend; they knew each other from the Sun Valley conference and other events. But Crowley was also a star in the MAGA firmament, MAGA was reascendant, and Karp's effusive greeting seemed emblematic of a change in attitude. This time around, he and Palantir were going to accommodate themselves to Trump unapologetically, even enthusiastically.

A few hours after seeing Crowley, Karp headed uptown for a live interview on Fox Business. Two days earlier, not far from the Fox studio, the CEO of UnitedHealthcare had been shot and killed, and his assailant was still at large. Karp's security detail was bigger than normal that day, and his bodyguards were noticeably on edge. They weren't thrilled when Karp, frustrated by Manhattan traffic, got out of the car and walked the last few blocks. Karp used the interview to reaffirm Palantir's patriotism—"Palantir exists to serve this nation"—and to crow about the company's success. "To all the people who hated on us, enjoy your coal," he said, eliciting laughter from Liz Claman, the Fox host. Asked about Trump's appointment of Elon Musk to head up a cost-cutting initiative called the Department of Government Efficiency, or DOGE, he was ecstatic. "I wholeheartedly support what they are doing, and God knows, you could not have a better person than Elon doing it," he replied.

From New York, Karp traveled to Los Angeles for the annual Reagan National Defense Forum. He was joined in California by Shyam Sankar, who was reportedly under consideration for a senior job in the Pentagon. Joe Lonsdale was also there, as was Doug Philippone. The conference was crawling with defense tech people, who seemed ebullient: the consensus among them was that the second Trump presidency was going to be good for business. Karp took part in a panel discussion. Claiming that Trump had won "a massive mandate," he heaped his usual scorn on the Democrats, whom he referred to as "my sometimes former party." He said the Democrats had lost the election in part because "people don't want to hear your woke, pagan ideology" but instead "want to know they are safe, and safe means that the other person is scared. That's how you make someone safe. The average American person understands this. Unfortunately, many of the intellectually captured institutions . . . intellectually owned by the Berkeley faculty, do not." On X, Musk reposted a clip of Karp's comments with an approving one-word summary: "Based."

A few days after the Reagan event, Trump rewarded Jacob Helberg for his $1.25 million campaign contribution by picking him to serve as under secretary of state for economic growth, energy, and the environment. In mid-December, Karp quietly made a $1 million personal donation to the Trump Vance Inaugural Committee. He skipped the inauguration, however, even though the festivities included a party that Thiel hosted at his Washington mansion. It drew a number of notables, among them JD Vance, Mark Zuckerberg, Sam Altman, Joe Lonsdale, Donald Trump Jr., and House Speaker Mike Johnson. Separately, some senior Palantirians held a cigar party at a Washington hotel. But one company executive was left off the invite list because he was deemed insufficiently MAGA. Karp spent the weekend skiing.

In February, a couple of weeks after the inauguration, Karp published a book. It was called *The Technological Republic: Hard Power, Soft Belief, and the Future of the West* and was coauthored with Nick Zamiska, Palantir's head of corporate affairs. The book was an explication of Karp's worldview, a rehashing of some of his pet grievances (expressed less vituperatively than was normally the case), and a brand manifesto for Palantir. It took a lot of detours, but its central argument was that the cultural relativism that supposedly held sway on college campuses, coupled with Silicon Valley's consumerist focus, had undermined the American Project and that a new, tech-driven nationalism was needed to keep America, and by extension the West, dominant.

The Technological Republic received mixed reviews. *The Wall Street Journal* hailed it as a "new treatise in political theory." The conservative columnist George F. Will wrote, "Not since Allan Bloom's astonishingly successful 1987 book 'The Closing of the American Mind'—more than 1 million copies sold—has there been a cultural critique as sweeping as Karp's." But the book was savaged by others. The political commentator John Ganz, writing for *Bloomberg*, said that it was "full of bad ideas, ranging from the merely dubious to the execrable and disturbing. . . . It heralds a dark and disturbing future." Some critics regarded the book as a pitch for techno-authoritarianism that happened to arrive just as Karp and other Silicon Valley oligarchs had effectively captured the state. But the naysayers didn't hurt sales: *The Technological Republic* reached number one on the *New York Times* bestseller list. On Palantir's X account, the company celebrated the achievement: "The insurgents have broken through the gates," it said. The book also gained Karp a fan in the Oval Office. In February, as part of his publicity tour, Karp was the subject of a feature in *The Wall Street Journal*, under the headline "Alex Karp Wants Silicon Valley to Fight for America." A few days later, Karp received a copy of the *Journal* article autographed by Trump. "Alex—great!" Trump wrote just above his signature.

For readers familiar with Karp's dissertation—a very small number of people, to be sure—*The Technological Republic* contained a jarring passage. The book references Martin Walser's 1998 speech decrying what he saw as the continued use of the Holocaust as a cudgel against the German people. Karp, in his dissertation, had cast Walser's speech in a sinister light, citing it as an example of fascistic rhetoric. But in the book, he and Zamiska hail Walser as a free-speech warrior who had courageously pushed back against the thought police. "He had articulated the forbidden desires and feelings of a nation," they write, "and in doing so relieved an immense amount of internal dissonance for his audience, most of whom had been immersed in a culture in which speech had been tightly patrolled and monitored for even the slightest signs of deviation from the received wisdom, the national consensus."

Karp's reappraisal of Walser reflected what appeared to be a broader change in his thinking. It was striking to note that a book ostensibly about the future of the West had little to say about liberalism and completely ignored the rise of the populist right and the threat that it posed to democratic governance in the United States and Europe. In the past, Karp had said that defending the West meant safeguarding its political order. As recently as 2020, in Palantir's S-1, the company declared that its mission was "to support Western liberal democracy and its strategic allies." But *The Technological Republic* gave no indication that Karp regarded democracy and its underpinnings, such as the rule of law, as essential to the West's success and continued prosperity.

Instead, he now seemed to hold a different opinion about why the West had flourished. In a letter to shareholders in February 2025, he cited approvingly the late political scientist Samuel Huntington's observation that the West had become dominant not because of "its ideas, values or religion" but rather because it was more proficient at "applying organized violence." During an appearance on CNBC's *Squawk Box* to promote *The Technological Republic*, Karp suggested that Western civilization was somehow just innately better. "The West, as a notion and as a principle upon which it is executed, is obviously superior," he said. It appeared that Karp was now delinking the fate of the West from the fate of liberal democracy. Perhaps he had come to believe that the two were not, in fact, inextricably bound. Or maybe, with Trump back in the White House, he was just being a savvy CEO and bending to the prevailing winds.

As Karp promoted his book, Palantir was again mired in controversy over ICE. In April, the online tech publication 404 Media reported that Palantir had signed a $30 million contract with ICE to provide software for a new platform called ImmigrationOS, which would expedite deportations. 404 Media obtained an internal Palantir Wiki page that explained to employees the rationale for signing the contract. It said that the "national conversation around immigration enforcement, both at the border and in the interior of the United States, has shifted" and that this presented Palantir with "an opportunity to do good work." The site also published Slack messages in which Aki Jain, the head of Palantir's U.S. government business, said that the firm would be addressing any questions and concerns that employees had. "I recognize this is a topic of interest for a lot of hobbits," he wrote. "We recognize that as this becomes more public you will probably be asked about what's fact vs. fiction from friends, family, candidates and customers." John Grant, a member of Palantir's privacy and civil liberties team, posted a link to an internal FAQ titled "Can it be right to support a customer who you think is wrong?"

By then, videos of masked ICE agents grabbing people off the street were proliferating, and the individuals being apprehended included not just undocumented immigrants but also international students who had participated in protests against the war in Gaza or who had merely spoken out against it. Some U.S. citizens were reportedly also picked up by ICE. Those arrested were sent to ICE detention facilities. Immigration lawyers and elected officials who visited these holding centers alleged that they were overcrowded and unsanitary and that food, water, and medical attention were in short supply. Some detainees claimed that they suffered physical abuse at the hands of guards.

ICE also deported hundreds of men who it said were members of a Venezuelan gang; they were sent to El Salvador, where they were incarcerated in a notoriously brutal prison. However, investigations by *The New York Times* and *The Washington Post* found that many of those individuals had no gang links. A federal judge accused the Trump administration of defying his order forbidding the government from sending two planeloads of detainees to El Salvador because they had been denied due process. In an interview in July, Tom Homan, Trump's border czar, told Fox News that constitutional norms didn't apply when it came to enforcing immigration laws. "Look, people need to understand, ICE officers and Border Patrol, they don't need probable cause to walk up to somebody, briefly detain them, and question them," he said. "They just need totality of the circumstances, right? They just go through observation, get our typical facts." Homan also indicated that racial profiling was part of ICE's strategy—he said that it was targeting people "based on the location, the occupation, their physical appearance, their actions."

While ICE was expanding its dragnet, Elon Musk and DOGE were ransacking the federal bureaucracy, supposedly in an effort to cut government spending and to identify and root out alleged instances of waste and fraud. DOGE dispatched software engineers, most of whom were in their twenties (one was a teenager), to different government agencies. The engineers commandeered computer systems, in some instances gaining access to data they were not authorized to see. A number of lawsuits were filed challenging the legality of DOGE's actions. One engineer had previously interned for Palantir. According to *Wired* magazine, two former Palantir employees were helping recruit for DOGE. *Wired* also reported that DOGE was planning to use Palantir's Foundry to merge all the data collected by the IRS and to make it accessible to other government agencies.

Despite the controversy swirling around DOGE—and mounting evidence that it was a ham-fisted operation that was imperiling essential government functions—Karp insisted that it was performing a necessary service for the country. In another appearance on Fox Business, he said, "Palantir is very pro-DOGE, I'm pro-DOGE, I believe it is going to be great for America." Given that Karp had spent two decades emphasizing the importance of data protection, it was odd to hear him cheerleading for a massive data breach that was certain to sow even greater mistrust of the tech industry, and of Palantir in particular.

Karp also went out of his way to defend Musk. On the day of Trump's inauguration, Musk had addressed a rally in Washington and concluded his speech by giving what was almost universally interpreted to be a Nazi salute. Asked about that during an interview with CNBC, Karp didn't comment on the gesture itself but noted that Musk had traveled to Israel after October 7 to demonstrate his solidarity with the Jewish state and said that any suggestion that the Tesla CEO was a Nazi sympathizer or an antisemite was "completely absurd and a complete rewrite of history." Musk expressed his appreciation for the support. "Alex Karp is awesome," he wrote on X, adding a heart emoji.

Meanwhile, Karp's own rhetoric was becoming increasingly bombastic. During an earnings call, he said that DOGE was "a revolution" in which "some people get their heads cut off," an apparent reference to the tens of thousands of federal workers who had quit or been fired at that point. In February, while promoting his book in a talk with Andrew Ross Sorkin at New York's 92nd Street Y, Karp fantasized about humiliating the Wall Street analysts who had been skeptical of Palantir. "I love the idea of getting a drone and having light, fentanyl-laced urine spraying on the analysts who tried to screw us," he said. Palantir's marketing also took on a harder edge: the company's new tagline was "Software that dominates."

All this was too much for some ex-Palantirians. In May, thirteen of them published an open letter titled "The Scouring of the Shire," in which they accused the company of betraying its founding principles (the protection of democracy and human rights, the defense of scientific inquiry) and of "normalizing authoritarianism under the guise of a 'revolution' led by oligarchs." The signers included Ari Gesher, one of Palantir's original software engineers. In response, Palantir said that while the former employees were "certainly entitled to express their views on these matters," they should have spoken to current Palantirians to "better understand that which they sought to protest."

Around this same time, Palantir posted a four-minute video on its X account in which employees who had left the company only to return explained what brought them back. The clip was very odd, and all the stranger because of the creepy background music. One boomeranger said that "I made it roughly six months out of Palantir" before realizing that leaving had been a mistake. The video seemed clearly intended to stave off an exodus of employees troubled by the company's work on immigration and other issues.

But one Palantirian who quit over ICE encouraged others to follow suit. Writing on her LinkedIn page, Brianna Katherine Martin said that for "most of my time here, I found the way that Palantir grappled with the weight of our capabilities to be refreshing, transparent, and conscionable. This has changed for me over the past few months... with the erosion of due process and institutions, this is not the time to erect a Maginot line of justifications based on comfort and compliance. If it feels wrong to you, it probably is."

In late May, more controversy erupted when *The New York Times* alleged that Palantir was helping the Trump administration build a master database containing personal information on Americans. This effort was supposedly tied to an executive order that Trump had signed in March to consolidate data collection across government agencies. During his first presidency, Trump had made clear that he wanted to use the powers of the office to punish his perceived enemies; his thirst for retribution was even greater now, and the construction of a central repository of personal data alarmed not only Democrats but also civil libertarians and privacy advocates. Historically, much of this information had been kept siloed precisely to avoid abuse—and with Trump, the potential for abuse seemed vast.

Palantir reacted with fury to the *Times* article. On X, it said that the story was "blatantly untrue" and that "if the facts were on its side, The New York Times would not have needed to twist the truth." It took additional swipes at the *Times*, including one that said, "Democracy dies in ineptitude," a play on *The Washington Post*'s "Democracy dies in darkness" slogan. The company also published a four-thousand-word blog post rebutting the *Times* piece (which was less than half that length). Palantir said that the story betrayed fundamental misconceptions about the nature of its work and insisted that there was nothing nefarious about its role in helping merge government databases. The goal was simply to make the federal bureaucracy more efficient. The blog post did not address fears that Trump would exploit access to private information to hound his opponents.

In response to the *Times* article, a group of congressional Democrats, including Representative Alexandra Ocasio-Cortez and Senator Elizabeth Warren, sent a letter to Palantir demanding more information about the alleged database and advising the company to preserve emails and other communications "in anticipation of future litigation and congressional oversight." But the reaction on the left was of little concern to Karp; what alarmed him and other Palantir executives—and part of what prompted the very aggressive pushback against the *Times*—was anger among MAGA influencers who were dismayed that Trump, supposedly a victim of the so-called deep state, was now, in their view, ceding it even more power. Nick Fuentes, the antisemitic white nationalist who had dined at Mar-a-Lago, said on X that Trump's work with Palantir was "the ultimate betrayal of his own people," adding, "if Palantir isn't the Deep State, then what is?" The Palantirians were adamant that the *Times* piece was incorrect, but they were also seeking to prevent the far right's outrage from metastasizing into something that could threaten their business. One prominent MAGA voice did speak up in Palantir's defense: Alex Jones, the veteran conspiracy theorist, said that it was no more untrustworthy than other tech firms and was being singled out because it had been "supportive of Trump."

Indeed, Karp now seemed to be all in on Trump. In May, he was among some thirty U.S. corporate leaders who joined Trump on a visit to Saudi Arabia. There, he chatted amicably with Trump and Saudi Crown Prince Mohammed bin Salman and took part in a traditional sword dance. A few weeks later, Palantir was one of the sponsors of Trump's military parade in Washington, D.C., contributing $5 million to the event marking the Army's 250th anniversary but that also happened to coincide with the president's seventy-ninth birthday.

However, that was a small investment relative to what Palantir had gained during Trump's first months back in office. According to the *Times*, the company had already been awarded over $100 million in new contracts and extensions of existing ones. Its stock price had nearly tripled in value since the election, a surge driven by a belief among investors that Palantir was uniquely positioned to profit from the second Trump presidency. In the first two quarters of 2025, Palantir outperformed every other stock in the S&P 500. By mid-August, it was pushing $200 per share, its market capitalization had ballooned to around $430 billion, and it was among the 20 most valuable companies in the world. Karp's net worth was now well in excess of $10 billion.

I caught up with Karp over the Fourth of July weekend. There was a lot to talk about. Palantir was once again the object of protests. Demonstrators had gathered outside its Denver and New York offices, as well as in the lobby of Thiel's building in Los Angeles. They cited Palantir's work with ICE, but also its support for the war in Gaza and its alleged role in helping the Trump administration expand government surveillance. Musk, meanwhile, had stepped back from DOGE, reeling from the harm he had done to his own reputation and to Tesla's share price, and his relationship with Trump had promptly dissolved in acrimony. Trump wasn't much more popular: his approval rating had slumped to around 40 percent, and a majority of Americans now disapproved of his immigration policies.

But Karp was full of praise for Trump, lauding the president for the recent U.S. attack on Iran's nuclear facilities (an operation in which Palantir's software had played a part via Project Maven). He said that Iran's pursuit of the bomb was a "fork in the road" moment for civilization and claimed that no Democrat would have displayed the same courage and resolve. Karp told me that he was a single-issue voter now, national security was his issue, and preventing Iran from developing nuclear weapons was an existential necessity. Trump, with the help of Israel (and Palantir), had made the world safer, and Karp expressed admiration and gratitude for his decision to order the strike on Iran.

When I brought up ICE and immigration, Karp (ignoring the shift in sentiment reflected in the polls) said that voters, in returning Trump to office, had made clear that they wanted not only to secure the border, but to maintain America's demographic balance, and he insisted that nothing Trump had done to that point was unconstitutional. He suggested that concerns about the fate of democracy were overblown because the United States still had a "fully functioning judiciary." He said he had no patience for Trump's critics and that panicked and disconsolate Democrats had only themselves to blame for Trumpism. "I don't want to have endless conversations about Trump, because the other side is totally irresponsible," he said. "They won't do anything on immigration or Iran. They talk all the time about racism but won't talk about antisemitism. I'm sick and tired of left-wing people fostering right-wing populist movements because they won't be adults about these issues."

Karp acknowledged that liberals would probably hate him for saying that, but it was the hard truth, and he now welcomed their scorn. The left's contempt for Palantir seemed to be good for the bottom line. Even though the company had never been more controversial, it continued to attract new clients and its stock was at a record high and still climbing. "Being unpopular pays the bills," Karp said.

ACKNOWLEDGMENTS

A book is a leap of faith for any publisher, and I am so glad that Ben Loehnen took the leap on this one. Ben is a terrific editor, a sage guide with a wonderful sense of humor, and it was a pleasure to work with him. Thanks, as well, to Carolyn Kelly, David Kass, and the rest of the team at Avid Reader Press. Avid Reader is a dynamic imprint, and I am proud that this book is part of its stable.

I am fortunate to be represented by David Black and Gary Morris, two of the finest literary agents in the business. They are tireless advocates and indispensable sounding boards, and I am grateful for their support, encouragement, and friendship. Gary has been a partner on this project, and the book benefited enormously from his wisdom.

I appreciated the willingness of so many current and former Palantirians to speak with me and to share their thoughts and recollections. A special thanks to Lisa Gordon for all that she did to make this book possible.

It is a privilege to be a writer for *The New York Times Magazine*, and I am indebted to Jake Silverstein, Bill Wasik, Dean Robinson, and their colleagues.

A handful of people read all or part of the manuscript and offered valuable feedback. My thanks to Peter Steinberger, Tobias Rees, Joel Fishman, Eric Tagliacozzo, Virginia Van Natta, and Rahul Jacob.

Thanks, as well, to Brian Shames and other cherished friends: Wilf Jaeger, Bill Klapp, Dickon Pownall-Gray, David Vos, Julie Ma, Gary Rosenberg, John Stocker, George Nouaime, David Cox, and Bob Cox.

I would be remiss in not mentioning my tennis crew. They are excellent sparring partners and even better friends, and our hits were a welcome break from the grind of book writing.

I am grateful, as always, to my parents, John and Rita Steinberger, and my in-laws, Joseph and Keiko Brennan, as well as to the extended Steinberger and Brennan families.

My son, James, and my daughter, Ava, delight and inspire me every day, and they fill me with hope.

Even after all these years, I still get a rush whenever my wife, Kathy Brennan, walks in the room. I love her, and I love the life that we have made together.

ABOUT THE AUTHOR

MICHAEL STEINBERGER is a contributing writer for *The New York Times Magazine*.